MOVING THE (

Paul Wheeler was born in Rugby, Warwickshire in 1963. His early triumphs culminated in the captaincy of the King Henry VIII school under-15 B team. Such early sporting achievement was inevitably impossible to maintain and a series of reversals brought him at length to Manchester University where the academic study of Geography presented the most opportunities for idling on a beach somewhere.

After short periods spent posing as a retail manager, picking flowers in the English Channel and a year's holiday at Leicester University he found himself with debts of such significance that he was forced to take up a job teaching in Colchester. Since 1992 he has found himself back in Manchester, a mere stone's throw from the University and miles from the nearest beach.

In rare periods of activity he has managed to marry Cara and sire a son, Oliver, and a daughter, Isabel. He can occasionally still be found throwing stones at the University.

He has edited two Coventry City fanzines and has had short stories published in a number of anthologies nobody has read. This is his first full length book. The effort almost killed him.

FRONT COVER ILLUSTRATION BY JO DOBBS

MOVING THE GOALPOSTS

A tale of three cities, one town, a small island and Coventry City Football Club

Paul Wheeler

The Parrs Wood Press
MANCHESTER

First Published 2001

THE PARRS WOOD PRESS
St Wilfrid's Enterprise Centre
Royce Road, Manchester, M15 5BJ
www.parrswoodpress.com

© Paul Wheeler 2001

ISBN: 1 903158 21 4

This book was produced by Andy Searle and Helen Faulkner
of The Parrs Wood Press and Printed in Great Britain by:

MFP Design and Print
Longford Trading Estate
Thomas Street
Stretford
Manchester M32 0JT

For Mum and Dad, Cara, Oliver and Isabel

CONTENTS

PRE-MATCH

WE KILLED AN IDLE HOUR before the pubs opened by throwing stones at Bob. Although Martin was generally more accurate than me, I could tell that his heart wasn't really in it. To me it was a competition just like any other and I have always been a bad loser no matter how trivial the pursuit. What Bob felt is unlikely to be recorded but I doubt if he was bothered. He'd probably been dead for a couple of days. It could have been much longer, but then I'm no vet.

Martin was visiting me up in the grim North because Manchester United were playing host to Coventry City in the Fourth round of the FA Cup. It was a bloody cold day and as we had some time to kill before we were due to meet some other old friends in a pub, we decided to have a wander around the Ship Canal and Bridgewater canal, because the pubs next to them were always the first to open. I spotted the dog but Martin had the bright idea to try and make its bloated skin explode.

I don't know how Bob got into the canal. Maybe he had just reached that age at which dogs die. With a last exhale of foul pedigree chum perfumed breath he passed away quietly in the night, not realising that this would be the final resting place bequeathed by his beloved master. Obviously a domestic pet of such great bulk could not have been quietly flushed down the toilet by some grieving pensioner. It's possible he had fallen into the canal. Perhaps he'd been slurping at some discarded pints, had a bit too much, lost his way and went over the edge only to find he couldn't get out again; struggling at first furiously and then gradually more pitifully before succumbing to the numbing cold.

This is usually quite a busy spot though, underneath the railway arches and with two or three nearby pubs. These are popular hostelries so if he had fallen in during licensing hours somebody would have been sure to spot his canine exertions as they crossed the canal to reach the pub. As this is England, and we love pets more than the homeless, a concerned passerby would have been sure to raise the alarm. Then some 'have a go hero' with one eye on tomorrow's newspaper headlines would have given up his own comfort to pull the bloody thing out.

It happens every year doesn't it? Some bloke's stupid, ugly, dog runs into a frozen pond and the daft git, shit-scared of what he's going to tell the kids or his Mrs. dashes in to save it. So he drowns and the dog finds its own way out just before its balls completely shrivel up. A tragic lesson to us all. So the dog must have fallen in while the pubs were shut, another victim of the harsh licensing laws deemed necessary on our little rock in the Atlantic.

We called him Bob, because that was what he did every time a stone hit his expanded frame. Slowly he would disappear under the chill surface and then reemerge as if resurrected or baptised. Only he didn't appear spiritually or physically cleansed by his dunking. I couldn't tell what brand of dog Bob had been. He had very little hair like one of those mean bastards that bite kids just because they can. He was a skinhead dog and his final resting place was face down in freezing canal, surrounded by litter and sanitary products.

Still he had the last laugh because we never did get him to pop.

When the pub opened we were the first in and had to wait while the bar staff sorted out what barrels and pumps were on. A so-called service industry. They open up late and then seem surprised and totally unprepared for customers. After pouring us a couple of pints of flat, stale beer that had sat in the pipes overnight, warm and sugary, the perfect breeding habitat for flies and cockroaches, they then discovered that there was no float in the till and already the day was starting to look badly planned, which wasn't the impression I wanted Martin to get. He was my guest up here. I'd been in Manchester for more than four years and so I was responsible for ensuring everyone had a good time on their jolly day out up North. If everything worked out there would be four of us, which was a respectable drinking number for a cold weekend in January.

Although Martin was primarily here for the football, he wasn't an obsessive and we were determined to make a decent weekend of it regardless of the game's final result. Living in Manchester I'd got quite a bit of stick from work-mates who readily adopted the arrogance so commonly associated with Reds. Several bets were passed that United would win and go on to take the cup. Pride made me accept these wagers at great financial risk. I'm a Coventry fan but I'm not stupid. Things turned out pretty well though because Coventry surprised me and nearly everyone else, as this was 1987 and the Sky Blues won their first, and only, major trophy. I never grew rich out of those Mancs who'd been so confident when challenging me to a bet. Terrible losers the Reds, but then they haven't had the practice that we have.

The beer tasted of cleaning fluid and the pub stank of stale cigarettes and the ghosts of erstwhile incontinent customers. After a pint we pushed off to meet up with the others. It was good to get outside and we walked in silence to an old pub on the outskirts

Moving the Goalposts

of the town.

This was my favourite part of this oldest of all industrial towns. On the tow path by the Bridgewater canal you really felt you were in a piece of national heritage. These were the canals dug by Irish immigrants to keep the flow of textiles open, bypassing Liverpool, to the rest of the world. Liverpool was charging far more to transport the raw cotton to Manchester via the Mersey than it cost to bring it all the way across the Atlantic. So the Mancunians decided to build their own canal. That the Victorian Mancunians and Liverpudlians couldn't cooperate even back then seems quite a comforting thought from a modern day perspective. Nothing changes. The modern Mancunians and Scousers still hold each other in such vigorous distrust and contempt that it makes our rivalry with the Villa seem no more than a lovers' tiff. It is as though when the industry that spawned their symbiotic growth went into decline they took it as the opportunity for blaming each other for their financial fall and their whole region's decline. It is strange really that they should have such similar ancestries and personalities. Fiercely proud of their wit, their music and their leisure scene.

Both cities owe their development to textiles; Manchester as the manufacturer and Liverpool as its port. Both grew rapidly through waves of hopeful migrants seeking their fortune, or at least something better than was available back at home. What these bright eyed would-be Dick Whittingtons found was a new way of doing things, the factory way, with man working amongst machines far more powerful and valuable than himself. After moving here from some rustic paradise or unproductive marginal land, depending on the quality of rose tinting in your perspective, or in the case of the Irish, fleeing the Great Famine, they found a new home in the damp and overcrowded cellars and slums of the city. The flee from rural starvation had led them only to a quick death through disease or industrial accident. In 1842 Edwin Chadwick published his 'Report on the Sanitary Conditions of the Labouring Population of Great Britain' which revealed that the average life expectancy of a Mancunian working man was seventeen years. At the age of seventeen I hadn't done a decent day's work in my life.

The living conditions of these two towns were so poor that when they were inspected by Friedrich Engels it provoked him into writing that '...the race that lives in those ruinous cottages...in measureless filth and stench...must really have reached the lowest stage of humanity.' Heaven knows what he would have said if he had returned 140 years later and inspected my student flat. Probably that while the rest of Manchester had made progress there was a small pocket of the town where time had stood still and there still lived, as he put it, '... swine that thrive upon the garbage heaps and in the puddles..'

It wasn't all bad news. The labour of these migrants and their initiative led to

3

the building of some outstanding features. The canals, railways, the Corn Exchange, Town Hall and Free Trade Hall all pay testament to the wealth created at this time and they will all still be here long after most modern residents are forgotten and their homes pulled down.

Still it doesn't pay to brood on such things and Martin hadn't traveled up here for a history lesson. He was here to sample some Northern cheer and I knew just the place to take him. It was a complete dive of a pub, but it had character and decent beer. One of the victims of the moors murderers or Yorkshire Ripper was said to have been found in its car-park, so it had a certain local colour so to speak. It was also home to the biggest video game ever invented.

The electronic hunter had to stand on one side of the pub and shoot at ducks that were digitally flying across a screen that covered the whole of the facing wall. To enjoy the game fully it had to be played when the pub was packed to bursting, which was nearly all the time. Then the fun began as you tried to point the huge double-barrelled shotguns through the crowd of drinkers and pick off the fleeing fowl. As a pub marketing ploy it never took off, but it soon gained cult status in the local area. Strangers to the pub got the shock of their lives and rarely stayed for a pint after being confronted with a pissed up lad pointing a shotgun at them as they came through the door.

The reason the pub was rarely other than full was the incredibly low prices they charged. These seemed to defy all logic and commercial sense and attracted tramps and winos from miles around. It wasn't a pub for quiet contemplation. When we arrived a casual acquaintance of mine called Brian was there. Brian didn't really have friends but he was the most interesting bloke I'd ever met. He was a snail man, though others chose to describe him as a dustbin man.

In a former life Brian had been to be a computer operator for the local council but he walked out one day because he got pissed off with the orderliness of a nine to five job. He just swept the contents of his desk into his regulation, local authority issued waste basket and walked out one Monday morning, never to return. About two weeks later he left his flat and his girlfriend, again without offering any explanation. When speaking about his decision now, he says that he wanted to know what it was like to be a free man. All he took with him was a sleeping bag and a few photographs. In the end he even got rid of these meagre possessions as he hated the worry that they might be stolen. Now he owned nothing except the clothes he wore. I think the responsibility of clothes ownership occasionally got him down and that he would really have preferred to go around naked.

He was called a snail because he carried his home around with him. This was a 'borrowed' wheelie bin which he crawled into at night for shelter and a little security.

Moving the Goalposts

Apparently there are lots of snailmen about but Brian hadn't ever introduced me to any of them. Nowadays I suppose he could join the ranks of homeless who sell the Big Issue to raise a little cash, but its unlikely that he would have chosen such an option. That would be too much like an organised, controlled life rather than the total freedom he was searching for. I suppose he was a cross between a traditional tramp and a modern age, low capital gypsy. Despite his engaging personality and unique history he wasn't a bloke you would want to sit next to in a packed pub because he stank to high heaven of soil and burnt wood. I guided Martin to the opposite side of the room rather than risk several hours inhaling Brian's perfume.

The others turned up about an hour later, complaining about the cold and the crap directions I'd sent them. I felt a bit responsible for both the weather and the map as my reason for moving to Manchester had been to study Geography and so I might have been expected to send a reasonable map and advance warning of the high pressure system responsible for the freezing conditions of the day. Still I wasn't their Mum and they were both big lads who soon stopped complaining after a couple of drinks. As for the match, it was hardly a classic. Both teams struggled on the frozen pitch and the foggy conditions did little to enhance the view from our crowded away terrace. Coventry had one chance right in front of the visiting supporters which fell to Keith 'Roy of the Rovers' Houchen. He stabbed at the ball with every part of his body as it bounced awkwardly in front of the United goal until after his third lunge the Coventry supporters behind the goal collectively inhaled and sucked the ball into the net. At least that's how it looked to me. 1-0 to the Sky Blues and we were on our way to the fifth round and an exciting trip to Stoke.

1.

In the beginning

ALREADY I HAVE GOT AHEAD of myself. Let me start again. I came into this Earth on the 20th December 1963. The year of the Profumo affair, the Great Train Robbery and the year that Kennedy was shot in Dallas. It was also the year that Pope Paul replaced Pope John and Lennon and McCartney had their first number one hit. I like to think I was christened Paul John after the latter pair.

I was born in the parish of Rugby, home to Rugby school and also the birthplace of the sport named after it and played by a mixture of gentlemen and thugs. Rugby is now a suburb of the historic City of Coventry, and I had the great fortune of moving to live in Coventry at the age of three. This simple geographical relocation was to be a significant influence on the rest of my thinking life as through a slow process and after a long and flirtatious courtship I fell in love with my local football club. Had we stayed in Rugby who knows what my waking thoughts would be dominated by. Perhaps Gilbert's balls, Tom Brown's school days, Flashman and fagging, but who can tell? As it turned out my worries concern the occasional inhabitants of a small area in the Hillfields district of Coventry.

Coventry is a City with a difficult past and an uncertain future. It owes its beginnings to Leofric, Earl of Mercia, and his more famous wife Godiva, who together in 1043 founded a Benedictine monastery on the site of what is now our city. Coventry made its fortune twice. The first was based on the medieval textile trade when Manchester was still little more than a borough of Salford, a small market town with an annual Fair. Its crappy wooden castle was eventually replaced by a manor house, a mock imitation of the mighty and royally patronised fortresses of Warwick and

Kenilworth. The second was born out of engineering, in the form of sewing machines, bicycles and cars. Our three M.P.s are all Labour, which hints at the city's post-war socialist history.

On 14th November 1940 Coventry and its engineering factories were the target of the worst air raid suffered in the war, the German 'Baedeker raid' attack, romantically code-named 'Moonlight Sonata'. From 7 p.m. until almost 7 a.m. the following morning four hundred and fifty aircraft dropped five hundred and three tons of high explosive and 30,000 incendiaries on the city, destroying three quarters of the private housing and killing five hundred and fifty four people. Churchill's comment that it takes a ton of bombs to 'kill three-quarters of a person' provided little comfort to the grieving survivors, particularly after the later admission that the attack had been known about in advance but our city had been sacrificed rather than reveal to the Germans that their Enigma code had been broken. British counter intelligence had devised a jamming system capable of disrupting the direction-finding beams on the German aircraft, but on that night it was broadcast on the wrong frequency.

Coventry wasn't strong in defence with only forty anti-aircraft guns and her air cover was provided by a range of aircraft including the almost obsolete Gladiator biplanes. The Germans lost only one of their four hundred and fifty bombers and that was probably by misadventure. The bomber crews reported that they could smell the city burning from 6000 feet up. The wooden roofed cathedral stood little chance of escaping the rain of incendiaries. Heroic attempts to save the city's religious heart included people standing on the roof and throwing incendiary bombs off as they landed. Finally, however, a burst water main ended these attempts as with no pressure left in their hoses, firemen had to watch a minor roof fire spread and destroy their cathedral. Nearly 60,000 buildings were damaged including twenty-one major factories. It was estimated that seventy-five percent of the city's war output had been seriously damaged. The morning after the attack one survivor said, 'Coventry is finished'. However within five days production had restarted in the factories. A pair of charred beams found lying crisscross in the rubble of the cathedral was tied in the shape of a cross by Cathedral stonemason Jock Forbes. This was to become the symbol of reconciliation and it still stands in the ruins of the old cathedral. A modern city arose, Phoenix-like, from the ashes.

Moving the Goalposts

The new Cathedral was consecrated in May 1962. Designed by Sir Basil Spence, it is dominated by Graham Sutherland's giant tapestry of Christ enthroned among the Four Beasts of the Revelation. Attached like a Siamese twin to the ruins of the old one, the new Cathedral is a dazzling piece of modern architecture described in the 1960's as the building which most caught the imagination of the nation. Coventry was also ahead of the times in its reconstruction of its commercial centre. The pedestrianised shopping centre was another first, indicating a previously unheard of willingness to plan ahead for the benefit of its citizens.

The influence of the car industry is everywhere. Even the Polytechnic was named after a car, the Lanchester, although it has now reinvented itself as Coventry University. James Starley developed the differential gear here and the cathedral displays the former car badges of over twenty local firms including Hillman and Riley. The biggest manufacturer today is the French-owned Peugeot whose name has graced the shirts of so many City players. Even the club's latest sponsors Isuzu and Subaru maintain this traditional link with the motor trade.

Of course, Coventry is also famous for one who didn't wear her clothes with pride. The most popular image of Lady Godiva is that of her nude form astride a horse. A similar statue (only this time on side-saddle) has pride of place in the city between the Cathedral and the pedestrianised shopping precinct, appropriately dividing its commercial and clerical hearts. It is said that Godiva rode naked through the city's streets in protest at Leofric's harsh tax rises. The reality of the story is probably a bit less dramatic. It would seem that she was only naked in the sense that she wasn't wearing her robes and chains of office. The citizens of Coventry are said to have all averted their eyes out of respect for her stand, all except Peeping Tom who was rewarded by being struck blind, which seems a little harsh in the city that also spawned page three stunner Debbee Ashby (who I had the great good fortune of going to school with). It is interesting that when Debbee followed in Godiva's footsteps by posing in 'Men Only' magazine, the school showed little respect for local history by expelling her. It would appear that the citizens of Coventry had similarly forgotten their role as every issue in Coventry had been bought up within a week, resulting in a desperate aid mission to Nuneaton and Birmingham for extra copies.

This was the city that I moved to in 1966. Of course that year saw many other important events such as the death of Buster Keaton and the birth of the mini-skirt as Mary Quant put the King's Road and Carnaby Street on the World map, making London the city of the 1960's. England's World Cup victory at Wembley reinforced the spirit of boom and national pride.

Closer to home a long chinned man called Jimmy Hill was leading a revolution at the local football club that came to be known as the 'Sky Blue Era'. Jimmy Hill took over the club when times were not so good. The team was made up of aging players and the week before his appointment they had suffered the humiliation of a cup exit at the hands of Southern League King's Lynn. He took over totally, introducing progressive ideas, a new Sky Blue kit and even writing the Sky Blue song that has entertained so many visiting fans. By 1966 he had transformed a demoralised Third Division team into a side pushing for promotion to the First Division.

After an indifferent start to the 1966/67 season a local lad by the name of Bobby Gould led the way with his twenty-four goals making him the league's top scorer and helping City on a twenty-five match unbeaten run that was to see the Sky Blues take the Second Division Championship. Jimmy had led Coventry City from the football wilderness into the promised land, and I was still only three.

2.

First sight

Coventry v Derby, April 1973

I HAD BEEN TO FOOTBALL matches before. A couple of seasons earlier I had watched the Sky Blues take on Liverpool as an unwelcome added guest at my brother's birthday treat. He and I sat in the wooden Main Stand all resentful of each other. I was bitter that my Dad had forked out to take these strangers to the match when the money could have been put to far better use on me. My brother was suffering under the inevitable embarrassment caused by having to drag your little brother along with you when you are among your mates. I hate to admit this but the fact is that I can remember wanting Liverpool to win. In my defence I should point out that my brother and his cronies were all cheering on Coventry to win so I had to adopt a contrary position. I had no choice, it's a biological thing.

I have vague, haunting recollections that my very first match was a charity game between some unemployed T.V. stars and Aston Villa of all people. I remember being disappointed that no one from Play School was in the TV stars team. In fact the celebrities' team seemed to be made up of ordinary people off the street. I think I had probably expected to see a hard fought game between Villa and a squad selected from the fittest members of Camberwick Green, Pogell's Wood and the Herb Garden, managed by Bill and Ben (this was in the days before players were randomly tested for traces of Weed).

Fortunately this early exposure to the Villa left me unaffected and I felt no overwhelming desire to swear undying support for the team from Brum. This time I got my loyalties right and wanted to see Villa humiliated by the glamorous celebrities. In fact anyone taking a look at the Topical Times Football annual for that year (1969) might note that I have placed a

huge tick next to the only Coventry player to feature in it (Ernie Hunt, pho-
tographed while doing a bit of weights) while I have scribbled horns and
blacked the teeth all over Villa player Lionel Martin's face, clearly proving
that our hatred of local rivals is a product of nature rather than nurture.
Actually, it was my older brother's book and he liked the Villa kit, so sibling
rivalry probably goes some way to explaining my unprovoked attack.

My first real taste of football was a trip arranged by my Scottish
Uncle Rob who was down visiting us with my Auntie and cousins. As a treat
he offered to take my brother, cousins and I to see Coventry play against
Derby. We went into town by bus and Uncle Rob, who was a teacher, pointed out features of Coventry that we were unaware of. It is often said that
tourists see more of a town than its residents, and our uncle seemed to
know far more about our home town than any of our school teachers. We
were unaware that our home town might be a place people came to visit on
holiday and look at. To us it was just our home and holidays meant going
to the seaside. I felt a bit sorry for my cousins for missing out on swimming
and sandcastles merely to go to our shops and look at our cathedral. Uncle
Rob, however, described all the passing features as though he was con-
ducting a coach load of Saga tourists through Las Vegas.

We walked up our road, past our grandparents' house to the bus stop
at the top of what counts in Warwickshire as a hill, where we waited excit-
edly for the first stage of our trip. It's funny how waiting for a bus can seem
like fun when you are nine years old, but is one of life's greatest burdens by
the time you are seventeen. The bus pulled out and we passed the large
Memorial Park, where we liked to play football and go on the swings. This
recreational amenity was, Uncle Rob informed us, created in 1920 as a trib-
ute to those that had fallen in the Great War. After the Second World War
there was a proposal to build a dance hall on part of the park and to move
the Dome of Discovery here from the Festival of Britain. Both exciting
ideas, but the park was never to see them and remained the tranquil haven
that we all so enjoyed. There have recently been new 'Millennial' plans for
the development of a major feature in the park. Let's hope that they aren't
planning to dump the new Dome here.

As the bus approached the city centre bus terminal at Pool Meadow
Uncle Rob pointed out that although there was no pool now there had once
been a huge lake on the site of the modern bus terminus. He told us that

Moving the Goalposts

Coventry was built on three old lakes of which only Swanswell still remains. The third pool gave its name to one of the city's most famous schools, Bablake. His graphic geographical and historical account of Coventry was all the more strange for the fact that he was a lecturer in Physics. Scientists aren't meant to care about ecology, geomorphology, urban development and the growth of the factory system. Not unless it involves digging or blowing them up.

As we grew nearer to the Sky Blues ground in Hillfields he even showed us the large, walled building that our dad worked in. I had never seen it before and was a bit upset when I discovered that that was where dad spent all his time as it looked to me like a prison. I hated the thought that our dad had to spend all the time cooped up in there when we were out playing in the park during the long Summer holidays, or building dens and bike tracks in the woods during the wet winter and spring breaks. I have since realised that the building probably had a similar effect on my dad most of the time.

Like all young first timers I entered the ground with several preconceptions, none of which were true. I knew that football was an expensive sport to watch and so I had expected some rather special facilities for the supporters and while Jimmy Hill's five years had greatly improved the stadium, it was hardly up to the standards that my annual excursions to see the Christmas pantomime at the Belgrade Theatre had led me to expect. Instead of joyous, excited young people enraptured by the onstage activities, there were jostling undisciplined crowds and a totally obscured view of the proceedings. Instead of laughter and the sound of people enjoying themselves, there was only complaints and criticism. Disappointment and anger scarred the men's faces around me. I too was disappointed. League positions and all that weren't important to me, but I did expect to see Coventry score and I did want to see them win. We waited patiently for Coventry's first goal, but it refused to come. After a short time I was bored and even if Coventry had scored it would almost certainly have passed me by as I spent most of the game fidgeting, watching the people around me and longing to go home. Derby won 2 - 0, but I wasn't bothered. I just wanted my tea.

3.

All change

AT THE APPROPRIATE TIME I was torn from the familiar surroundings of my Junior school, where I had grown into a position of dominance, being a good inch taller than anyone else there, and relocated into a far bigger and more imposing educational establishment. Despite the fact that several of my fellow vertically challenged associates made the move with me, I found the transition daunting. The place was huge, the other kids were huge and it was also a much longer walk in the morning and at night. Although I was undergoing a crucial educational, environmental and social change, it was the long walk that worried me most. In the 70's the popular press and other forms of media made great play on the dangers to members of the public posed by the presence on our streets of mindless thugs and football hooligans. These were ubiquitous and contact with them, seemingly inevitable. Their habitat was by no means restricted to football grounds. In fact, by all accounts, this was one of the least likely places you would find them. Nor were their activities restricted to match days. No, these boys were thorough professionals, available twenty-four hours a day, 'We never sleep'. They were the modern day bogeymen and it seemed their mission was to get snotty nosed, knock-kneed school kids.

As part of my walk home I would come to a crossroads where each day I had to make a choice of which path to take. The first choice was the furthest, a sinuous trek along side streets followed by an endless stretch down what seemed the longest road in the city. This was the least favoured path. An alternative shorter route meant passing through a rather grim wood and that was a bit scary for a youngish lad with a fertile imagination on his own during the darkening winter evenings. The wood had a reputa-

13

tion for providing a refuge for sexual deviants, most specifically flashers, and no matter how sexually curious I was at that age I had no great desire to have someone else's inflated toilet parts displayed for my education/benefit. After all it would have put me off my dinner.

The final option was by far the shortest but it involved a long hike down a curved and extremely high walled alley. The curve ensured you couldn't see what was coming up the other way and the walls made any escape, should it ever be necessary, impossible. The problem with this way was the fear of entrapment and it was not without substance. At this period in the 1970's there was a growing number of incidents of unprovoked attacks on children on their way home, attacks often attributed by the local press to the aforementioned football hooligans. One young lad lost an eye, another committed suicide after repeated bullying and a friend of mine was hospitalised after failing to keep up with his fleeing mates as they were pursued. The local gang, who sported the name of 'E-Troop', had allegedly been associated with a couple of racial attacks and were said to be involved in the stabbing to death of an Asian doctor in the doorway of my local chip shop. Consequently, I was always anxious of this unseen but ever present threat.

My feelings of vulnerability were exacerbated by the fact that I was unusually lanky and consequently the ideal target for any short kids with a chip on their shoulder about their own delayed growth spurt. In my life as a tall person I have learnt many important lessons, but perhaps the best advice I could pass on to younger generations is keep an eye on small people, they bring trouble.

I suspect that it is not surprising that ancient literature portrays imps, elves and hobgoblins in such a bad light. The tricky scheming elf or mischievous imp so popular in fairy tales may apparently have disappeared during the dark ages but they have left their legacy behind, which possibly hints at some cross breeding with normal, noble and peasant folk during the twelfth century. As a result, modern day short people retain many characteristics of their sub-human forebears - namely cunning, selfishness and a bitterness at their reduced perspective. This is the only feasible reason for the number of short people who tried to pick fights with me as a child. It surely can't have been my attitude or anything I said. I've always been tolerant and diplomatic.

To these people of restricted growth I can only offer the following apology, yes I am bigger than you, but your life need not necessarily be crap, after all you could always get a job cleaning hubcaps, ranching Shetland ponies or picking fruit in a Bonsai orchard.

This Big -Small conflict was most evident on the school sports field. For some bizarre historical reason the school I went to didn't play football, only Thugby. The tall players would be in the forwards and they would fight and wrestle and bite each other while the shorties in the backs would stand around making daisy chains and kicking the ball away if it came near them. Both groups seemed more than happy with their appointed role. This difference manifested itself both on and off the pitch as after Saturday matches against other schools the forwards would go off to Coundon Road to watch the then mighty Coventry Rugby Football Club play, while the backs went to Highfield road to either stand on the terraces and look at the bloke in front's back, or sit in the Sky Blue Stand and watch the game.

This arrangement appeared to have some genetic background as all the tall kids also had tall Dads and brothers who went to the rugby with them, while all the short kids had short and embittered Dads who stood at Highfield road for a good old rant at the vertically advantaged players on the pitch. 'Oi, Jim Holton (6'2", eyes of blue) - you donkey'.

So between 1972 and 1978 I was a rugby fan and really quite enjoyed it. I went with my big dad and big brother and presumably felt some sort of male bonding experience. Coventry at the time had a number of internationals including the leader of the successful British Lions tour to South Africa, Fran Cotton, who had taught me sport at my previous school. I use the term 'taught' very loosely, as what he actually did was physically cajole all the pupils and administer non-verbal punishments for the last to get changed every week. We were all terrified of him and the potential consequences of any lateness. In the end this resulted in more and more bizarre attempts to avoid being last. I used to go to school with my P.E. kit on under my uniform. One lad who was a notoriously slow changer used to skip off the lesson before (French, with a weedy teacher) to give himself a sufficient head start. I may still be crap at sport, but nobody is quicker at changing into their kit than me.

The year 1977 saw something of a renaissance in England. The Queen celebrated her Silver Jubilee. Virginia Wade won at Wimbledon at thirty-one years of age. The space shuttle made its maiden flight as Star Wars appeared in the cinemas. Elvis died on a toilet, Bing Crosby expired on a golf course, whilst on the Thames the Sex Pistols introduced a new direction for music, dragging us from the sequined haze of glitter rock into something new and unpredictable.

Even as an egocentric thirteen year old I could see that these were exciting and changing times. Family photograph albums show that although this was a dynamic period in modern English history I had not been caught up in the whirlwind of change, remaining as I have done for most of my life a good two paces behind the cutting edge of current fashions. So the picture of me on Jubilee day shows a lad in brown crimplene flares, a brown tartan shirt and a Val Doonican jumper. The photo must have been taken by my mother as it has cut off my feet and most of my head. I dread to think of what shoes I might have been wearing, but I can see enough of my greasy hair (underneath my aluminium foil Royal crown) to recognise a little Jimmy Osmond cut at its worst. A quick rifle through my record collection would reveal such all time classics as Boney M, The Wombles and Brotherhood of Man. My idea of anarchy was to squeeze the toothpaste tube in the middle, or leave my homework until Sunday night.

Events at Highfield Road also demonstrated the spirit of rebirth exhibited everywhere else in the country except in my wardrobe. The season before had finished with a typical position forged out of atypical conditions. The Sky Blues had avoided relegation on the last Saturday of the season, thanks to a two all draw with Bristol City. This score line meant that both Coventry and Bristol survived in the top flight at the expense of Sunderland who had lost away at Everton. The result was rather controversial as crowd congestion had delayed the kick off at Highfield Road by some ten minutes. When news came in of the result at Goodison it was broadcast on the scoreboard and both teams settled for a dishonourable draw, as Bristol passed the ball around in their own half for the final five minutes of the season. Sunderland lodged a complaint and an enquiry was carried out by the football league, but the consensus of opinion was that we were too good to go down. The following season seemed to bear this out. It was a fantastic year in which Ian Wallace and Mick Ferguson scored forty goals between them and City finished the season in seventh place, their second highest ever final position, which meant we just missed out on a second helping of European football.

I, however, was down at Coundon Road watching Coventry play Pontypridd. It is almost uncanny, my penchant for being in the wrong place at the right time.

By 1979 even I had heard of punk and everybody around me seemed to be rebelling. The only move I made towards the adoption of an anarchistic lifestyle was to take up with a different group of friends. Cheeky, sarcastic, immature little gobshites who were always getting into futile arguments and needless punishments. I felt right at home in no time. This great new peer group taught me all my social skills and it is only right that I recognise in print their invaluable contribution. True, their influence led to great parental dismay, atrocious reports and the alienation of most of the other people around me, but that is the price you have to pay for moving forward. 'The masses will not assume control without bloody revolution', or some bollocks.

The greatest gift that they endowed upon me was my reintroduction to the delights of Highfield Road. It only took one visit for me to realise what I had been missing.

4.

Ole,Ole, Ole.

I MUST HAVE SENSED that I was missing out on the great sporting occasions just around the corner for the following year I wisely swapped my sporting allegiances. So I abandoned my Coventry Rugby club membership card in favour of the thrills and glamour of the city's other sporting heroes, - the Coventry Bees.

I first went to the Brandon Stadium to watch Coventry's highly successful Speedway team in 1978. I don't know if it was the smell of the engines, the roar of the bikes or the grit flung in my eyes by the spinning rear tyres, but I immediately became a devotee and while my visits to Highfield Road were very irregular, my support for the Bees was unwavering.

My devotion may have been encouraged by the unusual situation of seeing a team I supported actually win trophies and my players win international honours. Coventry at this time were captained by the great Ole Olsen, and the riders included Mitch Sheera, Gary Guglielmi and Tommy Knudson. For several seasons they were virtually unbeatable at home and swept the board in terms of trophies. One evening I even saw them win two major trophies in two different ties, back to back. No worries about end of season fixture congestion for these boys. As soon as they had won the British League Title by defeating a Hull side that at the start of the evening were level on points with them, they were back in the saddle to beat Leicester for the Midland Cup. To be honest, although I am sure that these are the two teams the Bees defeated that night, that is all I remember, and perhaps that helps to explain why my support for them was so short lived. They were a very successful team and it was an exciting time, but it has left

18

no lasting impression upon me. I can't remember anything about what it felt like to be at Brandon cheering the Bees on to another inevitable victory. I have still got the old score sheets in a box somewhere but unlike my old football programmes I never get them out to reminisce about the good old days. So one season I missed a speedway fixture and I haven't been back since. Is Ole still racing?

In the meantime my occasional visits to Highfield Road saw two rather indifferent seasons, with the Sky Blues rarely looking like pushing for a place in Europe, nor really threatening a last day relegation thriller. Our cup performances were even less significant. In the F.A. Cup we were knocked out after one game in 1978, while the following year saw us defeated in the third round yet again, this time after a replay. 1980 saw a fourth round exit, while in 1981 we managed a run as far as the fifth round. Heady stuff. Our performances in the league cup were scarcely more impressive, dumped out by Liverpool in 1977, mighty Chester in 1978 and West Brom 1979.

1980 brought an unexpected anomaly to this usually most consistent of patterns and Coventry City found themselves one game away from a cup final. Was our name going to appear on the League Cup? Previous rounds had seen us defeat Manchester United at home and away. We had then squeezed past Brighton and Cambridge before comprehensively beating Watford 5-0 in the home leg after a draw at Vicarage Rd. The only thing keeping us from our first final was West Ham. At that time they were top of the Second Division, on one of their upswings in fortune. We were having one of our better seasons eventually finishing well out of the relegation zone at fourteenth.

At Highfield Road an all ticket crowd of 35,468 saw West Ham take a soft two goal lead in the first half (both bad mistakes involving a certain Les Sealey) which they kept until eighteen minutes from time. Thompson finally got one goal back for City and four minutes later Gerry Daley scored the equaliser. With five minutes left the Hamsters had a goal disallowed for offside and then in the ninetieth minute Thompson scored City's winner. In school the next morning everyone was in a state of shock. Everyone claimed to have been at the game, even people who didn't know where Highfield Road was. An American exchange student in my class had been there with his dad, enjoying their first taste of English football. They had been sitting in the better seats in the Main Stand and as they cheered City's winner a Hammer fan in the row behind punched the lad in the face, splitting his lip and giving him a black eye which he impressively sported at school the next day. Everyone felt a bit embarrassed that he should see such a shameful expression of supporter behaviour during his stay, but these feelings were tinged by an embarrassed pride that we had been at the game and not been beaten up, as though it was his American-ness, his obvious aura of not belonging there, that had brought this downfall. Well, we were only kids.

Other than this all conversation was about whether we could hold on to the fragile lead. My limited experience led me to doubt it, but I sat in my bedroom listening to the match commentary on the radio with all my fingers crossed, hoping against hope for a Coventry win. The second leg was far less exciting, a Paul Goddard shot brought the tie level and Neighbour scored from an offside position in the final minute to make it 4-3 to West Ham. They lost the final to Liverpool after a replay and we returned to our usual habit of early cup exits for the next five seasons.

This throws open another point I ought to share with you. I am not a great one for doing excessive research. The facts and match details I have presented are, as far as I can remember, correct. Results and league positions I am reasonably sure about. Goal scorers and attendance figures have been easy enough to confirm. Some of the other details may have suffered from reinterpretation during the retrieval process from my long term memory. While I am pretty happy that I have got the crucial information right, some expert may yet choose to question my recall on one or two other minutiae. In my defence I can only say that the facts are correct as I remember them, however, I also remember being quite a good all-round athlete at school and yet the only record I have of my achievements is a A.A.A. one star certificate, which rather puts me into the 'has trouble walking' category. Ahh, the tricks of memory.

5.

Ghost town

A FAVOURITE MOAN AMONG PARENTS and grandparents is that in their day they had to make their own entertainments. In their day there was no DVD and alcopops, just VD and pawnshops. They are keen to conjure up images of themselves singing around a piano all laughing and joining in rousing choruses of popular and risque variety show songs. This is despite all the evidence to the contrary, namely that they never laugh, can't hold a tune nor remember any lyric other than a trill 'la, la, la', have never owned a piano nor shown any evidence of any musical ability. The truth is that this is another example of older generation bluff and bluster. They didn't really stay in all the time. They went to dances, pubs and the cinema just as their offspring do. But then they are only passing on a moaning mantra that they too would have heard their grandparents chanting, which may have had a bit more truth to it.

Then again, old black and white films such as Love on the Dole and A Taste of Honey present a slightly different picture. These film archives and our history books have shown us that at any one time a small two up two down would be home to as many as three or four generations of the same family, all living together in disharmony. It is totally beyond my comprehension that they would all chose to sit in the same room of an evening, chatting about the day's events or having a sing-song. They would all have stayed out as much as possible, away from prying eyes and ears. They would have been on the street playing as children, courting as teenagers or hanging around in threatening gangs as youths, looking for new faces to court or challenge. They too went to picture palaces, dance halls and pubs when they had the cash and cruised the streets when they hadn't. Though mass entertainment was rare at the turn of the last century, the desire for social interaction was presumably just as strong as it is today. If the means and opportunities were more scarce and there was no access to cheap rapid transport, as today, then the sights just had to stay more local and the community was all. At the heart of most districts there would be the twin foci of the corner shop and the pub, and for major urban centres the local football team.

While poverty may have proven an obstacle to social activities it certainly doesn't remove the urge. The greatest attendances for many top football clubs occurred in the times of greatest austerity, particularly in the inter-war depression years. Birmingham City, Leicester, Spurs, Wigan, Manchester United, Newcastle, Sheffield Wednesday, Wolves and even Colchester United all recorded their record gates in this time. (An anomoly is Coventry's record gate of 51,455 which occurred in April 1967, a crucial Division Two fixture against local rivals Wolves, during a time of prosperity and growth, both in economic and in footballing terms). People may have had no jobs and few prospects but an afternoon at the football with friends or a night at the pub at least offered temporary respite from the harsh realities of day to day life.

At this time Temperance societies flourished in tandem with the brewers. That our towns could give birth to so many Temperance societies and Temperance pledgers suggests that there must have been more than a few intemperate people about. Engels wrote about the general drunkenness he witnessed on the streets of Manchester in the 1830's and the great Temperance drives intended to put working men and women back on the straight and narrow. Thousands took the pledge but apparently found it hard to keep. Engels comments, 'If one counts up the immense numbers who have taken the pledge in the last three or four years in Manchester, the total is greater than the whole population of the town.'

Clearly young people's hedonism in the 1990's was no new phenomena. It's just that your modern youth has more of it to choose from, more money to spend on it and more time to take part in it. With the development of the transport revolution (which was itself also a key midland employer from Crewe in the north with its Rolls Royce engineering and its railways, through Coventry the car and bicycle manufacturing centre, right down to Morris's Oxford and beyond) changes were taking place that resulted in greater personal freedom and an increase in each individuals sphere of influence. No longer were people tied to the local community, now there was the means, and with the introduction of regulations on the length of the working week, the time to travel and experience further afield. People no longer had to be insular. The time was rapidly approaching when residents of Torquay could start setting up the Devon Reds Manchester United supporters clubs, and the transport manufacturers of the West Midlands are directly responsible!

In 1979 something special happened in Coventry. Like most children and many adults I subconsciously believed that I was the beating heart of a slowly revolving Universe; that the major events of the day all occurred on my doorstep and their shockwaves dribbled out to influence everyone else. The big-world rarely touched my self-world, relegated as it was to half hour news slots and the front pages of boring daily newspapers. In 1979 and 1980 the self-world and big-world collided as Coventry found itself at the core of a global movement. As popular uprisings go it was relatively short-lived, having burnt itself out by the mid 1980's, but the 2-Tone revolution temporarily put Coventry on the trendy map. In so doing it brought national attention to Britain's own Motown.

Given the ephemeral nature of pop music it is perhaps inevitable that every town will have its Warholian fifteen minutes of fame. Fortuitously Coventry's glory years coincided with my peak in interest in the music scene. (Even inspiring me to form a group that shamefully operated under the name of 'The Black and White Menstruals'). The Punk era of the late '70's became superseded by a more laudable music cause in the early '80's, as The Specials, The Selecter and the Two-Tone record label came to embody the spirit of the times.

Coventry has had other musical success stories. Paul King, Hazel O'Connor and (ahem) Vince Hill all had loose ties with the city. Before the Specials the only chart topper was Lieutenant Pigeon's 'Mouldy Old Dough' which didn't appear on many 'Classic Hits of the 70's' compilation albums. Amidst this treasury of mediocrity The Specials are the one chequered highlight. If music reflects the zeitgeist then Ska was a revealing phenomenon. Taking its roots from Jamaican Ska and reggae the Coventry Two-Tone record label gave the movement a base and identity. 2-Tones founder, Gerry Dammers, wanted to create something new and chose Ska as it was easier to play than reggae. Needing a B-side for their first single 'Gangsters', Gerry decided the track called 'The Selecter' written and performed by Noel Davies and John Bradbury was perfect, so the pair formed a band of the same name. The 2-Tone label was up and running. Playing to packed houses in The Locarno and The General Wolfe their popularity and reputation soon spread. This fame gave rise to a new fashion and dance craze symbolised by the combination of black and white in clothes, in the band and in some sections of society. This racial integration took place at a time when the country as a whole was demonstrating rather less tolerance. The Thatcher government came into power in 1979 and one of its most enduring legacies was the resultant rising unemployment and social unrest. Specials concerts often became battle grounds between Rock against Racism supporters and the National Front, as both groups targeted the skinheads and Rude-boys as potential recruits.

In July 1981 riots erupted in Brixton, Bristol St.Paul's, Manchester Moss Side and other major inner cities including Coventry's Hillfields, as unemployment broke the three million mark. The protests were most violent in the regions most affected by the polarisation of wealth and as the inner cities burned The Specials found themselves topping the charts for a second and final time with 'Ghost Town'- a modern urban anthem for a doomed youth, in a summer of simmering tension. Within the band there was also friction and discontent which finally saw them split into the upbeat and lightweight Fun Boy Three and the more politically motivated Special A.K.A.. Dammers wrote Ghost Town while touring some of the country's most deprived areas and drew his main inspiration from the deprivation he witnessed in Liverpool and Glasgow, but he was partly motivated by the closure of Tiffany's nightclub in Coventry, where the band had recorded their first number one, the Special A.K.A. Live E.P.

Following on from the over-publicised, media fuelled Mods and Rockers antagonism and the anti-everything Punk revolution Ska was a movement preaching tolerance amidst the economic ruins. The 60's Beat scene had developed in times of full-employment and a youth with disposable income burning a hole in their Carnaby Street pants just begging to be conspicuously spent in a cafe or some exclusive Chelsea boutique. This era is often portrayed as youth's 'Golden Age', but it was commercially controlled and managed by big business who quickly came to realise that there was a new consumer in town. In contrast Ska grew in hard times in which nobody was preaching love and peace man, when a homogeneous youth was dividing itself into clearly delimited groups such as Mods, rockers, punks, skinheads and new romantics, all with their own look and culture. On the outside of this lay population clusters who didn't need to create a new exclusive culture because they had been born with one. They often felt the worst excesses of the new, manufactured, sects.

Ska was independent of the mainstream and commercial control. The uniform may have been sharp suits and pork-pie hats but it was easily imitated by those on more limited funds. Trips to jumble sales and charity shops would unearth a treasure trove of grandad suits and hats just ripe for modifying. The new trend was unpromoted, unhyped, under-invested. The People's music - the Skiffle of its day. It too may have had its roots abroad, but The Specials and their followers adapted it. Few could reasonably argue that 'Ghost Town' or 'Friday Night - Saturday Morning' are anything other than expressions of the local scene and its people at that time. Ska may have been a transatlantic import but Two Tone certainly wasn't.

Inevitably the media soon caught up with the new fad and it became a national rather than regional phenomenon. Ultimately Madness from London had the greatest financial and chart success after joining the band-wagon. Gerry Dammers never sold out. The Fun Boy Three may have split away into more obvious pop directions but Special A.K.A. kept to the orig-inal pattern, their ultimate achievement being the universally embraced anthem 'Free Nelson Mandela'. The Selecter too stayed true to Ska. The band had been offered their first record deal by The Specials 2-tone label. The £1000 deal to record three tracks resulted in their first single On My Radio/Too Much Pressure which entered the Top Ten in November 1979. By 1980 the 2-Tone movement was at its peak and had cultivated a huge following and cult status demonstrated in the Ska film Dance Craze. Dammers wanted to disband the label before it grew into a monster he could no longer control. As the movement grew it lost its initial drive and cohesion. Concerts became a target for violence and the Chrysalis record label proved a difficult partner. It was the beginning of the end and many of the bands broke up in acrimony, or reformed with new faces.

Ska's popularity may have been ephemeral but its' significance should not be underestimated. Though 2-Tone was licensed by Chrysalis, it was an independent label, often working from the now demolished Horizon Studios near Coventry railway station. Ultimately music in Coventry had become less passive. The message was get involved, take part, don't be a spectator. New labels started up. Music was recorded locally, rather than in London. Many of the bands still remain, often enjoying great popularity in a new generation of Ska fans. The Selecter and Specials continue to enjoy cult status with the rise of Third Wave Ska in the USA. Many of the old venues have now gone; The Locarno is now Coventry City Library, Tiffany's has been demolished, The General Wolfe on the Foleshill road has fallen into disrepair and been refurbished as bedrooms, but there are signs that the ghost town is preparing to be reborn.

A report in the Coventry Evening Telegraph Friday April 11th 1997 decried the fact that Coventry's city centre was a wasteland after 6 p.m. At the end of each day the city went home to have its tea and to watch television. The only bright lights or venue for young people to visit had been a Burger King restaurant and now the lack of any passing trade had forced even them to close their doors in the evening, earlier than any other branch in Britain. The president of Coventry University Students Union compared the behavioural habits of Coventry's night life to that one might expect 'in a quiet rural market town.' Happily the picture has since improved. As Coventry's student population has grown, so has the demand for evening entertainment. New clubs began to appear. 'The Planet' won national praise if some local criticism. 'Irish 2000' in Spon Street opened and catered for a more local custom, often resembling the last hour of a particularly drunken wedding celebration. New pubs and bars like 'Browns' (on a former public toilet) and 'The Varsity' opened to cater for the growing student population. Old favourites have begun to reappear, such as 'The Pink Parrot' in Tower Street adjacent to the Post Office main sorting office.

Manchester had its parallels. When the Buzzcocks released 'Spiral scratch' E.P. on the New Harmony label in January 1977 - all four tracks recorded and mixed in five hours, and then put in sleeves by Pete Shelley himself - they were kick-starting a Manchester music scene that was to involve and inspire such names as The Fall, Magazine, Joy Division, The Chameleons, New Order, Anthony H. Wilson, Cabaret Voltaire, O.M.D., Inspiral Carpets, The Hacienda club, James, The Smiths, Oasis, M-people and infinitely more. The Buzzcocks launched independent music and as a result spawned the whole 'indie' scene. Music became D.I.Y. and London with its A+R executives and patronising attitude found itself on the periphery, a spectator. That the Buzzcocks then went to sign up with United Artists, Factory records collapsed in 1992, and the Hacienda club is currently being demolished and replaced with flats and offices, is less important as the wheel had already been set in motion. It may ultimately have resulted in the creation of Simply Red and Sad Cafe but the movement had its roots in the Punk scene of the 80's.

That so much of the early music was about misery, poverty and hardship reflected the environment that fostered it far more eloquently than the standard fodder of Euro-pop and cover versions. The story of Coventry and Manchester music is one of getting involved rather than merely standing on the touchline.

To many outsiders the perception of Coventry as a ghost town was the most enduring image of that time. Our industrial base seemed to have been mortally wounded by the twin evils of the excessive union activity and co-incidental industrial unrest of the late 70's and the lack of investment and poor management in the 1980's. The physical dereliction of the old industrial sites brought into focus the boom of the 60's as stark contrast to the gloom of the 80's. It was an image the city had trouble displacing during the long wait until the arrival of the next piece of good publicity in 1987.

6.

When Saturday comes

IN HIS STUDY ON THE EFFECTS of football grounds upon their local residents John Bale remarks that for some people 'football provides a kind of psychic income which enhances the quality of their life'. There is nothing new in that idea of course and you don't have to spend too long looking at the faces in the crowd at Old Trafford or Anfield to witness the process. To many people football grounds have replaced churches as their chosen place of worship. Icons and religious trappings can be seen all around the stadia and the biggest clubs have been almost as successful at extracting tithes from their supporters via bond schemes and merchandising as the most materialistic evangelical TV preacher is from his flock. At least as importantly football clubs act as a focus for a town or city's collective identity.

Highfield road provides a setting for the people of Coventry to express their communal spirit and perhaps even civic pride. Terrace chants such as 'In our Coventry homes' and 'Pride of the Midlands' express this sameness and sense of belonging and it is shared even by those who don't go to watch the Sky Blues. Any reader of the Coventry Evening Telegraph would have to be a sufferer of severe selective myopia not to be aware of the activities of the local football club. Pubs in the city are full of citizens discussing how 'we' did in the league or cup and supporting the local team is perhaps the most visible expression of civic pride.

The existence of club and fan can be said to be symbiotic. The club depends on fans for its revenue (although television and marketing may have reduced the significance of the money taken at the turnstile). The fans depend on the club in all sorts of emotional and social ways. Football is classed as a form of entertainment and occasionally it fits this title. More regularly though it is anything but, yet serves its paying public with far more than mere entertainment. It forms an outlet for all the emotions that we would otherwise unhealthily bottle up. At work if I shouted 'you wanker' at my boss I would be sacked. If I spent my lunch break chanting for the removal of the firms Directors and Management staff I would be sent for psychological assessment, and then sacked. If in my social life I derided my friends and family's every mistake (what do you mean I do?) and heaped scorn at them constantly, I would soon find myself living a solitary existence. However, at the football ground the expression of such unreasonable and unchallenged observations is as normal as queuing for the toilets or a lukewarm pie at half time. So Highfield Road provides a setting for a sort of group therapy session where we pay to share our feelings with each other in their most basic and unreconstructed form. Here we are; this is our primal scream; hear my inner angst and personal rage, doctor.

However, to look at the weekly matches as purely positive well-being clinics with a real role to play in the treatment and alleviation of stress is perhaps to ignore one rather important factor. Rather than relieve my stress these visits are more often than not the cause of a large amount of it. For example, when I started writing this book the Sky Blues had just completed their thirtieth year of top level football. Yet again they had to wait until the final game of the season to secure this status. A week previously our survival had seemed impossible. To stay up we had to win our last game away at Spurs. Also Middlesbrough, Sunderland and Southampton had to fail to win their own final games. Only if all these criteria were satisfied would we stay up, and then only if Middlesbrough didn't win their appeal for the reinstatement of the three points that were deducted from them for their failure to field a team for their fixture at Blackburn earlier in the season.

Just writing this seemingly impossible escape clause has got my adrenalin pumping again and that season has been over for nearly three years. Last night I had a strange dream. I dreamt that the season had not really ended and we still had our last game to play. We had to win and were a goal ahead with only minutes left. Then in the final minutes we conceded two atrocious goals which barely trickled through the Coventry keeper's hands (It wasn't Magnus Hedman nor Steve Ogrizovic). And so we were relegated in a pathetic and farcical finale to our great three decade battle to remain a top club. The feebleness of our final minutes added fuel to my terrible disappointment. Inexplicably in my dream the City keeper is Peter Barnes. Why? I have attended lectures on dream interpretation and read many theoretical books on their meaning but the important message behind this one is beyond me. It seems just to be an extension to my waking worries, overtime for my relegation fears. So my claims that football is a cheap and effective cure for stress may be a little overstated. If nothing else it does provide an opportunity to scream obscenities at whoever you feel deserves it and, thus, it plays an important role in our modern society.

To some extent the success or failure of the club mirrors the spectators feelings of well-being and self-image. During particularly bad relegation dogfights, when there seems no chance of City staying in the top flight I too begin to feel worthless and unsuccessful. I become morose, inactive physically and mentally and a bit depressed. But during the good runs, or when we stay up against all the odds, I feel on top of the world and a huge asset to mankind. My sense of worth takes off and if it were not for the rapid onset of the next bout of Coventry City failure I would become unbearably arrogant and overconfident

And it is not just me. During our famous FA Cup run of 1987 the whole city took on a brighter countenance. Folk smiled constantly, the whole ethos of the place changed. Pensioners forgot to grumble that the new decimal coins were confusing and far worse than the old ones. People joked with their dentist and bank manager. Customer complaints departments had to lay workers off. This feel good factor had economic consequences too. Consumers spent more and we had a mini economic boom. As we progressed further in the cup, word of our success spread projecting a positive image of the city far and wide. In terms of P.R. the cup run was second only to Lady Godiva in enhancing our image. Consequently investment in the city grew and many supporters benefited either directly through the new job opportunities, or indirectly through their spinoffs.

It must also be recognised that for many people football is perceived as a nuisance and something which diminishes their quality of life. Many people have justifiable worries about their personal safety on match days. For the supporter there is always the risk of violence from opposing fans, or the danger of being crushed into inadequate terrace areas. Although this is less likely since the Taylor report, there are still plenty of smaller clubs where this still remains a possibility. A study by the Sir Norman Chester Centre for Football Research showed that over 70% of FSA (Football Supporter's Association) members expect to be crushed or feel uncomfortable at matches and felt that some grounds were dangerous to visit. The perceived threat from hooligans is also an anxiety for many supporters and local residents. As modern stadiums have become more and more concerned with safety measures based upon segregation of rival fans and the surveillance of their spectators, for many people this has merely shifted the focus for fear to outside the ground before or after the game. For some, however, the measures designed to make grounds safer have contributed to their anxiety. For many the act of paying to be confined within a cage for two hours or more has undoubtedly fuelled feelings of resentment. The tragedy at Hillsborough in 1989 was a direct result of the measures designed to protect supporters from trouble and danger.

In recent years football has moved away from these negative images. The fences are down, grounds have been improved, better facilities provided and a different audience courted. That the atmosphere at grounds has suffered is undeniable, but for many it was a reasonable price to pay for a safer environment in which to spend their leisure time.

I have lived in the shadow of three football stadiums for short periods of time. In Manchester I have sat in my backyard and listened to 'The artist at that time known as Prince' and 'Guns 'n' Roses' concerts taking place at Maine Road during the close season. In Stretford I have opened my curtains one Sunday morning to find three Celtic supporters having an early picnic of Special Brew in my front garden before Bryan Robson's testimonial. Another five were lined up singing on my wall and kick off was still several hours away. In Colchester I lived close enough to Layer road to hear the fans opening their half time bags of crisps.

All these houses were structurally very similar. A long Victorian terrace with a small backyard or rear garden and no garage or driveway parking. The houses close to Highfield Road are also very similar. In my albeit limited experience, hooliganism was never a problem. Any graffiti was done by students or locals rather than the influx of supporters on a match day, and the only real problem was that there was nowhere to park your car if

Moving the Goalposts

you came back from the shops while there was a game on. Obviously there was more litter, but this hardly kept me awake at night in a cold sweat of fear. If I had been a parent with young children I might have worried about the danger posed by the extra traffic and if I was elderly and in need of medical attention I may have worried about the difficulty of access for my health visitor or any emergency vehicles, but I was neither.

For me the greatest nuisance caused from living close to the ground was the afternoon that I had to listen to bloody 'Guns'n'Roses' rehearsing all morning and then playing the same set again in the evening. In the end I had to go into town because the strain became too much for me and I found myself singing along to songs I didn't want to learn. I left the house and waited for public transport to whisk me away. And were there any buses? Were there buggery, they had all been diverted.

7.

In Exile

IN 1982 I WAS FORCED OUT of my closeted environment as I had reached the age where I had to either go out and get a job or seek further education. I chose the latter and after a minimal amount of research decided that I would spend the next three years of my life in Manchester studying Economics. I had a vague idea that this might lead to some well paid job in 'The City', wherever that was. I had visited Manchester on one of the University open days and it looked a decent enough place with plenty of attractions. Word of its fantastic clubs and its reputation for hospitality had even filtered down as low as this anoraked and spotty schoolboy.

I have to admit I loved Manchester as soon as I got off the train at Piccadilly station. It was incredibly busy and I wandered through the town centre in an apprehensive daze. The buildings were tall and imposing, the people loud, and the shops different. Nowadays when every town centre contains exactly the same shops selling exactly the same goods it is hard to remember how exciting it could be to go and look at the different stuff on sale elsewhere. I was amazed that my dietary staple of Walkers crisps were unheard of up there, yet they had Vimto for sale as a cordial. What a crazy mixed up world this was. There were also a large variety of cheap and cheerful shops where even a financially challenged consumer like myself was spoilt for choice. Best of all was the labyrinth known locally as the Arndale Centre, in which it was easy to get lost but where the persistent explorer could buy a week's supply of dodgy mince, choc ices and burgers for a couple of quid. There was no danger of me starving up here. I had a quick look around the Economics Department and took part in a nominal interview and then there was just time for another look around the town from the top of a bus before I had to board my day return trip home. As I gazed at a foreign landscape from the comparative luxury of a Second Class British Rail carriage passing mysterious towns like Stockport, Macclesfield and Crewe, I knew that if I really had to leave Coventry, then Manchester was where I wanted to go. With hindsight I can't help thinking that my view was slightly rose-tinted because I had been to Reading the day before, and after Reading even Keele service station looks architecturally and socially exciting.

A quick flick through the University prospectus resulted in my selection of some accommodation in digs as close as possible to where I would be studying and having finished the last of my exams with a resigned whimper rather than a flourish I disappeared off to Guernsey with a group of friends to spend the Summer picking roses with the aim of earning a bit of extra cash.

Guernsey is a roughly triangular shaped island, six miles wide and six miles long, situated just thirty miles off the French coast of Normandy and about one hundred miles south of the Dorset coast. Despite this geography it is a British Dependency and has been so since William, Duke of Normandy, became William the Conqueror of England in 1066. Despite numerous arguments with the French since then the Channel Islands have remained loyal to the British Crown even after Normandy was returned to France in 1205. Though loyal to the Crown the islands 60,000 inhabitants form a self-governing community. The islands' distinctive history is reflected in the unique character of its people.

The island's current prosperity is largely based upon finance, with tourism and horticulture also employing a significant proportion of the local population. Given the large number of people who live on such a small island she has always had to seek other ways of feeding her inhabitants. Privateering and smuggling in the Eighteenth century established the island's reputation as an off-shore financial haven. One that many Chairman of Coventry City have since sought refuge in.

Arriving by air in Guernsey gives an immediate impression of the physical importance of horticulture. Flying over the island is the best way to appreciate the vast expanse of commercial greenhouses that cover about three and a half percent of the island's surface, some five hundred acres in total.

34

Moving the Goalposts

Glasshouses have been on the island for over two hundred years. Originally little more than hothouses for the recreational cultivation of delicate flowers by delicate horticulturists, the heated greenhouse soon became an important feature of the local economy. Grapes were the first major crop grown for export and dominated until after the Second World War when tomatoes became more important. Tomatoes initially struggled to find a market and were treated with some suspicion by locals who refused to purchase a fruit that many believed to be poisonous. After tomatoes were cleverly remarketed as 'Love Apples' they grew in popularity and became a fashion accessory with tomato plants covering well over one thousand acres by 1950. Like all trends it came to an end and the crops profitability declined until, by the 1990's, flowers were the most important horticultural crop.

Picking roses on the 'Island of Flowers' sounded quite an attractive prospect. One of my A levels had been English Literature and I fear it may have left me with poetic pretensions. I was in for an early and rude awakening.

Very early, in fact, as rose beds are not designed for those intending a lie in. During the summer roses need cutting early in the morning before the sun causes the head of the flower to open too much. This necessitated a 5:00 a.m. start for those of us expected to harvest our crop at its peak. After picking they had to be graded, sized, bunched, chilled, boxed and sent for distribution on the English mainland. Then the greenhouses needed weeding, the bushes disbudding, the equipment cleaned and then it would be time for the afternoon pick. Like most things in nature, roses seemed to work on a monthly cycle. At their most productive growth periods the work and overtime could see us still packing the bloody things at 10:00 p.m. My friends and I soon discovered the harsh realities of rose vineries. Far from being a summer of fresh air and healthy outdoors we discovered that roses grow in greenhouses, that their thorns will remove a nipple if given half a chance and that the scars they cut into you last a whole year.

The traditional Guernsey greenhouse is an old wooden frame-built glasshouse whose design was said to have derived from the skills already possessed by the island's shipwrights and carpenters who turned from ships to glasshouses when shipbuilding went into decline at the end of the nineteenth century. These old structures were as solid as a galleon and, despite being over sixty years old many are still standing. The larger, more modern, glasshouses are made of aluminium with a steel frame. Their design allowed for greater expanses of glass which encourages even faster ripening and blooming. Guernsey regularly records the British Isles record sunshine total which is why flowers do so well. It also explains the island's popularity as a tourist venue. Unfortunately these long hours of blazing sun are less welcome if you are spending the whole day working in a greenhouse.

Needless to say we all had a great time. Saturday afternoons were a half day off and to make the most of our free time we bought a car to see a bit of the Island. This sounds a rather grand gesture but at the time Guernsey had no equivalent of the M.O.T. and our little Hillman Imp only cost us a fiver each. Obviously we weren't the first owners and there were one or two little problems. Namely that the bonnet would fly off if a velocity of twenty miles an hour was achieved and that the radiator needed refilling with water every two miles. These were mere teething troubles and while they did cause some hair-raising moments that was all part of the fun.

Two notable incidents spring to mind. The first arose because of the radiator problem, which would sometimes cause the car to cut out and it would take ages to restart. This happened once as I was driving. I had taken a bit of a gamble by pulling out across the lanes of a T-junction. There were cars approaching but I had estimated that we would get across without any problems. Unfortunately the car cut out just as it straddled both lanes in front of the oncoming traffic. I would like to brag that I managed to start it up and drive on, or that I pushed us all out of danger. To my shame I did neither. With three passengers in the car I adopted discretion as the greatest form of valour and I got out of the only working door, leaving the others screaming in the car.

Fortunately, the oncoming cars slowed down in time and one of the passengers got the car started, but I never thought of a reasonable excuse to explain to them why I bailed out. I have now. I was going for help. A pretty good excuse but a little late to retain any credibility.

In time my little misdemeanor, call it cowardice and treachery if you will, was forgotten partly due to our second incident. We were driving along through the tranquil green lanes of the island when suddenly the bonnet took off, flipped over the Hillman and over a cyclist who was travelling in our slipstream before landing behind him. We did what any responsible driver would do and immediately sellotaped the bonnet back on. Fortunately the cyclist was too shocked to complain. After Guernsey it was a full ten years before I ever bought another car. And when I did I made sure it was one assembled in Coventry. These other carmakers were clearly a bunch of cowboys.

It was shocking how much the prices had risen in that time.

In Guernsey I met for the first time a lot of people who were dissimilar to me. Everyone I had previously had close contact with had had broadly the same background and experiences as me, so I found this close knit community fascinating; with their deep mistrust of anyone from a neighbouring parish, yet warm welcome for strangers from off the island. The people we worked with were all characters worthy of their own novel. They were kind and good-humoured but most of all they were different. Eric was the most different with his bizarre patois language which took us the whole summer to understand. He had fallen out with his wife fifteen years previously about something incredibly trivial such as whose turn it was to make a cup of tea and they had never spoken to each other since. They still lived together, worked together, ate together and even slept in the same bed, they just never spoke to each other.

Bill was a fifty year old man whose greatest pleasure in life was his kettle. It was perfect because after he filled it and turned it on it gave him just enough time to go for a shit before it boiled. This was science at its best for Bill. We had a series of interesting discussions which usually ended with Bill's admission that he had never done it or been there himself, but that he knew a bloke who had. He told me that the world was over ten thousand years old. When I said that I'd read it was supposed to be forty-six thousand million years old, he looked quizzically at me and said that it was nowhere near as old as that but that he was prepared to raise his estimate to twenty thousand years. Bill was also fascinated by the Bible, in which he had discovered an important mistake. He refused to believe that Mary was a virgin because it just wasn't possible. His argument hinged upon the key idea that if she had been a virgin she couldn't have had Jesus. This was the fatal flaw in the Bible. Theology made simple. Bill, like Eric had never been off the Island, not even on the annual staff trip to the neighbouring island of Herm on a booze-cruise, but he knew someone that had been. His real claim to fame was that he had met Oliver Reed. In fact Oliver Reed had gatecrashed his daughter's wedding, taken one look at the bride and collapsed at her feet. Then he had got up and collapsed at her feet again. Finally, after a third collapse Ollie spoke to the bride saying 'When I fall in love, I really fall.' Most people I met in Guernsey had Oliver Reed stories and I was a bit disappointed not to have met him before we left. Particularly as I was to spend the next three years trying to emulate the wilder aspects of his anti-social behaviour.

Jim was the youngest of the full timers at the vinery. He had been off the island to do a horticultural management course and was scathing of all things academic. He had dropped out in his first term due to dissatisfaction with the course tutors. His ten years' practical experience in greenhouses had already taught him the folly of much of the theory being preached by those leading the course. We didn't quite know how to take him. If our textbooks had told us that the sun was cold we would have held it up as a universal truth. We weren't going to university to think for ourselves - that was what the lecturers were paid for.

In Guernsey we found people wiser and more affectionate towards us than we had any right to expect. It gave us a false series of expectations about what real work, when it finally reared its ugly head, would be like. The summer invaders who descended with their patronising views and then proceeded to take work that would have earned the locals huge sums in overtime were made to feel as welcome as family. They took us into their homes, took us to see their island and even nursed us and covered for us when virus or victuals made us too sick to work. Like most urban visitors to rural idylls, we took all we needed and then went home with all we could carry.

As luck would have it the Sky Blues first fixture of the 1982/3 season was against Southampton who were sort of the local team for the Channel Isles. To be honest nearly all the islanders I spoke to were Manchester United supporters, which shouldn't have come as too much of a surprise, but we didn't let that detract us from building the game into a sort of Coventry versus Guernsey grudge match. Sadly the game was at home in Coventry which prevented us sending a representative by ferry to the match. We didn't let this small matter detract from our gloating when Steve Whitton scored the only goal of the game for a Coventry victory. Our metropolitan superiority had been reinforced and we weren't going to let a little thing like not abusing our hosts' kind hospitality spoil our celebrations.

The couple of months I spent in Guernsey was the first time I had been away from home for more than a fortnight's holiday and there were times when I grew desperately home sick. At such times I would wander down to the nearby coast of St. Saviours and stare at the vast expanse of sea and crashing waves. Even on such walks it was impossible to get away from flowers. The cliffs were covered with Primroses and Ox-eye Daisies, Gold Samphire, Yellow Gorse and Yellow Horned Poppies. The meandering lanes are edged with Broom, Violets, Pink Campion and Sheep's Bit. It was an undeniably beautiful spot.

On the cliff top there was an old watch tower, a relict from the German occupation of 1940. It was an impressive structure of three or four stories height, though only the ground floor was accessible to all but the nimblest of climbers. This lower level was clearly well used by young couples. Either that or it was the site of an emergent rubber recycling business.

Despite this evidence of recent visits I rarely saw another soul as I sat contemplating my own misery and feelings of dislocation from home. Once I did spot a family group in the distance coming my way. They were mere specks on the horizon but I could make out that there were four of them and that they had a dog. As they got closer I could see that they were a family with two children and a Labrador. In fact they looked just like my own family. Then I realised it was my own family and I was so elated I could have cried. Then I wondered how they got to Guernsey, and how they had found me. I hadn't told anyone back at the rose vinery that I was coming to this isolated spot. It wasn't possible was it? And I realised I had imagined the whole thing and I was miles from my home on an island near France and all I wanted to do was go home and stay there forever.

8.

Manchester, North of England

ALMOST AS SOON AS WE FINISHED working in Guernsey it was time for my friends and I to split up and head off to different parts of the country. I had decided not to study economics after all and plumped for a geography course at Manchester instead. I was partly swayed by the staggering coastal scenery in Guernsey and the realisation that geography books have more colourful pictures and photographs in them than the rather dull looking economics text books. After all if I was going to spend three years reading academic journals I might as well choose nicely illustrated ones.

Manchester is analogous to Coventry in that it too has had a turbulent past and Coventry's post-war socialist history is in many ways a result of Manchester's social history. The factory system, the rise of the trade unions and the development of Chartism, three modern developments which have shaped Coventry's social and economic face, all originated in Manchester.

Most people are aware that Manchester owes its growth to 'King Cotton' and the city still displays its mills with pride. Many have found more contemporary uses and a satisfyingly large proportion of them are now in some way linked to the world of leisure as clubs, bars or restaurants. The internationally renown gay-village has grown up along the mills of Canal Street. While the Factory records spawned Hacienda club was born into the shell of an old textile warehouse.

As Manchester grew it acquired a status as the emblem for all things new. This was partly because of its unprecedented urban growth and partly because of the spread of goods from 'Cottonopolis'. What was also significant in the city's growing status was the way it increasingly embodied the new social order and released upon an unsuspecting gentry the unwanted forces of working class activism.

Manchester's symbolic role as the core of the Industrial revolution and the heart of the factory system strengthened its position as the voice of the provinces against the dominance of London. The city was the home of the Anti-Corn Law League and grew as a centre for middle class radicalism. However, although Manchester became host to those wishing to bring about social reform and the empowerment of the masses, it did not always do so willingly. It is interesting to note that in 1792 a group of one hundred and eighty six publicans signed a declaration banning radical societies from meeting on their premises. A common sign in pubs at the time read 'No Jacobites admitted here.' In 1817 there was the 'Ardwick Plot' to make a 'Moscow out of Manchester' by setting the city ablaze to signal a local revolt . The final act of public protest resulted in the Peterloo massacre of 1819 when a series of different groups calling for power to be controlled by the people through universal suffrage met on St. Peter's Field. Magistrates called in troops to clear the meeting and the resultant chaos killed at least eleven people and injured more than six hundred. Manchester then passed on the mantle of political radicalism to other champions, but the city still prides itself as a spokesperson for that part of England north of Watford and, like Coventrians, it has little time for any claims from Birmingham for that position. Whereas Birmingham has until recently taken the route of dull mundanity, producing such cultural icons as the Bullring shopping centre and the spaghetti junction, Manchester has always aimed slightly higher and its city centre, its night life and its reputation for precociousness are features about which it is justifiably proud.

That isn't to say Manchester isn't without its problems. When I first arrived in the city it was still smouldering from the civil unrest of the early 1980's.The areas at the heart of the protest were those suffering mass unemployment, such as Moss Side and Hulme. In 1986 Moss Side and Hulme had unemployment rates of 44% and 59%. In 1986 youth unemployment in Hulme was officially 68%. Resentment was rife and Moss Side had gained the reputation for lawlessness that it would keep for the next decade, while its nearest neighbouring district of Hulme seemed to visibly decay before your very eyes. The modern housing development of Hulme was acknowledged to be the worst of its kind in Western Europe. The huge six-storey deck access crescents were factory-built and fraught with structural and design faults. To save cash they had been built on top of the cellars of the Victorian terrace slums they replaced, leaving the perfect breeding ground for rats and other vermin. They soon became damp, cockroach infested, asbestos walled hell holes. At the time the local Baptist minister, the Reverend Alec Balfe-Mitchel, described his parish with these words. 'It's a brutal architecture, a brutal way of housing people'.

In July 1981 the people of Hulme and Moss Side registered their protest in the most striking way. Hulme, where Henry Royce (co-founder of Rolls-Royce) built his first motor car in 1903, hit the headlines with pictures of burning vehicles and mob rioting. Perhaps the most arresting image was of the icecream vans and hot-dog vendors serving the Moss Side protestors.

I first saw Hulme about a week after I arrived in Manchester and was frightened by it. Staring at the infamous flats, mocking caricatures of the Georgian crescents in Bath, I could see burnt out windows and dereliction on each of the unpoliceable levels. Children were stripping a car abandoned at the entrance of one of the gangways. The walls had an impressive gallery of graffiti that made the Berlin wall look like a 'Vision On' display. The higher levels could only have been done by a team of creative abseilers. It appeared that the many coats of aerosol paint were the only thing preventing the walls from crumbling. On a later visit I went to buy a record that was being produced locally for the Cherry Red label and sold from the singer's flat in one of the crescents. The song was called 'It's a fine day' and I had to presume the singer 'Jane' had sought inspiration elsewhere. The stink of piss was overwhelming and the sense of personal security zero. I never found the flat despite wandering through the maze of crescents for most of the morning. God alone knows how the post office staff operated but clearly the area was still within the reach of the rest of the civilised world as my postal request for a copy of the record managed to find its way through to the flat.

As a geography student my course started with a week in the Lake District learning how to survey and map landscapes, a skill I have never had to use in my normal day to day activities. Most of the students were very keen to make a good start and there was much feverish clamouring for first use of the theodolites and surveying equipment. This gave me plenty of time to pursue my own interests which at the time were little more than eyeing up the girls and finding somewhere to go for a drink in the evening. Fortunately I almost immediately stumbled upon someone with very similar goals in life. He was a Stoke City fan called Graeme and our mutual admiration for beer, curries, girls and our local football teams (although not necessarily in that order) managed to get us through those difficult early days and in fact the whole three years.

As luck would have it, it turned out that he had also been accommodated in the same flat as me. Small world. I also came across another Sky Blues supporter from Leamington who suggested that we go to the games together. Small, small world. Too small, in fact, as unfortunately he was the Geography department bore and I had to spend most of my time avoiding him. His intervention did help me to cultivate the art of being able to conjure up an excuse for not doing something at only a second's notice. This was possibly the most useful and frequently used skill that I learnt at University.

During only my second week in Manchester the Sky Blues had a match against Manchester City at Maine road, which was a mere five minute walk from the flat I was staying in. I couldn't persuade Graeme to accompany me and there was no way I was going to go with Mr. Boring so I went to a match on my own for the first time. I felt a bit of a fraud joining the City supporters after their trek up the M6. After all I had been in bed until almost 2.00 p.m. City unfortunately lost by the odd goal in five. The first of many disappointments I was to endure at Manchester grounds in the next few years

After the match the police decided that I represented a bit of a threat to local residents and refused to let me loose in Manchester despite my pleas for freedom, so I was marched back to Piccadilly Station with the other Sky Blues supporters. Just when I thought I was going to have to take an impromptu voyage home the escort evaporated and I slunk off, feeling a bit of an infiltrator. As the real Coventry fans went back to the Three Spires of home I was left with strange and mixed feelings, a bit like a refugee or displaced person. An illegal immigrant deserted by his brothers. It is a feeling that has nagged away at me ever since.

When I left home in 1982 little did I know that I would never return as a permanent resident. My base since has always been some other foreign town. But this absence has to a great extent nurtured my sense of being a Coventrian, albeit one in voluntary exile. It would have been very easy for me to shift my allegiances to some nearer club. Manchester United would have been a cheaper and far more successful club to pin my loyalty upon. I have now lived in Manchester as long as I lived in Coventry and could perhaps justifiably claim that the Reds were my team. The prospect of this, however, appalls me. I am from Coventry and this is a source of great, if perhaps misguided, pride to me. My isolation from home has made me more hungry for indirect contact with the city and Coventry City F.C. was the most obvious vehicle for that contact.

Many of my friends in Manchester did slowly switch their allegiances from Luton, Spurs or even Liverpool to one of the Manchester teams. For me though absence made the heart grow fonder.

People have tried to compare football and popular music, often claiming that it was the Rock'n'Roll of the 1990's. Some players have even tried to combine the two. Alexi Lallas of the U.S.A. World Cup team looked like a rock-star (albeit Catweasel from the early 70's) and played in a rock band. Unfortunately he was apparently no better at music than he was at 'Soccer'. Sky Blues Old Boy Stuart 'Psycho' Pearce is renown for his love of Punk and plays the Sex Pistols before matches, Presumably 'No Fun' and 'Bodies' are his favourites. Evergreen (and that probably means mouldy) Pat Nevin has written regularly for the serious music press. I don't believe that football is anything like music appreciation. We tend to alter our music tastes as we age, otherwise I would still be listening to The Wombles L.P.s and dancing along to Boney M. With football supporting usually once you have started the habit you are hooked for life. Otherwise we would all be Manchester United fans now, we would have been Liverpool fans in the 80's and 70's and supporters of Tottenham and Ipswich in my early youth.

Loyalty in football is a very complicated matter. People may pick a team for a huge variety of reasons but I would guess that it is mainly because of either geographical proximity, current success, or some family history of support running back many generations. I support the Sky Blues because this is where I was born and bred. But I do also keep one eye on the Luton result because I've a mate who lives there, and a peek at Stoke as its my wife's home town, and at Colchester United as I worked there for three years. With football when you are born with a team or adopt a team you stick with it. There can be no updating and reassessing. You can never change. While players, managers and even directors may come and go, such fickleness rarely extends to the terraces. The paid servants are mere mercenaries, the fans are the true continuity of the club.

9.

Home from Home

WHEN I DECAMPED IN MANCHESTER I found myself sharing a flat with seven other students from the four corners of England. Mark was from Bedford and supported Luton and was studying Aeronautical engineering. He was standing in the doorway as I arrived wearing a sweatshirt bearing the logo 'Bullshit'. Clearly he was some sort of intellectual.

Next to appear on the landing was Trevor from Birmingham who turned out to be a supporter of the hated Villa. His course was law so I decided to watch my step with him as my father had always warned me about lawyers and Villa fans. Tom was the oldest, having already dropped out of a degree course in Medicine. He was from Beverly, which turned out to be near Hull, and he supported Leeds. His current course was in mechanical engineering. After a year he dropped engineering for a go at information technology. Needless to say he never finished this and the last I heard of him he was making a fortune in the U.S.A. as a computer programmer.

There was another geographer in the flat. Graeme and I had already met on our field trip, a sort of pre-season friendly for geography undergraduates. His presence meant that we could operate a job-share scheme to increase our leisure time and pool our resources. What it really meant was that we both almost got kicked off the course for doing far less than the absolute minimum requirement out of fear that the other might think we were a pathetic swot, desperate to come top. There was also a medic in the flat. Adam was an Arsenal supporter from Baker Street, home of Sherlock Holmes and that crap Jerry Rafferty song. He had the largest collection of pornographic material I have ever seen. Curiously he also had a girlfriend with unfeasibly large breasts, so it came as no surprise to any of us that this was the area of medical study he chose to specialise in. Many years later we all met up for a reunion in London. Eddie Izzard was hosting a comedy show in the Raymond Review bar in Soho and we decided to spend the evening in his capable hands. On the way Adam insisted on stopping at a few peep shows to look at some new breasts. What a thorough professional, always on duty.

Adam was a medic of a different breed to Dr. Kildaire. His family background was all medical and he rather saw following in the family footsteps as an inevitability. His compassion was nonexistent and his knowledge of the human body extremely patchy if the subject strayed away from mammary glands. Whenever I have taken any exams I have always adopted the same procedure. First of all I get my hands on as many past papers as possible. Then work out which questions recur with greatest frequency and revise just those topics. It has always worked for me. However I was horrified to discover that medics follow exactly the same procedure for their exams. This conjured up horrific images of turning up at an accident and emergency department with severe chest pains only to find the Doctor on duty had never bothered to learn about the heart as questions on feet were far more common. My friendship with this trainee doctor had such an impact that I have rarely visited my own G.P. since.

There were two other flat mates. An Ulster man from Northern Ireland and a Geordie from Newcastle. Both had totally incomprehensible accents and the rest of us spent our first few weeks trying to work out who they were, where they were from and what they were at Manchester for. Geordie's lilt was so strong we thought he lived in 'the Castle' which impressed us no end and gave the image that we had Geordie monarchy living with us. You can imagine how short changed we felt when we learnt he was actually from Byker Grove. The Ulstereman's accent worsened when he had had a few drinks and consequently he was totally incoherent for most of the day. It was his suggestion that we should get to know each other by sharing a few bottles of scrumpy before the pubs opened and it worked so well we spent the next three years repeating the procedure. It eventually turned out that the Ulsterman was studying computer science while the Geordie was a physicist.

So here were eight naive young lads away from home and all parental influence for the first time. You can imagine what a mess we lived in. The bathroom was so matted in hair a visitor might reasonably think that they had miraculously stumbled upon the nest of a yeti. The kitchen looked like a penicillin factory, while the communal lounge was a sea of cider bottles, lager cans, chip wrappers, stolen road signs and street furniture. It operated much like the Bermuda triangle in which things would disappear for months at a time. On the last day of the year after everyone else had buggered off home and I was left to tidy up I made discovery after discovery in the lounge. It was a bit like an archeological dig as layer after layer of accumulated sediment was painstakingly removed. The first revelation, after I had cleared about twenty bin liners full of detritus from the floor, was that we had a carpet. Such was my shock I immediately ran off to the phone to ring my A.W.O.L. flat mates to share this news. Such was Mark's disbelief he insisted that I take a photograph of it to substantiate my outrageous claim. Sadly it never came out, just like the vomit stain I found under the ironing board; that I found under a sign for the local Hospital; which I found under a huge collection of free newspapers in one of the corners of the lounge.

Much as these communal rooms were untidy it provided scarce preparation for the scenes of apocalyptic destruction which lay behind my bedroom door. There was mess everywhere. It was so bad that I couldn't leave my window open in case any passer-by mistook my room for the local tip and dumped all their domestic refuse through it. Once, as a witty student prank, the others broke into my room and left behind three bin liners full of all our kitchen waste. The scoundrels. When I hadn't noticed this present of rotting garbage after two days they admitted what they had done and offered to help me search through the wreckage to retrieve it.

During this first year (1982-3) I saw a wide variety of football games in Manchester and on my occasional visits home I got to see the Sky Blues, the highlight being a win over Stoke by a Mark Hately brace on the weekend of my Birthday. That gave me something to crow about after the Christmas break, as Graeme had kept telling me what a great team Stoke had and that Mark Chamberlain was the next Stanley Matthews. When I saw him he played with the pace of the current one.

The return match at Stoke saw our only win in our last fourteen games that season and was enough to just keep us up. As the Sky Blues had lost ten and drawn two of their previous twelve games Graeme felt quite confident of exacting his revenge on that penultimate weekend of the season. It was my first visit to Stoke and though I have made many visits since it is the one that sticks in my memory. The whole day was perfect; our poor run of previous form which had left me pessimistic for any success; the train down from Manchester after a few drinks at a pub near the station; a pint of Springfield bitter and a pie at the ground - the same bitter my local pub, The Burnt Post in Coventry, served. Surely an omen. And finally a great result which secured us another season in the old First Division. If only all Saturdays could be this fulfilling.

This satisfying win left me free on the final Saturday of the season to watch one of the Manchester teams. In those days City and United were both in the top flight and played on alternate weekends at home. Both were easy to get in. You just poured out of a nearby pub, paid your four quid at the turnstile and in you went. No queues, membership cards, season tickets or mortgage needed. The final Saturday had City at home to my friend Mark's beloved Luton Town. Manchester City or Luton would be relegated depending on the result. City only needed a draw, Luton had to win. My girlfriend at the time was a season ticket holding Manchester City fan and had been all her life. In those days that made her a bit of a rarity, I think her dad had probably wanted a boy. My closest friend was a Luton fan. Did this present divided loyalties? Did it bollocks! And off we went to join the huge crush of Luton fans packed into one tiny section of the Kippax.

A rather dour game ensued and I was beginning to think I would have been better advised to have invested my four pounds in the pub when David Pleat made one of his greatest ever decisions, he put Raddy Antic on with only seventeen minutes to go. The rest as they say is history. Raddy scored, the Luton end went berserk and their celebrations were like nothing I had ever seen, only eclipsed by Pleat's own pitch invasion at the final whistle. Raddy built on this solitary playing success and went on to become a very successful manager, notably with Athletico Madrid, so there is hope for us all.

For our safety and convenience we were kept in after the game and when we were finally allowed outside the ground I saw a Manchester City fan burn his shirt among the many season tickets tossed on the floor. The abject misery and loss of hope on the faces of the Mancunians in the streets around Maine Road has stayed with me and comes back to haunt me during the latter stages of those many seasons since then in which we too have seen ourselves involved in last day relegation battles. Fortunately, though we have regularly stared over the edge of the precipice into the horror that is lower division football, so far we have never tumbled.

As soon as we got back to our digs, Mark and I went straight round my girlfriend's to gloat in such an ugly manner that it just about ended that relationship. Come to think of it all my relationships have ended during the close season, perhaps there is some deep psychological reason for this. Maybe only after a season ends can I make decisions about other parts of my life. Or perhaps that is just a load of pretentious, Hornbyesque crap.

10.

On the field

MY DISLOCATION TO THIS NORTHERN TOWN also resulted in a change in my relationship with the game of football. As I increasingly used the game to reinforce the ties with my distant family and home I began to take an active role. For the first time I started to play football and I was staggered at my lack of ability.

I was relatively fit for a student and still regularly ran and went training although this appeared to have no reducing effect on what was becoming an admirable beer gut. My years of enforced participation at Rugby had strengthened my puny physique slightly and had encouraged my hand/eye coordination. As a rugby player I had had some success rising from the level of complete uncoordinated dosser to the heady heights of Third team captain (there was no Fourth team). At University I also took up mixed Hockey without revealing myself to be completely feeble and managed to score a couple of goals in what appeared to be unfeasibly small nets defended by a Sumo wrestler covered in cricket pads. I feel there is an important message lurking here somewhere along the lines that with a little perseverance and effort it is possible to find teams of people even crapper at sport than yourself. This sporting history of occasional minuscule success made my complete abject crapness at the game I loved harder to take.

My flat mates and I played five-a-side football most nights with no noticeable improvement in any of our abilities. In fact Ulster man seemed to be getting worse with every bottle of cider. For the eleven aside game I attended trial after trial with the inevitable 'Don't call us, we'll call you.' conclusion. Finally I got my big break. The Geography society team was a player short and as their captain was my flat mate Graeme, and as he didn't have any other geographer's telephone number, I was in. It meant letting the mixed Hockey team down but, hey, you have to seize your chances. Graeme told me I was to forego any sexual activity the night before the game even though he knew I had no hope of getting any even if I had trawled the city's bus terminal in seek of those ladies who sell such favours to desperate students.

We got changed. I was handed a different shirt to everyone else and it dawned on me I was going to have to play in goal. Graeme's final advice before kick off was to do my best which summed up just what low expectations he had. During the first few minutes I had little to do. I had a couple of goalkicks which I just about managed to get out of the goal area, and I soon became quite bored. When I used to watch Les Sealey, Jim Blyth, Raddy Avramovich, Steve Ogrizovic and Magnus Hedman in goal for the Sky Blues they were all constantly active, even if the ball didn't come into their half for twenty or thirty minutes. Les Sealey would keep his mind and body active by screaming foul obscenities at his defenders, shattering their confidence and causing the mum's of our younger players to write to the manager to request an immediate transfer. Jim Blyth was big on stretches. All match he would pull himself this way and that. I used to think he was either arthritic or desperate to grow more. I vaguely remember that one game he was stretching during the pre-match kick in and strained his back resulting in his substitution before kick off (this might have been Oggy but I always picture it as big Jim). God alone can imagine what went through Raddy Avramovic's mind during a game but according to Bobby Gould it probably wasn't football. Gould pilloried Raddy after a disastrous performance in a 3-2 home defeat by Stoke and he vowed that Raddy would never again play for the Sky Blues. Raddy took the hint and obviously sensed that the grass was greener on the other side of the advertising hoardings and went back to Croatia to become a coach. Oggy always took his guardianship of the Coventry goal very seriously. He, too, was a stretcher, but also spent a fair bit of his Saturday (or Sunday or Monday, cheers Sky TV) jogging for a few moments or making strange markings on the pitch with his studs, possibly in the hope of attracting a sponsor. I reckon for a few hundred pounds Oggy would have been happy to carve the McDonald's golden arches big 'M' logo in the six yard box. For a thousand he would probably have carved 'Pepsi - the choice for a new generation'. In contrast Magnus Hedman adopts the cool composure of a professional who has no doubts about his own ability and the peace of mind that comes from having a stunning pop star wife waiting at home. He exudes confidence and, by clapping and chatting to his back four, passes on this confidence through the team.

However as I stood between the posts I did nothing. I hardly even drew breath and could easily have been mistaken for a scarecrow. During one corner kick I did jump up and I very nearly sprung into action when the opposition were awarded a penalty. Unfortunately I was still deciding which way to dive when the rest of my team were kicking off for the restart. To my credit I didn't let them blame me for the team's defeat. With a single mindedness that would have drawn an appreciative nod from Les Sealey I told Graeme 'The defence are fucking crap, you want to get them out training.' I comforted myself with the reassurance that I was really an outfield player.

Meanwhile back in Coventry as the 1982/83 season drew to its close, big changes were afoot. Dave Sexton's two year reign as manager was coming to an end and most of the City team were at the end of their contracts. The team list was a mixture of battlers destined for the lower leagues, players who were to flourish elsewhere and the rare gem who shone at Highfield Road.

Players like Brian (Harry) Roberts and Gerry Daly would find themselves relegated at the beginning of the following season, Daly to Leicester and Roberts to Birmingham. Other names, such as Hortmanshuk and Jacobs, seemed to disappear altogether.

For Garry Gillespie, Danny Thomas and Mark Hately, their departure coincided with their greatest fame. The never popular Hately, on the verge of the full England squad, had made no secret of his desire to leave us. Pompey of the Second Division offered an insulting £50,000 and he was away for a tribunal fixed fee of £190,000. Within a year he had won the first of over thirty England caps and had scored against Brazil in the Maracana. His returns to Coventry have never been particularly warmly feted. In contrast Gary Gillespie's departure was seen as a fitting reward for a player who had tried his best in an indifferent team. Few fans begrudged him his opportunity of a little glory at Anfield and this soon arrived in the shape of three League Championship medals and a European Cup runners-up medal. Danny Thomas was also determined to leave at the end of the season. After Dave Sexton's dismissal Thomas won two England caps in the tour of Australia and completed a transfer to Spurs. Sadly, a serious knee injury sustained after a bad tackle prematurely ended the promising career of the twice-voted City player of the year.

Other than the gifted Danny Thomas, the other real player of outstanding ability in the team at the time was Steve Hunt. Hunt was signed from the New York Cosmos where he played alongside Pele and Beckenbauer and was voted the NASL's most valuable player. How he managed to readjust to playing alongside Coop 'the scoop' and Don Nardiello is a testament to his professionalism. He was one of City's most gifted midfielders and was on the fringes of the England squad for many seasons. Naturally his only cap came after he had departed from us and moved down to West Bromwich Albion where he suffered the indignity of swift relegation. The following year he was relegated again, this time with Aston Villa, which kind of makes you think he was still really working for us as an undercover agent.

So in season 1983/4 Coventry City had a new manager, Bobby Gould. Bobby's playing career at Highfield road had been characterised by a combative spirit that more than made up for any shortcomings in his ability. The team he inherited from Sexton was in a mess with eight first-teamers out of contract and with no interest in re-signing. In their place Gould assembled a squad of players much in his own mould. He bought twenty five players in eighteen months, a rate which makes even Ron Atkinson seem thrifty. The big difference was that Gould's team was made up of players that nobody else wanted. The majority of them came from the lower divisions and by December this team assembled on a shoestring budget were fourth in the league.

Many of Gould's players (Peake, Pearce, Gibson, Gynn, Bennett, Adams, Ogrizovic, Kilcline and Regis) went on to have successful careers in the top league. What was more surprising was that for most of them that success was achieved while still playing in the Sky Blue of Coventry City.

Sadly, despite their excellent start, the Sky Blues faltered and once again we had to win our final game to stay up. Coventry only escaped because, in that final game against Norwich, a Robert Rosario header struck the inside of the City goal and came out again. That is how slim the margin of success and failure can be. The following season also began badly and Gould was sacked, leaving behind a squad of players that eventually went on to win the FA Cup. Gould himself had to wait an extra year, leading Wimbledon to the cup the season after Brian Kilcline had raised it for the Sky Blues.

11.

Final year

ALMOST AS SUDDENLY AS MY STAY in Manchester had begun it seemed to be ending. Already I was into my final year and my prospects for extending the delaying tactics I had used so far to postpone the need for me to find gainful employment were, unlike my steadily developing beer gut, slim. As if to soften the blow the University had a whole careers department whose task it was to push unwilling graduates into the job market. Each final year student was invited to an interview with the career guides and an extensive questionnaire was completed regarding your interests and qualifications. This material was then fed into an impressively large computer which could suggest the most suitable career path, individually tailored for each student. All my friends took their turn with this procedure and we were all duly sent the computer's verdict. Without exception the computer always came up with the same conclusion. A degree in geography and interest in economics? Then your ideal job is accountancy. A degree in chemical engineering and a love of dogs? Your ideal job is accountancy. History of Art and an active interest in Mediaeval churches? Accountancy is for you my lad. Medicine and numerical dyslexia - accountancy. Maths, further maths and a hobby of trainspotting - have you considered puppeteering?

A number of us weren't entirely convinced by the computer's verdict and went to seek some careers advice face to face. The ensuing discussions were fruitless and my questions remained unanswered. Why can't I be a pop star? Whose job is it to check for tan lines on the Baywatch babes? What further qualifications could I possibly need to read the Weather on TV? In the end I did the same as everyone else. I filled out a standard application form, got my dad to type me a curriculum vitae and sent it out to all the banks, manufacturers and retailers in the Directory of Employers. After the first dozen rejections I began to rethink my strategy. In the box asking you to state preferred location I replaced my first answer 'anywhere warm' with 'no real preference'. I also widened my target area and eventually got an excellent letter from Cambridge United F.C. explaining that they did not wish to interview me for the vacant position of team manager to add to my growing collection. As these rejections continued to arrive I decided to concentrate on more immediate concerns, namely whether Coventry City would ever win a match in Manchester.

The previous two seasons, 1982/83 and 1983/84, had seen us lose at Old Trafford by three goals each time and this season had started in a familiar way with United beating us 3 -1 at home. Lady luck was determined to give my ambition of seeing a Sky Blue victory up here a helping hand and arranged for City to be drawn against both Manchester clubs in the third and fourth rounds of the FA cup. Terry Gibson saw off the challenge of Manchester City with a brace of goals at Highfield Road. The reward was an away tie at Old Trafford. In between the Sky Blues were due to play United in a league match and I made the short trip across to Stretford try-ing to decide whether I would prefer City to win the cup or the league fix-ture.

Naturally I wanted them to humiliate the Reds in both games, but I was well aware that it didn't do to wish for too much. In the end I decided I could stand a City league draw if we would win the cup game. Back in Coventry Jim Holton, who had played for both teams during his career and was currently the landlord of a popular Coventry pub was asked what results he wanted. Jim made a similar deal. Not wishing to offend his clien-tele, he opted for a City cup win if United could win the league fixture. He said at the time that he thought City would be safe from relegation by May, while United needed the points if they were to build on their dream of win-ning the League. As it turned out Jim and I had got the picture completely wrong. City won the league fixture by a solitary Terry Gibson goal, United won the Cup game and failed to take the league title yet again. For the Sky Blues however the win was critical because at the end of the season City found themselves needing to win their final three games to avoid relegation. Had we lost the United game we would have already been down. Instead the stage was set for one of the greatest escapes of all time.

Norwich had already completed all their fixtures and, after an unexpected away win at Chelsea in their final game, sat a fairly comfortable eight points ahead of Coventry. The first of our three games in hand was on a Friday night at Stoke. The Victoria Ground had become quite a rewarding venue for me and for the City as Coventry had won convincingly in both of the two preceeding years. This time there was more at risk as any slip would mean the dreaded drop. Stoke were already relegated having had a terrible season and having only managed three wins in all their other fixtures. It turned out to be a game of two penalties, both were in the second half and both were slightly dodgy, but Salford referee Neil Midgely's decisions ultimately favoured the Sky Blues. He awarded the first penalty to Coventry after Cyrille Regis headed onto George Berry's hand. Pearce hammered it home saving his big miss for another time and another place. From then on it was a battle of nerves until, with only five minutes left Paul Dyson, one of Bobby Gould's rejects, had won Stoke a chance to seal our fate. Ian Painter's penalty was well struck, but hit the underside of the bar and bounced down on the line until Oggy finally grabbed it. Midgely immediately blew his whistle and I thought he was going to order a re-kick, or even worse give a goal. Instead it was a free-kick to us and the first stage of the great escape was over. Now it seemed a far more realistic hope as the Gods were surely on our side.

There was a crowd of 14,833 for the visit of Luton on the following Thursday. This apparently low number was in fact a huge rise on our normal gate that year which had rarely topped 10,000. We saw the Sky Blues win by an unconvincing single goal scored by a Brian Kilcline free-kick through Luton's defensive wall with only six minutes of the match left to play. Surely Sunday's final visitors, Everton, would be a far more difficult hurdle to clear. After all, they had only lost one game since Christmas.

As luck would have it Everton had already won the league title by this stage of the season and they were in as much of a party mood as many of the Coventry supporters. The attendance was over 21,000 and those wearing Sky Blue colours were able to enjoy most of the game as City took the lead within the first five minutes through a Regis header. Fifteen minutes later Micky Adams doubled the lead, but Everton pulled a goal back before half time to postpone the celebrations. When Cyrille Regis scored again only seconds after the restart the party really began. Terry Gibson got the final goal in what turned out to be an easy 4 -1 win in the morning sunshine. Coventry City had done it again and Norwich were doomed to the drop.

So that was the Sky Blues sorted out. Now all I had to do was get a job. After months of rejections and with no means in sight of paying off crippling debts to my relatives, my prayers were eventually answered. Just like the corporation buses, nothing comes for ages and then along trundled three opportunities all at once. The three jobs seemed to be exactly the same. All were in retail management of one flavour or another. The three companies that had decided to employ me were John Lewis, McDonald's and Littlewood's. I decided that I would take the Littlewood's job as they had said that they would let me stay in Manchester and work in their store in the heart of the city. I wrote my acceptance letter and waited for the information to arrive about pay, start day, holidays etc. I was in for a shock when I got their reply telling me to report to Swansea the following week for my first year's training. I wasn't sure if this was a joke or perhaps some initiative test. If it was a joke it was very elaborate, as they had even included a one way rail ticket. I thought it might be a joke because in their recruitment questionnaire I was asked if there was anywhere in the U.K. that I didn't want to work and I had answered Wales. Then by return of post I received this one way ticket to Swansea. It was a nightmare. I decided to phone them up. As I had no phone of my own this meant using a pay phone. So I stood in the phone box with a small stack of ten pence coins and I got my first taste of how frustrating a career in retailing was likely to be. My pile of coins steadily reduced as I was connected to department after department at the Personnel H.Q. in London. Eventually I was down to my last coin and I still hadn't been able to speak to the right person. Finally, as the seconds ticked away, I realised that we weren't going to sort the problem out so I told whoever I was talking to at the time that I was on my last ten pee so could she tell whoever was in charge that I wouldn't be coming. The last words of our call was her reply, 'Oh, do you want us to ring you back....?'

So by default that left a choice of McDonald's or John Lewis. John Lewis had promised that with their accelerated management scheme I could reasonably expect to be running one of their stores within twelve years. McDonalds said I could run one of theirs after ten weeks. So McDonald's it was and I found myself wearing brown crimplene again for the first time since Jubilee year.

12.

All work and no play

LIKE MOST PEOPLE FORCED FROM the protected environment of education into the harsh realities of making one's own way in life, I felt a certain resignation in my fate. I'd had a good run in my attempts to avoid working for my living, but now adulthood had caught up with me and any further struggling was futile. All I could hope for was an easy passage through the next forty years of my life. Maybe, with good behaviour, I would be granted parole through early retirement. Perhaps, I would win the pools or some other windfall would bless me and save me from this fate worse than debt.

Then, to my surprise, I discovered work wasn't that bad. OK I was employed by a glorified chip shop with megalomaniacal dreams of world domination, but that didn't mean I couldn't have fun. Also after a ludicrously short training period I was left in charge of a million-pound business. At McDonald's there is this continual training scheme where employees build their skills while working. The most obvious indication of this is their badges with a number of stars for different skills, such as working the till, cleaning up mess, fending off complaints, that sort of thing. It probably has enormous merit, but it did serve to show just how short term most of their employees' careers lasted. If they survived a whole week their badge had a constellation big enough to keep Patrick Moore interested for a few hours. Fear of litigation prevents me from spending too long sharing the many adventures I enjoyed during my eighteen months with McD's, but I did get to meet a boyhood hero while in their flame retardant uniform.

One evening I was working my usual evening shift, trying to stop the local disenchanted youths setting fire to the bins and gobbing on the mirrors when who should walk in but the great Terry Gibson. The same Terry Gibson that had knocked in nineteen goals for the Sky Blues on each of the previous two seasons. This man, all five foot four inches of him, had scored fifty-one goals for Coventry City in the two and a half seasons between Bobby Gould buying him from Spurs for £100,000 and Ron Atkinson buying him for Manchester United for £650,000. It was largely Terry's goals that had kept us in the top flight for the last two years and our chances of staying up without him seemed bleak. Particularly as his replacement was Alan Brazil.

I approached him as he waited for his food to be assembled by my highly trained staff. What do you say to the man who once scored a hat-trick against Liverpool and this very season had scored in seven consecutive games for City? I could have asked if he was sad to have left Coventry, whether he missed the city as much as I did? I could have asked him to corroborate the rumour that he had left the Sky Blues because his wife was unsettled in the Midlands. I could even, with one eye on the future, have asked him what working with Ron Atkinson was like. I might even have asked if his meal was alright, after all I was the manager.

Instead I resorted to the most basic instinct one feels when finally coming face to face with your hero. I asked him for his autograph. I managed to claw back a little credibility with my follow up question by asking how things were at United. What I really wanted to do was grab him like one of the pissed up old farts who sit around the Arndale Centre drinking Special Brew and say, 'You and me Terry we're the same. We are both in exile from the beloved Three Spires. Mercenaries who have prostituted ourselves in the search for employment in the grim North'. Fortunately I realised that this would mark me out as a nutter and so I left him in peace with his McFries, McPie and McDrink. I did feel that I had squandered an important opportunity. As though on meeting Dr. Livingstone I would have said 'Ah there you are'. Or if it was me instead of Neil Armstrong that had descended the steps of Apollo 11 then the oft quoted first words on the moon would have been. 'We're here'. That I would have been the one on Scott's expedition to the North Pole attributed with the quote 'Are we nearly there yet?'

Poor Terry, however, was not destined for great things at Manchester United. He scored only once for the Reds in twenty-nine matches as Big

Ron chose to play him in a system totally unsuited to his poaching skills. Salvation was at hand for Gibbo in the form of Bobby Gould for the second time in his career. He joined Wimbledon in 1987 and was part of their FA cup winning team the following year. If he had stayed at Highfield Road his medal might have been a year older.

I also met Bryan Robson under quite special circumstances while managing the Altrincham McDonald's. On the very day after he had led England to defeat in the Mexico World Cup he was in my store with his family to celebrate his return to England. And as at McDonald's we prided ourselves on regular inspections of our washroom facilities I can also say with some degree of authority that Bryan had not been adversely affected by his Mexican diet.

After a year and a half at the cutting edge of hamburger assembly I was ready for a move - anywhere. An unfortunate incident with a depraved staff member and the milkshake machine resulted in my speedy transfer into the heart of Manchester at Oxford Road. I was back in my old student drinking grounds, next to the Tommy Ducks pub which drew crowds to look at the hundreds of pairs of knickers pinned to the ceiling and the even busier Peveril of the Peak, which didn't. Lunchbreaks got longer and wetter and my bosses were beginning to suspect that I might not go all the way in the big burger building empire. For me the only attraction of work was the train journey from Altrincham to Oxford Road that took me past the derelict canal side industries that were yet to be gentrified into clubs and restaurants. It was a bleak and stunning landscape that was only spoiled by the twelve hours work that broke up the inward and outward journeys. The Oxford Road store was housed in an old theatre and it had its own beauty that wasn't totally hidden by the imported golden arches that signalled the presence of the new industrial revolution. My disinterest was clear to all as I broke with conventional management wisdom by not bothering to develop any rapport with the other staff. This was a bit of a shame as otherwise I might have discovered that the guy called Gerald, who shared a taxi with me on the late shift and was the best regular grill chef we had, was actually 'A Guy Called Gerald' who made it big as a D.J. in clubs on both sides of the Atlantic after his single 'Voodoo Ray' had stormed the dance charts. It turned out that he flipped discs even better than burgers.

Like Gerald I'd seen more than enough of hamburgers to last me a lifetime and I began to dread every minute at work spent fending off complaints from the customers, the staff, the bosses. I was ready for a greater challenge. I needed stretching in a way that would utilise my many undiscovered skills. Then, just as I was becoming desperate I was head hunted by Sainsbury's. They were looking for some new managers, invited me for a interview and offered me a job stacking shelves at a far greater salary. Could this be my vocation? Just in case emptying cases of beans turned out to be less glamorous than it sounded I also began to look around for a complete career change. Perhaps longing for just one more year in the idle luxury of further education I decided to apply for a teacher training course back at University. In order to keep my travel costs down a bit I decided to look for a University a bit closer to Highfield Road. Ironically this resulted in me applying to our local rivals Leicester for a place on their highly regarded course. As my application went through the necessary procedures I resigned myself in the meantime to the new job in food retailing. They started me off in the meat department where I nearly took off my own hand with a bandsaw, was shuffled around into the bakery where I ate into their profits and finally, in what was probably a damage limitation exercise, was settled into the grocery department. As the computer did all the ordering, Personnel did all the hiring, staff training and firing and Customer Services dealt with any problems, the extent of my managerial input was to stack the shelves with tins and biscuits, which inevitably I buggered up.

Back in Coventry Don Mackay's reign as manager of the Sky Blues was as brief as my own at McDonald's. The 1985/86 season had started without a win in the first five games. By April we looked relegation certainties once again. An unbroken run of eight games without a victory climaxed with a five goal mauling at Anfield. Mackay was put out of his misery and George Curtis was brought in to save us from the drop with only three games left. George's first game brought a vital win against Luton. However, a defeat against West Ham in the penultimate fixture meant that for the third successive season Coventry City had to win their last match to avoid relegation. As I had a rare Saturday off I was able to join the Sky Blue faithful gathered to see the City's fate. Though we were all used to this, now familiar, situation our nerves were in shreds when the visitor's Q.P.R. took the lead via a Trevor Peake deflection. Our prayers were answered when Killer Kilcline thundered in a free kick and then Dave Bennett gave us the lead with a brilliant solo goal, just before half time. The second half was just a battle which City somehow managed to survive. A late QPR shot beat Ogrizovic but rebounded off the crossbar. At the final whistle the Sky Blues had not only secured a twentieth season of First Division football, but incredibly they had been propelled to their highest position for four years. Little did we know it at the time, but this was the dawning of the golden age of Sky Blue football.

13.

The Class of 86/87

'It is a comfort in wretchedness to have companions in woe'
Christopher Marlowe, *Doctor Faustus.*

AS THE 1986/87 SEASON STARTED, expectations were not high. During the summer break George Curtis had hardly been overactive, only bringing in two new faces. Keith Houchen arrived from Scunthorpe for £60,000 but all anyone knew about him was that he had scored the goal when York put Arsenal out of the FA Cup. David Phillips arrived from Manchester City in a swap deal that saw Perry Suckling travel up the M6. On paper this did not seem the sort of transfer dealing to bring about a revolution in our fortunes. Fortunately George knew best. Despite some excellent league performances, which saw us achieve a final position of tenth, and some great games at Highfield Road, the season will always be remembered for just one thing. The FA Cup.

Our cup run began about as unglamorously as is possible. City were drawn at home to Bolton in the third round. This turned out to be the only home tie on the way to the final. It was a miserable afternoon in all but the football. The temperatures were sub-zero as we took a three-goal lead by half time. As the pitch froze in the second half neither side looked interested in trying to change the scoreline. Bolton's manager Phil Neal blamed his keeper Mike Salmon for all three goals, but he might have been better advised in directing his hot air onto the pitch.

Our reward was a home tie for me, although most Sky Blue supporters greeted the trip to Manchester United in the fourth round with less enthusiasm. I invited old school friends up for a beer and football weekend and we all had a great time thanks to Houchen's winning goal. The Sky Blue Army were already making plans for the next round. I could hardly believe my luck when we were drawn away to Stoke. Another tie almost on my doorstep, at a ground upon which I had never seen City lose.

As Stoke were still in the Second Division this did seem like a dream tie. If we won this game we were into the quarter-finals for the first time since 1982. Then fate conspired to throw a spanner in the works. I was scheduled to work on that Saturday. I had not been employed there long enough to be entitled to any holiday leave and the schedule, I was told in no uncertain terms, was not flexible. Sod's law. Fortunately, not only had I not been at Sainsbury's long enough to qualify for holidays or the employees profit sharing scheme, I also hadn't been there long enough to feel any company loyalty, and it was a very small matter for me to phone up that Saturday morning with suspected gastroenteritis. My reward was an unscheduled weekend off and a trip down to Stoke to sample the Springfield bitter, Stokie pies and another Sky Blue victory.

Just like me, City rode their luck at times with Greggy Downs making one clearance off the goal line and Stoke having a penalty appeal turned down. For the second cup match in a row our winner was scored by a player who was only on the pitch due to the unavailability of the manager's first choice. Keith Houchen had only played at Old Trafford because of an injury to Dave Bennett, while the scorer at Stoke, Micky Gynn, wouldn't have found himself in the team if Dean Emerson and Lloyd McGrath hadn't been ruled out with suspensions. Players and supporters alike dared for the first time to believe that fate was conspiring to help us and that this might really be our year after all. There were over eight thousand Coventry fans at the game and I was surprised that quite a few of that number got on the train back up to Manchester with me. I felt a bit less of a Coventrian in solitary exile that evening, and as the icing on the cake I had all weekend off to celebrate. It was the quarter finals next. Another away tie at Hillsborough where the Sky Blues hadn't won in seventeen years (that season we had managed a draw with a goal by Steve Ogrizovic!). It looked as though the dream might be over for another year.

At the time I was living in a third floor bedsit in Stretford. I had been fairly itinerant for the previous eighteen months and my current abode was the cheapest I had ever found. Of course you tend to get what you pay for in this world, unless your name is Ron Atkinson, and so cheap in this instance also meant nasty. The other tenants were either the mentally ill who had been released into the care of the community or former tramps who had decided to settle down for their last remaining months on this planet. The day I moved in was also the day I quit working for McDonald's and at the time I felt a huge sense of liberation. My previous address had been a house shared with friends I had made whilst working for the multi-national beef burger cookers and so on that day I had severed all my ties at once and burnt all my bridges behind me. Now I had moved to an area in which I knew no one and I was starting a job where no one knew me. It was a great opportunity to reinvent myself and possibly out of fatigue, apathy or some degree of mental instability I chose the lowest possible standards.

The flat possessed few facilities. There was no wardrobe or chest of drawers so I had to pile my clothes on the floor. The carpet had no discernible pattern and its original colour would have proven even beyond the restorative powers of the Eastman Studios. There wasn't a bath or a shower and the tiny sink had to double up as my area for food preparation as well as my washroom. There was a two ring electric hob to cook on and an electric fire that seemed to work by warming through discharging a series of electric shocks whenever I passed too close to it. The main characteristic about the flat was the appalling stench. I thought at the time that a dead dog must be buried under the floor boards. I later discovered from a neighbour that the previous occupant had died and remained undiscovered in the room for quite some time. The smell quickly invaded all my clothes and it never left them even after I had moved on to more salubrious shelter and subjected them to multiple boil washes. I found the compactness of my new habitat surprisingly comforting. I could reach everything from the bed, which was useful as there was no other furniture to sit upon.

Reflecting upon the six months I spent in these surroundings I can see all sorts of warning signs. I shut myself off from all my friends by not passing on my new address. I moved away from the people I was working with and for the only time in my life I made few visits home to Coventry. This is also the only place I have lived that my family have never visited. I didn't bother to have the telephone connected and made no attempts to contact other people. I can't imagine what I used to do after work. I didn't socialise with my new colleagues and I lost contact with my old ones. My girlfriend and I stopped seeing each other as she refused to visit me in this squalor. I don't blame her as the final straw came when she went to visit the communal toilets on the second floor. These do not need any description other than a comment that they were in no way pleasant. As she opened the door an old man fell out at her with his trousers and underpants round his ankles and his age withered genitals exposed. He groped at her moaning and grunting. She managed to push him aside. I heard her shouting 'Get off you dirty bastard. Fuck off and die.' Which he then proceeded to do. He hadn't been making sexual advances, he was dying from a stroke. She never came back and that was one less person for me to worry about.

At around about the same time a friend called Mike, who was a former work mate of mine at McDonald's, sought out my address and came to visit me but was chased away by 'Psycho Billy' who lived on the ground floor. Billy had a bit of a reputation for violent behaviour. His flat had no electricity due to persistent non-payment of his bills and most nights you could hear him, shouting in the dark. Billy's problems were rumoured to be the result of an altercation in a police cell which had left him needing surgery and the insertion of a steel plate into his skull. This plate was said to cause him pain and confusion from time to time and the rest of the tenants knew to keep a wide berth of him. Mike's big mistake was that when he had bought his car, two years previously, he had chosen a blue mini-metro. I am sure that it did good mileage and had a full service record but he should have chosen something, anything, else as blue mini-metros may easily be mistaken for panda cars by psychopaths with a deep resentment of the police who inhabit dark ground floor flats. Billy's attack was short and mercifully inaccurate. The axe he was wielding found itself embedded in the door of the flat opposite and in no time my friend was reversing down the road at a rate that would make a World War Two Italian tank commander envious.

The only other thing I remember about those lost months were Coventry City's amazing cup run. As the quarter final against Sheffield Wednesday approached I had a real sense of dread. I had invested all my dreams in City reaching Wembley for the first time in history. The last time Coventry City had appeared in a quarter-final was in 1982 when I was still at school. On that occasion our progress was thwarted by West Bromwich Albion and in particular by a certain Cyrille Regis. This time Cyrille was on our side as I joined 15,000 other Sky Blue hopefuls in the Leppings Lane end. History favoured the Owls, who had not lost a home tie in twenty-three matches. The Sky Blues had recorded their last FA Cup win at Hillsborough in 1911.

On the day Cyrille showed he still had that touch of cup magic and put us a goal up with a thumping low drive after a quarter of an hour. At half time City still held the lead and I just wanted the game to end. My worst fears were realised when Wednesday equalised half way through the second half. But this was a City team raised on three successive years of hard fought relegation battles. They knew how to fight in the key games and eventually their persistence paid off. Ultimately the glory went to Keith Houchen who got two goals in the final fifteen minutes and City were into the Semi-finals for the first time in their history. Now the City of Coventry and one rather subdued castaway in Manchester seized this opportunity to revive their flagging fortunes and develop a new sense of direction and purpose.

At Highfield Road it was announced that tickets for the Semi-final would be made available to all those who had a ticket stub for the forthcoming evening tie with Oxford United. It was a game I just could not make. As always in times of need my mum and dad came to my rescue without me even having to ask. They queued on the night for tickets to their first ever match at Highfield Road, and they queued again with the ticket stub the following day for a piece of history, a ticket for the semi-final against Leeds.

Between the nerve wrecking quarter final and the epoch-making trip back to Sheffield, which had been allocated as the venue for the semi, there was a whole month to idle away. After the Oxford game, City's next four fixtures were all away, which probably put them in good stead for the Leeds tie. Although the three losses and a goal less draw did little to inspire much confidence for the fans.

In the meantime Coventry as a city decided to make the most of this unique occasion. The enthusiasm that was shown by shops, offices and individuals was inspiring. Window displays for consumer goods were replaced by sky blue ribbons and models of the FA Cup. A real sense of local pride developed as the City was in the media spotlight for a piece of good rather than bad news for once. We all knew these were historic times and I prised myself out of my Stretford hermit's cave and back into the spring sunshine of Earlsdon and South Coventry. I became a social animal again and my visits home became far more regular.

By the time of the semi-final I was already filled with enormous excitement and joy. Almost overnight I found myself changed from a miserable, gloomy bastard into a child anticipating a great adventure just around the next corner. The tie coincided with my acceptance on the teacher-training course at Leicester. I was going back to University and Coventry City were playing for a place in the FA Cup final. The Gods must have been shining on me through that dirt encrusted third floor skylight.

Super Sunday finally arrived. I rose early and set my video so that I would have a permanent record of this unique day, and then left Stretford for the trip to Sheffield. I had given the spare ticket from the two my mum and dad had earned by going to the Oxford game to a friend called Jacko. He had been honoured with one of these rare parchments because he offered to drive me across the Pennines to Hillsborough. Leeds fans' reputation for a somewhat unconventional approach to showing support for their local club meant the Yorkshire police were not merely satisfied with a Sunday morning kick-off and strict segregation of the two sets of fans. They insisted on segregating the whole of Sheffield so that the Coventry fans were directed off the motorway to the ground through one half of the town, while the Leeds supporters found their vans shepherded through the other half of town. It was an impressive piece of work and few City fans even spotted a yellow and white scarf outside the ground. Its only flaw was it assumed all Leeds fans lived in Leeds and all City fans lived in Coventry. So any fans not approaching from the right direction found themselves corralled into a more and more hostile environment, a bit like haddock swimming into a trawler's net. And just like the haddock, any fan who found himself approaching a destination he would rather avoid had no opportunity to head back in the direction from which he had come. All the side exits were sealed and your fate was out of your hands.

I was as blissfully ignorant of the situation that lay ahead of us as your average kipper heading for a future of gutting, smoking and shrink-wrapping. As we sat in my friend's tiny Fiat that Sunday morning on a pilgrimage to seek the Holy Grail, his car bedecked with Sky Blue scarves ancient and modern, we cut a solitary path through the Yorkshire countryside. Much chanting was taking place and all the sheep in the fields were taunted with anti-Leeds songs. We were having such fun that I got us lost and the resulting circuitous route brought us into the City of Sheffield along the exact flight path the Yorkshire constabulary had intended. He surely works in mysterious ways.

Inside the ground the Sky Blues were celebrating the occasion as though it alone was the pinnacle of our possible achievement. In the pre-match interviews the Coventry players had said that this was their FA Cup Final, expressing a widely held view that all reasonable ambitions had been satisfied in progressing this far. Anything else was a bonus to be enjoyed. This was despite the fact that City played their football in a league above Leeds. Before the match our ancient Lady Mayoress was paraded around the ground and fortunately we were all making so much noise that any Leeds comments about her desirability were too masked to get through.

Before the kick-off the Leeds manager Billy Bremner had said not to expect a great spectacle as the result was everything, thus making no attempt to hide his tactics. He must have been very disappointed afterwards as the game was a thriller from start to finish.

As the match kicked off Jacko was quick to point out from his position of neutrality all the deficiencies he could spot in the Sky Blues performances. After a short time he was beginning to get on my tits. It was true that we had started nervously, and but for a great display by big Oggy we could have been a couple of goals down in the first few minutes. Even he couldn't stop David Rennie giving the City fans a few headaches by putting Leeds ahead in the fourteenth minute. This spurred the Sky Blues on and gradually we took command, though failed to score before half time. The second half was much the same with us creating chances up front while looking vulnerable in defence. None of the above had any affect on Jacko's continuous monologue of gloom and failure. It went on and on until in the end he seemed to become the source of City's unimpressive display rather than a mere commentator upon it. As another Leeds attack was only just thwarted Jacko piped up with the comforting reflection that 'It won't be long before one of those goes in and then it's game over.'

It became clear to me at that moment that he was the Cuckoo in the nest, the fault line from which the avalanche would fall, the hole in the dike that had to be plugged to save the rest of us. He was making us lose with his stream of negative Karma. I turned to my chauffeur for the day and requested him in language far bluer than the Coventry kit to cease his monologue or suffer a life-changing physical assault. This silencing of their greatest critic had just the desired affect on the Sky Blues.

John Sillett followed my lead and changed things around. Nick Pickering went off to be replaced by 'super-sub' Micky Gynn. Gynn managed to do what the others had failed by taking his chance when it came. His 68th minute equaliser turned the whole tie. Ten minutes later a move by Gynn presented Houchen with a chance and we were in front. Regis had an opportunity to make up for his earlier misses and seal the tie but again hesitated too long. Perhaps it wouldn't matter. Then just as we were getting ready to celebrate the greatest day in City's history, Leeds equalised. The players seemed a bit deflated, but as the 27,000 Coventry fans urged them on in extra time Dave Bennett popped up to tap in the winning goal. Steve Ogrizovic had one more crucial save to make before the final whistle and Sky Blue heaven. All our prayers had been answered and after cheering our heroes until we were hoarse, we turned for home to celebrate in the usual manner. Jacko and I found ourselves locked in at a pub we had never before frequented, surrounded by new friends, all of whom were singing Coventry's praises and most of whom we had persuaded to have a shot of Blue Bols in their pints. That night we all toasted George Curtis and John Sillett's players and we did it with Sky Blue coloured beer.

The only downer was that I hadn't allowed for extra-time when setting the video that morning and so missed out on recording our great moment of triumph. Well you can't have everything.

14.

The Final

LLOYD MCGRATH IS MY ALL-TIME favourite player. He did what no sane Coventry City fan had dared to hope for - he scored the goal that finally won us the FA Cup. Admittedly the record books fail to note Lloyd's name and choose unromantically to name the scorer simply as Mabbutt, own goal, but that does little justice to the occasion.

The rest of the world has annual carnivals in which normally sane people behave in an insane way. The carnival was traditionally a pre-Lent festival in which people could express their anti-authority urges and latent anarchism as beautifully captured in Brueghal's picture, 'Battle Between Carnival and Lent'. It was a time of year characterised by overindulgence to the point of vomiting and public defecation. A time when the world became inverted with fools crowned as King, where good was bad and bad was better. A time of nudity and of dressing up as devils. A period of pageantry in which the nobles and under classes would share disguises and hide their true identities behind masks and costumes. In England we don't have carnivals to rival Mardi Gras or Semana Santa. In England we have the FA Cup.

On the sixteenth of May Martin and I joined a long queue outside Coventry railway station at an ungodly hour and waited to board one of the Sky Blue specials to Wembley. Everyone in the line in front and behind, like me, had already bought their rail ticket and most had safely hidden somewhere on their person a cherished ticket that would let them be part of an occasion that no other Coventry fans in history had ever witnessed. We would see the Sky Blues run out onto the Wembley turf. So Wembley might be an old ruin, more like a urinal than a national monument but until its demolition it remained every football fan's Mecca (well except followers of the Saudi national team, obviously). We rose early that morning but without complaint, because this day would be far too short no matter how early we got up and how late we returned. Coventry City playing Tottenham Hotspur in the cup final at Wembley, who would have believed it?

As I was still working away at the time my father was emotionally press-ganged into joining the longest and slowest queue in the world - the one snaking around Highfield Road in which hopefuls gathered to get a ticket. He tried on two successive days and after getting up one morning while all the birds were still stacking zzz's and worms were frolicking on lawns without a care in the world, he brought home the treasured passport to Wembley. I was to be one of the lucky ones.

We caught the train and sang all the way to London. Spurs fans missed out on this bit of ritual as they rose from their London beds and meandered to the ground. This was a treat for the Sky Blues only. Now, finally, at Wembley and beneath the Twin Towers I saw a father handing his tickets to the three children with him, only for some scum to rip all four out of his hand. He stood open-mouthed in disbelief. His dream over. His family's day destroyed. I felt terrible for him and buried my ticket even deeper into my pockets.

Outside the ground Martin and I split up. He had got his ticket off someone in the legal office where he was now working and consequently had a seat just on the fringe of the Royal box. I was luckier and my ticket placed me right in the heart of the Sky Blues end. In the ground at last and the terraces soon filled with colour and noise. Thousands of Sky Blue flags, balloons and scarves indicating a mini-revival in the local textile trade. We were all here and we wanted everyone to know. It might have taken a hundred years but it was here and now and the rest of the World could just look on in envy.

Then the game started and within minutes my whole world crashed down around me. Chris Waddle skinned Greg Downs and Clive Allen got in front of Trevor Peake to nod the ball past a helpless Steve Ogrizovic. Spurs went wild. I felt sick and stupid. It had taken only two minutes of play for the dream to shatter. How foolish we had been to hope. We had lost control of our expectations, of course Coventry City - a team of nobodies, couldn't beat Spurs - a team of players that were always in Shoot or on Top of the Pops. I felt embarrassed for letting my dreams run away with me.

But then it all changed. Seven minutes later Downs crossed, Keith 'Roy of the Rovers' Houchen flicked the ball on and Dave Bennett left everyone standing to guide the ball past Clemence. I screamed myself hoarse with joy and hugged a huge and bearded stranger whose celebratory leap had synchronised with my own. One all, now we would show them. This was the real start of the game and despite my longing for it to be over and for City to have won I could see it was a great game of football. Lloyd McGrath was getting control over Hoddle, Downs was finding his way with Waddle and Gynn almost put us in front but was thwarted by Clemence. Just before half time the City defence got in a mess and Oggy was left standing as a scramble saw Kilcline and Mabbutt together put the ball into City's net. They do say that it is a good time to score. This time I felt less dejected, after all we had been coming from behind to win all season. We'd done it at Hillsborough in the semi-final against Leeds and we could do it again.

The second half was as fast and exciting as the first, but City seemed in control. They fed Bennett time and time again and he led the Spurs on many a merry dance. Then Houchen laid the ball off into Dave Bennett's path who took it on before placing a teasing cross just beyond Gough and tantalisingly in front of Houchen. Somehow his diving head made contact and we had scored one of the greatest goals in cup final history. I screamed and hugged the bearded man again. Now we would really see what Spurs were made of.

Inevitably extra-time was needed. This was far too important a game to be played over just ninety minutes. Ninety minutes was for normal matches. This was our special game. Kilcline had to go off after a clumsy challenge and the team captaincy had passed back to that great City servant Trevor Peake who had only lost the job because he'd dared to air some of his team-mates grievances to the former manager Bobby Gould. Now he had the captain's armband back and the fairy tale seemed almost complete.

Graham Roger was 'Killer's' replacement and he probably couldn't believe his luck, playing in the cup final in only his sixth top class game. Luck was certainly on his side when he released the ball to send McGrath clear down the right wing. Lloyd wasn't accustomed to such a forward role.

Moving the Goalposts

He was a stopper rather than playmaker and all day he had done just that. This Wembley occasion was supposed to be Glen Hoddle's swan song before going to seek his fortune abroad. Before the game Brian Clough had said it was a disgrace that Hoddle should be allowed to stage manage his own departure from the club. Cloughie had said that if he was in David Pleat's position he would leave him out of the team. In the end Lloyd had prevented Glen from starring in his own farewell and now Lloyd was beating him at his own game as well. As Lloyd completed his run there was little obvious support but the Sky Blues were gradually arriving at the edge of the Spurs box. Only Mabbutt was in front of him. From the right wing Lloyd took a last look and crossed the ball off Mabbutt's rising knee and arcing majestically into the Tottenham goal over a flatfooted Clemence. The bearded man and I didn't hug or even cheer. We were too knackered. Instead we just shared a smile. We cheered at the final whistle though and we cheered when 'Killer' lifted the cup. We even cheered all the way home on the train back to Coventry.

The winning goal; a local lad Lloyd, from Brum; had been at City since he was a kid; Sky Blue through and through, always gave his all; promised his fiancee before the game he would score for her (quite a brave statement as in his eleven seasons at Highfield Road he only netted five times). He won the cup for City. I always knew he would. The Sky Blues were Sky high.

Martin and I returned in triumph back to Coventry. We caught the last of the Sky Blue special trains home and were hoping that we might just make it to the pub before last orders to continue the celebrations. Whenever the rail route ran alongside the motorway we could see that the M1 was packed almost as tight as our carriage. Many of the cars were bedecked with Sky Blue scarves and there was much friendly signing from rail to road. As we approached Rugby, the town of my birth, we got our first sign of the celebrations started by those who stayed at home. In the gardens by the rail track there were parties and barbecues as people had gathered together to watch Coventry City's biggest day. Pissed up part-time fans waved their congratulations at the sober returnees on the train whetting our appetites for some liquid celebration. Truly the Sky Blues were the pride of the Midlands.

Back in Coventry the 'The Rocket' was packed to bursting with those who had returned before us on the earlier trains. We were never going to get served in there. The only alternative was a dash to our local 'The Burnt Post'. It seemed crucial to finish the day with a pint in a Sky Blue pub, celebrating with our neighbours, but time was against us and of course there wasn't a bus or taxi in sight.

We did try to flag down one of the passing cars, all blaring their horns and covered with City flags, scarves and streamers. One, a Jaguar, that potent symbol of Coventry's prestige engineering, stopped and we asked for a lift but the driver just wanted to know what it had been like at Wembley. 'What did it look like on TV?' we replied. 'Fantastic' said the driver. 'It was much better than that!'. We started running towards the pub and arrived about five minutes before last orders, but the bar was packed. Somehow we got served just in time and then turned to share our experiences with those who hadn't been fortunate enough to get a ticket. We looked around at all the ecstatic revellers and neither of us had anything left to say, so we grinned instead. What a day.

The morning after and we all waited in the city centre for a sight of the team returning in triumph with the Cup. Martin and I decided that the Council House would be the best spot as that is where they would end up and show the trophy from the balcony. They were very late. Nobody had anticipated just how many people would want to turn out to congratulate the team and the open-topped bus could make little progress through the streets. Nobody minded waiting as it merely prolonged the moment. I bet the celebration banquet for the players was spoiled though.

It wasn't really a long wait, not compared with the one hundred and seven years the city had waited to celebrate their team winning any real trophy of value. The Sky Blues had been to Wembley and achieved a goal that even their most loyal supporters had felt was beyond their reach. They had taken a huge step forward and now it was my turn.

15.

Goodbye Piccadilly, Hello Leicester Squares

I RETURNED TO MY STRETFORD BEDSIT, with its Sky Blue flag hanging out of the third floor window and packed up my tramp scented belongings. The following morning I handed in my notice at Sainsbury's and in a couple of weeks I had left Manchester, opting to spend the Summer sweating among the roses of Guernsey rather than yawning among the frozen peas in Altrincham. An ideal rest before the next stage of my nomadic existence.

If I had fled Manchester in haste I was to repent in Leicester.

Leicester is only twenty miles from Coventry, but the East Midlands is very different from my own Western counterpart. While the west has become an engineering heartland, the home of the screw and the camshaft, the east is more of a rural idyll. The sort of mental picture an American conjures up when you mention any part of England outside London. While people from Hereford and Worcester may be scratching their handkerchief bedecked heads and comparing me with their own local village idiot at the notion that Leicester is a rural place, the contrast struck me as that extreme. Leicestershire has less industry and the whole pace of life seems noticeably slower. People appear to be in less of a hurry in thought and deed. This is the biggest city in middle England and you notice immediately how clean and bright East midland towns are despite their industrial heritage. There is little evidence of factory smoke in the air. The nearest heavy industrial works were over in Northamptonshire in the shape of Corby steel works. The East Midland industries were generally not mechanised until the gas engine had been developed and so the earlier phase of steam and smoke that blackened the northern towns had no place here. Consequently Leicester and its environs looks prosperous, clean and healthy externally. To some extent this first impression is not deceptive as the East Midlands gives off an aura of regional prosperity. It has never shared the mass unemployment and poverty experienced on such a large scale in areas to the north and west. When Manchester was the sweatshop of the world, Leicester was still a market for straw sucking agricultural types. The only industry around was lace-making in Bedford and whip-making in Daventry and though these remain essential components of the erotic clothing market, they are hardly the sweaty furnaces of heavy industry.

The arrival of canals, passing through to more dynamic areas of the country, brought about a number of changes during the late eighteenth and early nineteenth centuries. Their proximity stimulated the local economy and Leicester grew on the back of two manufactures. The great bulk of workers were employed in the hosiery trade and most of the rest in footwear, with Leicester specialising in ladies' and children's shoes. So the town's economy was dependent on knickers and cobblers. As the great bulk of workers in hosiery were women and in footwear men, it meant that most households had two incomes. As the two industries were rarely depressed at the same time there was always someone at work and thus some income, even in bad times.

As a city I could begrudgingly see that Leicester had a more interesting array of shops and more accessible sports and leisure facilities. Although Leicester City are only second to the Villa as local rivals I found myself very impressed with my temporary new home. The fact that they played in the Second Division meant that I had no need to feel any great rivalry with the indigenous population. The beer was bit more expensive than I was used to paying in Manchester, but it wasn't at all bad. Ruddles County bitter and I soon became the closest of friends, particularly when I was sent to Rutland sixth form college on my first teaching practice.

Rutland is to counties what Coventry City are to the Premier League and I enjoyed travelling to its county town, Oakham, every morning, even though it meant I had to get up an hour earlier than my colleagues, who all had school placements nearer the University. Rutland shared my misplaced refugee status. The county had woken up one morning to find it no longer existed. A map of England's counties in 1973 has Rutland, the country's smallest county, nestling comfortably in middle England, between Leicestershire and Lincolnshire. A similar map of 1974 has no mention of such a place. Like Atlantis it has disappeared into the stuff of legends with few pieces of physical proof to show it was ever really there. In an attempt to hide the evidence a huge chunk of the county was flooded under a reservoir to satiate the thirst of Leicestershire. When Leicester drinks deeply a church steeple can be seen breaking the surface of the Rutland Water reservoir, revealing incriminating evidence that people did once live there.

Rutlanders never forgot their true individuality. The dictionary of human geography defines the term 'sense of place' as 'the consciousness that people themselves have of places that posses a particular significance for them, either personal or shared' and 'placelessness' as 'people who feel personally or culturally separate from an area'. We had a lot in common Rutland and I. We both had the belief that we belonged elsewhere. Rutland even went so far as to issue its own passports. It mounted a continual campaign through the media to reclaim its status. It wasn't just a desire to control their own finances and services that prompted people such as the 'Value Rutland Group' to battle for the reintroduction of county status. It was to preserve their very identity.

Oakham is a calm place. It is dominated by its private boarding school, although the state school I was at just up the road seemed to bear it few grudges and little rivalry, rather enjoying the reflected glory of its more famous neighbour. During free periods I would browse the town's shops and occasionally frequent one or other of its excellent pubs and I was rather sad when my teaching practice there came to an end. The school was understandably less sorrowful as my clumsiness was rather eating into their not unlimited educational budget. Whilst I was on my placement there the course tutor made two visits to assess my ability and suitability as a future teacher. It was made pretty clear that the only way to fail the course was through a poor performance in these assessments. The threat of a return to stacking beans or cooking chips inspired me to meticulously prepare a lesson on rivers, a topic I wasn't particularly confident about, for the first inspection. As my tutor entered the classroom all my props, exercises, extension work and open and closed questions were ready. The notes and tasks had all been painstakingly copied out in five attention grabbing and interest generating colours on to plastic sheets for projecting onto the screen behind me. The professor took a seat at the back. I turned the projector on and there was a loud bang followed by a shower of glass as it exploded. After the initial shock the realisation dawned upon me that this was a tricky situation as the whole lesson had gone up in smoke along with the projector. Not possessing either the wit nor the wisdom to teach from my own knowledge after a few attempts at ad-libbing I was reduced to reading the sheets out while the students copied down my words. I had a feeling that I hadn't done enough to earn a pass just yet.

For the second and final visit it would be fair to say that the atmosphere was a little tense. My preparations had already resulted in one broken photocopier and the lesson before had been spent practising turning the projector on and off. I had even scouted out the location of a spare one in case lightning struck twice. The professor entered and we began the lesson by making a big show of turning on the projector and joking about it not exploding. As the light came on the whole class heaved a huge sigh of relief and then I turned to pull down the screen from its ceiling mounting. On my first tug the whole mounting and screen came crashing to the floor in a pile of plaster, dust and rubble and it seemed an appropriate time to consider what career path to choose next.

Outside of the classroom the good news about the course was that it left all the weekends and school holidays free which meant I could take full advantage of my first ever season ticket. I usually decline from buying a season ticket for much the same reason that I rarely book my holidays more than a month in advance nor buy concert or theatre tickets for performances in six months time. While this frequently exposes me to financial, physical and verbal abuse at the hands of touts and denies me any other early bird financial advantages, I don't really have much choice as the only alternative would for me to become organised and plan ahead. This is not something that comes naturally to me.

On the rare occasions on which I am forced through circumstances beyond my control to book something in advance it results in many nights' lost sleep as I am tortured by the nagging spectre of doubt of some other forgotten important engagement, or that something more important will come up in the meantime.

For years there was never any risk of not getting in to Highfield road. During the 70's and 80's the ground was rarely packed, even during one of its frequent conversions into an all seater stadium. Away games can be more difficult, with a number of clubs being notoriously mean with visitors tickets, but I have never failed to get in to a game I have gone to. At Manchester City and Stoke I have on occasions had to keep quiet as the only available seats were amongst the home supporters, but there has never been any problem at most other grounds around here. Bolton, Oldham and Blackburn even seen pleased to see you.

However, in 1987 I had my very own season ticket. Entry to all home games was guaranteed while I would be given special priority for away games. What luxury. Now I really was part of the set up at Highfield Road.

16.

On the field and off the peg

IN 1987 COVENTRY CITY WERE the cup holders, I had a season ticket and lived only twenty miles down the road. The only thing that tarnished all this glitter was the Sky Blues' decision to play all their home games in what appeared to be polyester pyjamas. Coventry have had more than their fair share of terrible kits. At times the club have seemed to gain perverse delight in choosing kits that even the most ardent fan would hate to be seen in. The marketing department clearly hadn't got the hang of this merchandising idea. Or perhaps they were all colour blind.

Since Jimmy Hill introduced the first sky blue kit in 1962 it has gone through many ugly stages of metamorphosis before finally resulting in our current decent strip. Some of the more horrific designs include such bizarre fashion statements as the chocolate brown 'egg-timer' ensemble sported by Steve Hunt and company between 1978 and 1981. This was eventually replaced by the worst kit anywhere in history - the infamous Talbot 'Big T' design. This was Jimmy's ahead of his time idea to get some sponsorship onto the kit. Rather than plump for a logo or small advert he selected a kit which had a huge Talbot car symbol printed on the shirt and even extended down the sleeves and the shorts. His attempt to change the club's name to Coventry Talbot for a bit more cash was fortunately forbidden by the F.A. Incredibly this big T period was followed by a season in which we were so bad nobody wanted their name seen on our shirts. Eventually that impressive multinational corporation Glazepta (who?) took pity and sponsored a quite sober all blue shirt. Subsequent high profile sponsors included Tallon pens and Granada bingo before Peugeot took pity and returned a little credibility to a our shirts.

The next strip was our cup winning white and blue deck chair style kit which survived until the Wembley final only to be replaced by the washed out pyjama effect hoisted upon an unsuspecting public by Hummel in 1987. This was positively pleasant compared with the yellow and black away kit that soon followed. Surely it was designed by a traffic warden with an acid habit as it had the unmistakable appearance of a juggernaut's skid marks through a set of yellow 'no parking' lines.

The following year we had a jigsaw pattern that appeared to have been assembled by some reception class teacher from his or her least able pupil's drawings. Worse followed with a blue and white flecked affair that made the players look like a whole flock of starlings had had the shits while flying over the ground. The matching red and white away number made Ndlovu and teammates appear as though they were actors in a particularly low budget slash and gore movie. Then, finally, good sense prevailed and we have recently had a more retrospective all sky blue kit followed by a couple of Inter Milan copies and the current snappy little number that today's heroes are wearing with such pride. But how long can it be before we fall back into our old habits of sartorial anarchy? Perhaps in the near future the team will be decked out in orange tartan, especially if Wee Gordon adds to the three Strachans he's had on the payroll.

So 1987/8 was to be a season played in pale pyjamas. Our preseason started in the best possible arena with another trip to Wembley, this time for the Charity Shield. City took a record visiting crowd to the game against League champions Everton and it provided us with our first look at John Sillett's new recruit David Speedie. His signing fee, a club record £780,000, seemed to echo Sillett's promise that we would no longer be shopping for players at Woolworth's and were now in the Harrods range. His added comment that 'We're going for everything. The title - the lot!' was refreshingly positive, but many wiser heads suspected that such pride might herald a fall, and that buying at Harrods wasn't what had won City their cup the previous season, it was hungry last chancers previously left on the shelf at Woolies. With the FA Youth Cup also newly in place in the trophy cabinet he might have been better advised to build on that base. How easy it is to preach with hindsight.

Although the day out at Wembley was another great occasion and a chance to enjoy the place rather than worry about the result, it was only saccharin after the sweetness of the previous May. On the day City played well enough but the whole game was a bit of an anticlimax, with Everton scoring the only goal. The overall benevolent atmosphere was summed up by Sky Blues fans taking the applauding of worthy opponents a little too far by singing 'we love you Everton' as the wrong sort of blues went to lift the trophy. It did seem that we were perhaps a little too sporting, as though the Sky Blues had been indulged with the cup win and now we were ready to resume normal service.

Nothing could have been further from Sillett's mind as he fuelled expectations with talk of Europe and great days ahead. Some quietly feared he might be digging his own grave. While David Speedie turned out to be a real asset and had the rare ability of being able to change the course of a game by a moment's inspirational play, he alone did not change Downs, Borrows, McGrath, Kilcline, Peake, Bennett, Gynn, Regis, Pickering and Houchen into a team capable of winning the League.

Fate was kind and we began the season with a home match against Spurs, the side we had so recently defeated in the Cup. A crowd of almost 25,000 turned up to rub their noses in it, with Gary Mabbutt coming in for special praise from the Coventry supporters. David Speedie scored on his home debut as we cruised to a 2 - 1 win and all left convinced that if we could play Spurs every week John Sillett's predictions for our football domination might come true.

The next home game brought us back down to earth. A four one thumping suggested that we still had quite some way to go before we could challenge the big clubs. The final home game before my move to Leicester was against Manchester United and it was a match without a goal. That season we had a record seven no goal games, six of them at home. Most people who go to games get a variety of emotional needs satisfied or denied at the ground, but the simplest and probably most important is the shared joy when a goal is scored. Even if it is a consolation goal during a hefty defeat it brings its own unrivalled wave of communal happiness, if only in the form of shared ironic applause. So no-score draws are the anathema of the football supporter. When they occur it means no one in the ground goes home completely satisfied. The visiting supporters may have the bonus of an away point, but most fans (except during crucial relegation run ins, and, I can only speculate here, during pushes for the title) would prefer to see their team lose two out of every three games that produced 5-4 thrillers rather than draw nil-nil week in, week out. It was certainly how I felt that season. At one point we managed three goal-less games on the trot, that is over two hundred and seventy minutes waiting for a goal to be scored in either net.

While some goal-less ties can be real thrillers, particularly in edgy cup games with the promise of a replay, these were largely dour and disappointing affairs. A goal changes the whole complexion of most games. The scoring team has attained a superior position and the losing team has to approach the game in a more cavalier and attacking way. It opens up otherwise stalemated matches. I saw all but one of City's no score bores that season. Fortunately I had neither the will nor financial means of taking the long trek down to Portsmouth on a cold December morning and you have to feel sorry for those that did. All that way for nothing. You should have been doing your Christmas shopping or have gone to the pub with your mates, or have taken your kid to visit Santa in Owen Owen's. But the long haul down to the South coast on icy roads or railways, well you didn't want to do that. I know that the alternative is to leave the players at the mercy of a totally hostile crowd, or worse, that you might miss the greatest Sky Blues match of all time. Obviously, the wisdom of a long haul to Newcastle, or Southampton, or Norwich can only really be assessed after the event.

Of course there are clubs with even worse transport problems. Few would envy Carlisle or Torquay's travelling fans the long hours they spend on the road. It is no coincidence that Carlisle are sponsored by Eddie Stobbart as nearly all their fans must be long distance lorry drivers. On a trip to Russia recently I saw Dynamo Moscow play a match against a team from the far flung ex-Soviet province of Kazakstan, which must be a five day rail journey away. Despite the lack of away fans the pseudo-Nazi Dynamo supporters presented the most threatening crowd, with the greatest likelihood of violence, that I had ever experienced. When the visitors tied the match with two goals in the final minutes you could see the frustration on the local skinheads' faces at not having any visitors to vent their anger upon. And before people holler that this is proof that hooliganism and football walk hand in hand I really should point out that it was an ice hockey match.

More recently I was in Barcelona and went along to see Espanol play a big relegation match against Tenerife. I must have really been missing Coventry to sit through a Spanish bottom of the table six pointer. There was no discernible support for Tenerife in the ground and that must be the normal situation for their players at away games. Why would any player want to sign for a club with no away support? Then there is all that travelling as well. A friend who accompanied me to the game said that he thought that Tenerife were forced to play their home games on the Spanish mainland, but that must be even worse. It is bad enough playing away games a thousand kilometres from your home fans but playing home games an ocean away is unthinkable. What is the point? If Coventry City played their home games on the Isle of Man, for me they would become the Isle of Man F.C. even if they kept the name Coventry. This throws up other questions about my own credentials as a Coventry supporter. I haven't lived in Coventry since the early 1980's, so do I really have any right to consider myself as a Coventrian? Does my self imposed exile make my increasing devotion to Coventry's football club more hypocritical? I drive a Peugeot that has been assembled in Coventry in the vague hope that my home industrial base will benefit, but perhaps an acknowledgement that I have become an economic migrant and an attempt to assimilate within my new environment would be more appropriate. As I currently live in Fallowfield, Manchester, a district with one of the highest car theft rates in Europe and whose population is made up entirely of students, does this mean I should dreadlock my hair, get up at lunchtime, smoke rollups and attend raves? Or maybe I should see the bigger picture and accept my position as a denizen of Manchester and dress in the ubiquitous uniform of Manchester United's latest shirt and shell suit bottoms and spend my evenings joy riding. But I fear that I am stereotyping. Just as many Manchester United supporters don't actually live in Stretford, so it is that many Sky Blues live out of sight of the Three Spires. My inner sense of belonging to Coventry is more than enough to justify my feelings for the club. Just as many Jews in north Manchester feel that their spiritual home is in Israel, and many West Indians in Moss Side see Jamaica and its culture as their birthright, so it seems reasonable for me to remain a Coventrian while temporarily resident elsewhere. I have just been displaced for the last two decades, little more than a refugee in foreign parts. On completion of my work here I will return home.

Moving the Goalposts

October 1987 was a bad month for the Sky Blues. In under four weeks we had lost five league games in a row. There were only two breaks in this miserable blanket of dark clouds. The first was home and away victories over Cambridge United in the League Cup while the second was the draw for the Third round which saw us paired with Luton Town. That in itself was little enough to warm the heart, but Luton at the time had a plastic pitch upon which they were not allowed to host cup ties. Consequently they were forced to play their home games at some neutral ground and as luck would have it the tie was played at Filbert Street, Leicester.

On the night of the game I managed to persuade a lad on the same teacher-training course to accompany me. He was a non-hostile Villa fan and somehow seemed to accept my argument that this had all the makings of a classic cup encounter, one he would rue missing. There was absolutely no problem getting into the ground as only 8,000 bothered making the trip and most of them were from Coventry, which put the Sky Blues in an unusual position, effectively having home support in Leicester. Of the Luton fans, most seemed to be citizens of Leicester who were just out for a night's abuse of their local rivals. You can't blame them because their own team was having one of their frequent spells in a lower division and they probably fancied watching a real game for a change. That evening they were given something to smile about because both teams were woeful and Luton came out on top aided by some not entirely impartial refereeing decisions.

At this stage my first season ticket seemed to be a totem of bad luck. After the opening day defeat of Spurs we did not win another game at Highfield Road all year and we only won five all season. Our final uncharacteristically elevated league position was more a result of good away form and a mean defence. In fact it had been so long since I had seen a victory that I organised a school outing to London for a tour of Nelson's flagship.

As we left the ground the trouble started. The Leicestershire constabulary seemed to bear any number of grudges against Coventry supporters and were less than courteous towards the taxpayers bedecked in Sky Blue. On the walk back to the University for a couple of beers, just so the evening wasn't completely wasted, we encountered many other hostile natives hoping to ambush any lost Coventrians. None of them had Luton scarfs, but the real give away came when they opened their mouths to ask, 'Do you want a fight - Me duck?'

Moving the Goalposts

As well as heralding the Sky Blues worst home form for years my new season ticket also made me a sedentary fan for the first time. Before then I had enjoyed sitting or standing in different parts of the ground depending on the weather, my feelings, the opposition, or even to avoid some boring bastard who had spent the whole of the previous game shouting shite. Now however I was fixed in the old Spion Kop and thus had few migratory possibilities. It being a stand in the old sense of the word I was allowed the luxury of picking my own viewing spot each game, but even at Highfield Road the grass always looks greener on the other side of the fence and goals always seemed to get scored at the other end of the ground. This enforced sedentary status inhibited upon my superstitious involvement in the proceedings on the pitch. Stuck for the whole season on the Spion Kop end I couldn't help the team break their poor run by my usual inspiring method of watching them play each match from a different part of the ground. In the past this simple technique had apparently transformed City's seasons and had kept us up in the top flight a couple of times. Now I was forced to look for some other ridiculous and unnecessary superstitious behaviour to try and influence an outcome I had no control over. Given our results I clearly failed.

The season petered out as my course drew to a close. It was time to find a job and pick a new part of the country to live in. My Sagittarian nature with its characteristic wanderlust encouraged me to choose somewhere completely different. I'd tried the North so now I turned southward. Having been born a landlocked Midlander from the English city furthest from the coast means the sea has always held a fascination and mystique for me. It conjures up images of holidays and fun, so I decided to look for jobs in a maritime vicinity. When a post for a newly qualified teacher in Colchester was advertised I applied for and got the job in the mistaken belief that it was a seaside town. Fortunately they didn't ask me at the interview whether I could point out on a map exactly where I was, or they may have realised that their new geography teacher was less than the finished article.

17.

Colchester

IF COVENTRY, JUST ONE MILE from the geographic centre-point of England, can make a reasonable claim to lie at the very heart of the country, then perhaps a case could be made for suggesting that Manchester, on the edge of the Pennines, lies at it's backbone and rural Leicester at its stomach. With Scotland as this figure's head and Cornwall as its feet it is not difficult to extend this picture to encompass Colchester. This oldest of all English towns can be found in the most northern reaches of that often maligned county Essex. As such, if we take East Anglian neighbours Norfolk and Suffolk to be the rump and seat of the country then it is hard not to see Colchester as lying at the exact point of this body's arsehole. The ferries fleeing from nearby Harwich to Rotterdam and Hamburg would appear from a satellite as the result of Colchester evacuating the nation's bowels.

This curious geography appears to have been influenced by the great planet shaping changes of recent geological history. To the north the country's impressive mountain ranges and sharp valleys carry the rugged scars of the four great Ice Ages that have shaped the major geomorphological features of Great Britain. When the huge ice-sheets grew upon the northern Highlands and combined with the Irish sea ice they formed an overpowering moving force that carved out a new British landscape.

Sweeping out in all directions from our highest peaks this mass of ice began a slow and unstoppable march south chiselling new, breathtaking scenery en-route. These ice-sheets and glaciers stripped away all the old earth, deepened stream channels into huge troughs and took fierce bites out of any hills unfortunate enough to be in the way. The ice showed no intention of stopping as it reached the Midlands, flattening out any irregularities in the surface over which it flowed, constantly abrading and scraping smooth the rocks over which it advanced, cleaning the surface like a super Ajax scourer.

Onwards went the irresistible ice, as it passed Coventry it left a reminder of its visit by permanently diverting the course of the River Avon. In Earlsdon it deposited part of the dirty moraine load it carried as a thick unsorted boulder clay which has made our family garden so prone to bogginess in winter, so heavy and hard to dig, a subject of various failed attempts at improvement by neighbours unaware of the mighty force they are battling against.

Finally the ice approached Essex. It paused for a while on the fringes of the region and then chose to progress no further, instead retreating back to the hills from which it had originated. There is evidence of four such ice advances in Britain and on each occasion the glaciers have turned back on reaching the Essex border.

And I felt I knew better, sailing into town without pausing for thought.

Colchester was the site of a Roman camp and has a Norman castle. It is officially the oldest town in England and it celebrates this fact and is quite happy to play the history card. All around the town there are reminders of previous visitors including Saxons, Normans, Dutch Weavers and Victorian developers. Much of its history was bloody. The town was originally built by the Romans as a physical reminder of their conquest and subjugation of the local tribes. The site was subsequently destroyed by Boadicea, queen of the Icaenae, in AD 60 as she took revenge on the Romans for their earlier atrocities on this ancient British tribal capital. Such was the extent of her rage at the rape of the land that she lay waste to huge tracts of the region eventually meeting her match at Mancetter to the north of Coventry.

Colchester saw more action during the Civil War as it endured an eleven week siege. The castle was even once an interrogation centre for the notorious Witch Finder General, Matthew Hopkins. Clearly this is not the most peaceful part of the country. Modern Colchester still retains a military role with its large garrison exerting an important economic and social influence in the town's growth. In contrast to Coventry's distaste for soldiers, which has been recorded for all perpetuity in the phrase 'sent to Coventry' (reflecting the lack of welcome soldiers based in the city had to endure, ostracised by locals who would even disown their daughters if they were seen fraternising with the soldiers. Consequently the military found themselves totally isolated and confined to their own barracks and company, excluded from normal intercourse and condemned to a solitary existence. Thus being sent to Coventry was not the favourite posting for a soldier), Colchester has depended on a military presence for its development since its first Roman camp developed. However the relationship is not necessarily any more harmonious than that experienced centuries before in Coventry.

In Colchester there exists a strange form of local apartheid. Squaddies and civilians share the same town and yet rarely come into direct contact with each other. Squaddies had their own three or four pubs where the landlord was more than happy to welcome the free spending and cash laden soldiers. Clearly the profits they made more than covered the inevitable breakages associated with military recreational manoeuvres. Meanwhile the rest of the town avoided these pubs and divided the remainder between themselves. Some were student grunge and drug holes, some were Essex man's brash and loud fun themed dens, the rest were probably much the same as most other local pubs. Nightclubs also exercised this apartheid and the big three discotheques in town all generally excluded squaddies. Young girls in the town all claimed that they always gave the uniformed lads a wide birth unless the uniform was that of an officer, yet all the squaddies proudly boasted that they pulled a different local girl every night and that the camp shop had always run out of condoms by Monday morning. Clearly at least one of these two parties was lying.

There was also a subtle racial dimension to this social avoidance. Colchester is very visibly a southern town. There is a lot of blond hair about, perhaps suggesting that some of the earlier northern visitors had had more success in courting local girls before heading back to the longboats. The locals drive Dagenham Fords and wear coins on their fingers. The shell-suit first found designer status here and the boys drink lager and the girls Malibu. People are tanned even in December. They speak southern and they look southern. They keep to themselves, even holding the students at arm's length on a campus a few miles out of the town. Most of the soldiers housed in the southern garrison towns of Aldershot and Colchester are from Northern English or Scottish towns and they betray their lack of homogeneity as eloquently with their voices as their uniform.

North-South rivalry is, like any other form of bigotry, rarely subtle and we Midlanders find ourselves with few allies. In Manchester my accent betrayed me as a soft-southern shandy drinker while to Colcestrians my brogue was that of a Durham collier or a thick Lancastrian navvy. Like the students safely ensconced in their hermetically sealed enclave, I found myself part of a third group - outsider. It is strange that a town whose workforce is divided into either imported mercenary or London commuter should be so unwelcoming to newcomers. On the day I started work I was told that it would take six years to make any friends here as that was how long it took people to acknowledge the presence of an outsider. Sadly, I only stayed for three years and so cannot comment on how precise that prediction proved to be, but after three years there were certainly signs that they were warming to me. My local newsagent had even started saying hello as I bought my daily paper. What was true was that the pupils I taught were anything but unwelcoming. They were bright, enthusiastic and fun to be with. I learnt much from our lessons together and can only hope that my teaching didn't hold them back too much. They all certainly gained a much better understanding of the role of the City of Coventry in the development of modern civilisation. Our geographical discussions took us in many directions and we confronted all the major geographical questions of the day.

'Is it true that the whole of the World's Population would comfortably fit standing side by side on the Isle of Wight?'

'Why does the bath water go round the other way in Australia?'.

'What about Australian shower water?'

'If everyone in China jumped up at the same time would the resultant tidal wave cover the United States?'

'Do one legged ducks swim in circles?'

'Who would win in a fight between a Rottweiler and its equivalent bodyweight of Chihuahuas?'

While some of our questions remained unanswered there was one thing on which all my classes agreed, namely that Colchester United (4th Division) would easily beat Coventry City (old 1st Division). No amount of logic or explanation could convince them of the folly of their deduction. City weren't having a great time, but Colchester were hardly awakening giants storming up the Leagues. Our academic battle seemed futile, their resistance pathetic. Then one day the pupils, as they had done many times before, provided physical evidence to prove me wrong. Coventry were worse than Colchester United because Colchester had never lost to non-league Sutton United of the Vauxhall Conference and on 7th January 1989 John Sillett's team, nearly all of them cup medal holders, were beaten 2-1 in front of a crowd of eight thousand at Ganders Green lane. That Sutton then went on to lose 0-8 up the road at Norwich only rubbed salt into the gaping wound. It was a moment frozen in time for all Coventry City supporters. In an interview in 2001 John Sillet revealed he still tormented himself by displaying a packet of Sutton seeds on his fireplace that some supporter had unkindly sent him many years ago. If sown they would have produced a crop of sky blue forget-me-nots. It can be a cruel game. The subject of football was subsequently designated an inappropriate topic for discussion in Geography lessons. Not that that stopped the little dears from bringing it up at every opportunity. With hindsight I can take some little comfort from the fact that a couple of years later Colchester finally tumbled temporarily into the conference. But to be honest that gives me little joy as I had shared the Colcestrians relegation worries during my years in the town, when only Darlington could save them from the ultimate drop. When Colchester finally did fall from the League they at least did it with typical style and for many Colcestrians the couple of seasons in the Conference were little more than a welcome break in which they enjoyed countless huge goalfests all crowned by a Championship trophy. A holiday away from the everyday pressures of League football. Now that's not something that merely avoiding relegation can ever provide.

Without wishing to add too many stereotypes to those that we all carry around with us no matter how hard we try, this bum bit of Britain is a tiny bit of a footballing wilderness. O.K. there is Ipswich twelve miles to the North, while another two hours' drive down country roads whilst stuck behind combine harvesters and trucks piled high with sugar beet will take you to Norwich. Or the really intrepid can take a trip south through the cultural wilderness of shell-suitland for Upton Park, but that means a train journey into London and then out again. This is hardly the football friendly time I had enjoyed at Coventry, Manchester and Leicester. Now a trip to see the Sky Blues took the whole weekend. In fact a trip to see any team took real effort, which just left....

Colchester United. They played in blue and white and weren't averse to the odd relegation battle. They also had the occasional familiar name on the team sheet. So this was where Tommy English had ended up. Could this possibly be a home from home?

Layer Road is a good place to watch football. More intimate than I was used to, with nice pies in the ground and decent access to local pubs. The only problem was that people who turn up at a pub on their own before a game on match days are carefully observed by all the other drinkers. My accent clearly identified me as an alien and therefore, probably, a rival supporter. This doesn't create the ideal atmosphere to enjoy a pint of the landlord's frothy finest and so I found myself abstaining from this important pre-match ritual.

In the ground there was very little unique on or off the pitch with the exception of the terraces themselves which seemed to be flexible reminding me of the dance floor of the Ritz club in Manchester. The Ritz was one of those nightclubs that earn cult status despite a complete absence of any obvious charm. Various nights of the week were filled with very different themed participants. Wednesday was Punk/Indie, Thursday was grab a granny, Friday was chart and Saturday was fight night. The reason that so many different sub-cultures were happy to share such a place was solely because the Ritz had a bouncy dance floor. I don't think it was designed that way, more it was a result of construction inadequacies when this former warehouse had changed uses. As soon as the floor filled up with pissed revellers all stomping to the same beat (well most - there's always a couple of people who seem to be dancing to some different tune that only they can hear) the whole floor would begin to bounce up and down like a trampoline. Great fun. Sadly Layer Road's terraces no longer vibrate so we will all have to look elsewhere for bouncy spectating entertainment. A lap dancing bar perhaps.

18.

Back in the jug agane

'But to go to school in a summer morn
O! it drives all joy away;
Under a cruel eye outworn
The little ones spend the day
In sighing and dismay.'
William Blake, *The Schoolboy.*

THE LACK OF ACCESSIBLE FOOTBALL provided me with ample opportunity to settle in and devote my energies towards my new career. Teaching is a funny profession. We all have our own opinions and memories of what school life is like based on various experiences. The archetypal best days of our life are hugely influenced by the teachers we get; a couple of good ones and life isn't too bad; a couple of sadistic power freaks and every day seems like Monday morning.

Teaching certainly seems to attract an interesting choice of people to it as a career. The general public's stereotypical teacher wears only Dr. Scholl sandals, nylon shirts (heavily stained under the armpits) and Stayprest trousers which are at least 2 inches short in the leg, with or without turn-ups depending on what is grossly out of fashion at the time. In winter this sartorial elegance may be further enhanced by either a tank-top of psychedelic design and/or a Packamac. Jackets (now only worn in the poshest of fee-paying schools) must always have corduroy patches on the elbow. Teachers never shower and use soap only for cleaning their cars, which are always crapper than the ones driven by their pupils. It is hard to imagine a profession so undervalued by society. We seem happy to forgive our Doctors and lawyers for their accidents that kill loved ones or lead to our financial ruin, but if a teacher ever slips up it is greeted with a huge knowing 'tut' as if to say, well what can you expect from a bloody teacher.

Schoolteachers themselves have a general distrust of all other so-called professionals, based on resentment at their perceived better pay. Consequently they never use their services and this is why people who work in schools always appear so stressed. It isn't the mountain of exercise books they take home every night (and bring back unmarked in the morning) that causes them so many sleepless nights. It is the anxiety that results from their attempt to sell their own house privately, or do their own major structural repairs on the subsidence that threatens not only their own house but the whole terrace, or because they have attempted to perform a minor operation using a razor blade, mirror and G.C.S.E. biology text book and the result has gone septic. This also explains teachers' notoriously poor dentition and halitosis and why they are so frequently absent from school but never have a doctor's note. One teacher told me that a friend of his was sacked when he used the school's chemistry laboratory equipment in a spectacularly unsuccessful attempt to manufacture his own aspirin. He apparently got a short custodial sentence for manufacturing banned hallucinogenic substances and now works for the government as a leading toxicologist.

I slipped into these traditions with great ease. It isn't hard to understand how such stereotypes have become so common. The reason teachers frequently take on a haggard and bizarre appearance may lie partly in the fact that they are too badly paid to be able to afford the luxuries of life such as nice cars, builders' services or toothpaste, but the main reason is that if the only people who see you all day are groups of thirty hostile and disparaging students you soon lose all self respect and critical awareness anyway. Arriving on the first day of term resplendent in a new Armani suit the novice teacher soon has the wind taken out of his sails by comments such as 'its only Emporio', 'that was last year's cut' or 'it's a knock-off from a Turkish market isn't it' and within a week he will have donned the uniform so preferred by her or his colleagues.

A recent government sponsored campaign to attract recruits to the dwindling numbers embracing education as a career drew upon the slogan 'No one forgets a good teacher' and while this may be true it probably isn't quite as true as 'nobody forgets that complete sociopathic bastard of a teacher that spoiled what were supposedly the best days of your life'.

Moving the Goalposts

Teachers are an unusual species with a number of very different breeds, all attracted to the job for disparate reasons. A colleague recently suggested that a number of distinct categories could be clearly identified.

Firstly there are the scholars who enter the profession in the false belief that it will enable them to follow their own selfish academic pursuits. These types almost certainly loved their own school days surrounded by books, tables and charts and hoped to use the long school holidays and numerous free periods to continue their research into 'rumen bacteria of the lower intestine' with a view to publication in some weighty academic journal. Sadly all too soon they discover that life at the chalk-face is not as they had imagined and the early lessons delivered in a tutorial style not dissimilar to the Dimbleby lectures soon give way to hours spent watching the class build papier mache models of their own genitals for submission as G.C.S.E course work.

A second and not altogether dissimilar group are the bureaucrats attracted into the profession by the large number of photocopiers available and schools' unique opportunities for generating meaningless mission statements, achievement targets and league tables of fatuous information. This group are soon promoted out of trouble to the lofty heights of senior management where they are rewarded with a secretary and photocopier of their own. Particularly prolific paper generators may be head-hunted by the civil service to act as school inspectors.

It would however be unfair to suggest that no teachers are there because they want to help young people on their journey through life. Teaching has always attracted its fair share of idealists, philanthropists and political agitators. Schools are fertile developmental areas and thus perfect for those who in previous generations may have sought a life as a missionary or revolutionary. This group in many ways prove the old adage that 'those who can do, while those who can't teach'. The classrooms of these teachers will either display posters from Class War demanding immediate execution of the rich, or Christian Aid pleading for a day of fasting for world peace. Both types spend the greater part of their free time in theological discussions on the meaning of life and whether a rich man can enter the kingdom of heaven.

Another type commonly attracted to teaching is the fascist who is drawn because of the promise of a position of power over hundreds of regimented youths. With their explicit internal hierarchies, clearly defined rules and unchallenged procedures schools are ideal homes for those who would prefer to live in a police state, particularly if they were allowed to rule it. In public schools the fascist can be found running the cadet forces and after many years they often forget that they are teachers and genuinely believe themselves to be Lord Kitchener. Those who remain sane bitterly regret that corporal punishment is no longer an option in modern schools but in many cases this has merely served as a springboard for them to develop ever new ways to humiliate and bully any freethinkers.

An equally terrifying subgroup are those with suppressed paedophilic tendencies who are happy to put countless hours of their own free time into a diverse range of extra-curricular activities just because it allows them to be close to the children. They are happiest when running a scout group at weekends which provides them with the opportunity to spend days at a time surrounded by their charges. They tend not to mix too well with the other teachers and are easy to spot because they are the only teachers not complaining about something. Headteachers are advised to pull the plug on any proposals for a field trip to Bangkok before it gets off the ground.

A less malign group are the cynics/exhibitionists. These are attracted into teaching because they realise that other jobs are even worse. Often they have worked in a 'real' job before deciding that schools offered shorter working hours, longer holidays and greater job security. They also enjoy the fact that to a class of twelve year olds it is easy to show off as either a know-it-all or ham actor. The pre-teens will laugh at anything (If you don't believe this just watch half an hours children's TV) and the exhibitionist can build up his or her own Walter Mitty world in which he is a combination of Eric Morecambe and Albert Einstein. Teaching also allows other delusions of grandeur. When coaching under-12 football most adults will soon slip into the false reality that they are even better at the job than Gordon Strachan, and after a session of double games there is always the warm glow to be gained from reflecting that for the last hour you have been paid to play football and therefore are officially a professional sportsperson.

The final type is the 'dusty old relic'. This is always a bachelor male teacher of indeterminate age who spends the largest part of each day asleep in the staff room. Other teachers seem unsure of his role, subject, or even why he is there, but he carries some suitably vague title such as school antiquarian. He may teach the odd option lesson to the slow reading group, usually on 'the history of the school', but his main use is as a resource for the under-funded history department who wheel him in to lessons to demonstrate a particular point or add flavour to a topic. He's far cheaper than a trip to the Imperial War Museum, never double-booked and invariably too deaf to hear any of the pupils abuse or questions. All the history teacher has to do is guide him into the room and wake him up then, bingo, a forty-five minute lesson of anecdotal information on the Boer War, Crimean War, Great Flood etc. Some progressive schools allow the art department to use their 'dusty old relic' as a life drawing stimulus because painting a nude form is far more interesting when the subject has weathered skin and interesting folds, while infant schools may enlist his help to demonstrate what God looks like.

Needless to say I have never come across any of the aforementioned types, nor do I fit any of the categories. My colleagues and I are all devoted educational enablers who are proud to serve the school, the community and our governors. Honest.

Teaching geography has been particularly good for me. It has provided the excuse, opportunity and funds to travel widely and has introduced me to the unique joys of travelling to many of the world's cultural centres and most romantic cities with a group of thirty youngsters whose own agenda rarely stretches beyond finding the nearest McDonalds. Visiting the Louvre, St. Basil's cathedral or the Vatican accompanied by thirty or forty youngsters is an experience everyone should share. Witnessing the expression on a couple's face as they realise their romantic meal in a Paris restaurant is over when you enter with a party of children, all shouting as quietly as they are able, is worth the hours spent in a German police station explaining why your charges don't understand that jaywalking is a crime. As an unmarried geography teacher I was a willing recruit for any trip that more discerning people had already rejected. The considerable efforts of colleagues have enabled me to travel through most of western and large parts of eastern Europe, the old Soviet Union, U.S.A. and even Africa and the main things that I have learnt from these educational and cultural visits are that;

a) Children get diarrhea upon setting foot on foreign soil.

101

Moving the Goalposts

b) The younger the child, the easier it is for them to find and buy Euro-porn, weapons and alcohol.

c) Pupils of all ages are outraged at the suggestion that they are not allowed to smoke. Cigarettes are like comforters for pupils on foreign trips. No schoolchild can withstand nicotine withdrawal of more than five minutes if in the company of peers, despite the fact that at home they only smoke on a Friday night. On one history trip to the monuments of Renaissance France I was lucky enough to witness an excellent interaction between a pupil and an aged member of the school staff. The boy, resplendent in bikers jacket, ripped jeans and offensive T-shirt, a model ambassador for his school and country, was caught by my colleague hiding behind a column in a picturesque Chateau, smoking a Marlboro. The subsequent conversation revealed just what different dimensions pupil and teacher occupy.

Teacher; 'Danny, you really shouldn't smoke.'
Pupil; 'Why not? It aids digestion.'
Teacher: 'Well for one reason it killed the king.'
Pupil; 'Yeah, but the king did drugs as well.'
Teacher, horrified; 'What ??? George VI used drugs??'
Pupil; 'Oh, I thought you meant Elvis.'

d) If you attempt to expand the horizons of any pupil beyond MTV or Tomb-Raider the response will always be, 'What have you brought us here for'. This was most tellingly brought home when I stumbled upon a young lad's diary which accidentally fell open revealing the following insights....

'Monday; Early start. Had burger at airport. Short pleasant flight to Paris, had a coke and part of the in-flight meal of scrambled egg, bacon and mushrooms. At hotel we had big row over sharing rooms, eventually I got to share with Tim (good) and Steve (bad). Hotel v. good but our TV didn't work. Everyone else's did. Face a whole week without any entertainment. Afternoon - Saw Eiffel Tower (big) and the Mona Lisa (small).

Tuesday;. Notre Dame, top shut for repairs, expensive ice creams outside. Bought big bottle of Coke from supermarket, much, much cheaper than rip-off vending machine in the hotel. Afternoon went to the Palace at Versailles. The train there was a double-decker and I sat upstairs at first, very good seats, but too hot, so sat downstairs and played cards. On way back from palace it was only a normal single-decker train so I slept. TV still not working !!!'.

etc. etc.

d) Tour guides are the real enemy. On a number of trips to the ex-Soviet Union our school party have been thoughtfully supplied with fully trained local guides who obviously had been instructed to provide a continual monologue cataloguing the weight of annual output of all local factories and intimate tours of an infinite number of monuments to the glorious patriots who died defending their country from other, less welcome, guests. Their uninterrupted commentary was possibly to prevent a suitable pause to allow our pupils to ask questions such as 'Why are the shops empty of food but full of alcohol?' Or 'Why do all Russian women under the age of forty feel the need to dye their hair urine yellow by soaking it in neat bleach?'. During one trip we plucked up enough courage to ask whether it might be possible for us to take a diversion to see what was probably one of the World's finest exhibition of Impressionist paintings that had been previously hidden by the Soviets since 1945. In response we were told in no uncertain terms that this would not be necessary as they were, after all, 'Only paint on canvas'.

The main benefit of travelling with a large number of children in tow is that it seems to open many doors. When locals see this group descending upon their town they take it as an opportunity to show off all that is best about their home and so at various times I have been invited to witness weddings, funerals, minor operations and even a birth, as though not to do so would have been to thwart future tourist prospects for the region. Accompanying foreign school trips taught me to never underestimate a child and their potential for outrageous behaviour. I have stared in wide-eyed disbelief as a boy picked up and then licked the skull of a plague victim 'for a bet' during a visit to the underground burial catacombs in Paris. Similarly, the best technique I have ever experienced for clearing a space to sit down on a packed beach took the form of another bet when a boy under my care and supervision stood barefoot in a fresh, still warm, dog-shit as a dare. The look of horror on the families who witnessed this act is burnt into my brain. As they packed up and left in disgust, their family Sunday outing rudely cut-short, I wanted to tell them that the boy wasn't a blood relative, that I wasn't to blame, that he was mentally ill and need-

103

ed sympathy rather than contempt. Sadly the truth was that he was a normal English twelve year old and that is how they like to behave. I suddenly felt very old.

As well as providing opportunities to visit and be humiliated in foreign countries, Colchester was also a good base for exploring that usually inaccessible rump of England that Midlanders only visit on family summer holidays - Cromer Ridge, the Norfolk Broads, Blakeney Point, the bustling port of Harwich with its access to Holland and Hamburg, Constable Country and, my personal favourites, the traditional seaside resorts of Great Yarmouth, Frinton and Clacton.

Frinton is a place where anyone under the age of seventy is viewed as a potential mugger. Activity in the town seems to take place at the speed of a slow motion replay as the retired gentlefolk who make up the bulk of the residents steadfastly refuse to meet their maker. The locals' daily routine revolves between the doctor's surgery and the pharmacy and the town's unusual demographic characteristics make it one of the world's most dangerous locations. Forget uranium mining in Siberia, prostitution in the Philippines or being a clerical officer at the American embassy in Baghdad. If you really want to look certain death in the face move to Frinton with its terrifyingly high mortality rate. Most of the local commerce is devoted to the residents' overriding concern about how to survive another day. Thus Frinton has frowned upon permitting any traditional tourist development and the local council was probably relieved when the package holiday revolution lured potential visitors away to more exotic locations in Spain and Greece. The local choice seems to be either to visit Harwich for the Continent or Frinton for the incontinent. There is no Pepsi Max Big One here, although EXIT, the campaign for legalising euthanasia, might like to consider subsidising the construction of some suitably cardiac arresting rollercoaster, not so much a Big Dipper as a Grim Reaper.

It is not harsh to say that Frinton does not really welcome tourists with open arms. It has actually passed by-laws forbidding ice-cream kiosks and whelk sellers, and many other peddlers of frivolous holiday pleasures. The one pub seems rarely to open as the residents choose not to mix alcohol with their prescribed medication. What it does have is two miles of clean gentle beaches topped by green, litter-free, open spaces, lined with hundreds of beach huts, which look as if they have been there since

Dickensian times, and one thousand free car-parking spaces, which clearly haven't. It is a place where holiday-makers must do exactly that as no one else is going to provide any entertainment for visitors to consume. While Blackpool has its illuminations, in Frinton on wet days people gather to watch the traffic lights change colour. This part of our own growing Costa Geriactrica is where the aged come to die but have forgotten what they came for. The shopping opportunities afforded compare unfavourably with an Albanian market town in mid-winter. The housing estates that fringe the town are really retirement homes. No one gets out of this place alive.

Clacton on the other hand welcomes one and all with its garish neon signs and adverts. Clacton has invested to lure visitors and the results are not entirely impressive. The pier is little more than a half hearted copy of the far grander ones found elsewhere. A stroll along it is about the only safe way to cross from the shore to the sea. Gazing down at the water carrying its heavy load of minced excrement, chemical spills and domestic refuse you want to shout a warning to those foolish enough to go for a paddle. With its fun pubs, chips, drizzle and Bingo, Clacton is everything a seaside resort ought to be and I found it an irresistible magnet.

The noise and smells have such a nostalgic feel to them that they have a romance all of their own. Shops are full of things that free the money from the tightest of pockets. It is impossible not to want to spend money here and I had finally found the resort I'd thought Colchester was going to be. Every time I drove to this part of the Essex coast I got the same excited, need a wee, buzz as soon as the car turned the corner that allowed a first glimpse of the sea. It is now almost a decade since I left this part of England but the memories of this resort are still among my strongest. Personally I can't wait for global warming to start picking up speed and I do all I can to aid the melting of the polar ice-caps in the hope that one day sea-levels will rise enough for me to live by the seaside again either in Manchester-Super-Mare or Coventry- On -Sea.

Despite these salty charms, and the fact that according to local legend I would only have to wait for a few more years to make any friends here I felt the pull of the north calling me back to the wilds from all this southern sophistication. A chance glance at the Times Educational Supplement ultimately resulted in the offer of a job back in Manchester and I was on my way.

Moving the Goalposts

The final year of my exile in Anglia coincided with Coventry City's best season since the cup win. My own attendances had declined dramatically as geography literally prevented a quick sprint home to see the team in action. Fortune favours the brave and hardy and I was able to witness CCFC leading the League after a 2-1 hammering of Manchester City in August.

To be top after only four of the thirty-eight games may be seen as peaking too early but it was heralded as triumph indeed in Coventry. This was, after all, the first time in the club's 101 years that they had reached the summit of the huge league pyramid in which the Sky Blues held the unique record of having played in seven different divisions, namely the Premier, First, Second, Third, Fourth, Third South and Third North. Beat that Arsenal. The expected rapid fall to the relegation zone never materialised and City were in the top half of the table for nearly all the season as Speedie, Smith, Livingstone and even Drinkell kept knocking in the goals. By March a second win in two years over Villa (who we previously had not beaten since 1937) had taken us in reach of the top five and erased all memories of another embarrassing cup exit, this time at the hands of Fourth Division Northampton. A now familiar trudge over to Norwich to witness a goal-less thriller was made worthwhile as we rose to fourth in the Barclay's League Division One, the only dark cloud being the fact that Villa were at the very top. Sadly the momentum couldn't be maintained and the joy of a first ever win at Anfield was more than erased by a 6-1 loss to them in May, the biggest home defeat for seventy years. As the season trailed off the Sky Blues could reflect on a successful season and anticipate even better delights the following year, while I could contemplate that I was returning to my old haunts of Manchester and its famous northern cheer and homely welcome.

In my absence the city had renamed itself as Madchester. When I had last been here it was de rigueur to don grey army coats and stuff daffodils up the arse in imitation of the style influences of Joy Division and The Smiths. Now it was all Stone Roses, James and Happy Mondays as depression had been replaced by mania. The spirit of the place was completely changed. Comprehensive redevelopment of the inner cities was well under way, the first of several bids for the Olympic games was being scrutinised by the relevant bung-seekers and the bulk of the population were happy to inform you that they were 'mad for it'.

While the South can feel rightly proud of its smog-free air and rural tranquillity, not to mention its clement climate that allows the wearing of T-shirts for eight months of the year, the North has the huge compensation that while you stand in the black, acidic rain, hacking up lung-fulls of froth corrupted colliery air, you do at least have the opportunity between wheezes to reflect on the fantastically low-priced and high flavoured beer.

Working with over privileged children from the GameBoy ghettos of South Manchester brought many rewards both physical and metaphysical but the greatest boon was that the school played football. Despite all the years I had spent in educational establishments as both a pupil and a teacher I had never before been in one that played football. All of the state and private schools that I had learnt or taught in were for ideological or geographical reasons rugby schools. So not only was I entering an exciting new role as football coach I was also going to get my first chance to play regular football as the staff had a team with fixtures every week. What bliss, my weekend timetable could be written in stone. Friday night play football, Saturday morning watch/referee under-13's football, Saturday afternoon watch football at Highfield Road, Maine Road or Old Trafford. At last true contentment. Was there ever a life or a time better than this?

Playing football, even at this lowest of all possible standards, taught me an important lesson. Namely that if you play enough football, against weak enough opposition then you will eventually win something. This certainly was true for the Sky Blues who managed to get their hands on the FA Cup after only a century of attempts. As for myself, after monotonous decades of sporting failure I found myself, like CCFC, suddenly in need of a trophy cabinet. This success was not the result of some late flowering of previously unnurtured ability but was simply because teachers love to win things. Perhaps this avarice derives from a need to compensate for other gaps in the academic lifestyle. Consequently in educational circles there are always so many cups, shields, rose bowls and medals on offer that everyone's turn comes round sooner rather than later. The entirely spurious nature of some of these awards seems not to matter in the slightest.

For example I am a proud winner of the South-west of England 4-a-side championship. This sounds a laudable achievement and the shield and medals that accompanied the triumph certainly looked impressive (not as good as the European Cup but certainly better than that plastic thing awarded to the ultimate winner of the Krypton factor). In fact they looked so impressive that our national success was heralded in the local press. One of the 4-a-side team who was applying for promotion headlined it in his curriculum vitae and after talking at length about his trophy and the 'culture of success' that he could bring to the new job found himself head of department at one of the country's more prestigious public schools. The sad truth is that the South West of England championship was won during a boozy tour to Weston-super-mare, when we managed to play a little football to justify getting out of bed in the mornings. It was 4-a-side because only four out of the twenty colleagues who promised to come bothered to turn up. We had the trophies made, travelled down to the seaside, got drunk, had a kick about with some locals and then awarded ourselves the prizes in the pub afterwards.

This isn't to suggest that all footballing teachers are crap at the game. Surprisingly many that I play with claim to have been on schoolboy books or have had trials with clubs as varied as Chelsea, Wolves and Port Vale. On some happy occasions a starry eyed first year, following up something another teacher has told him, has asked me if I really did once play for Coventry City, which rather says more about his opinion of the football skills of CCFC than it does about his assessment of mine. However we did discover one day that our staff football ranks were to be strengthened by the arrival of a current soccer international. Admittedly the international cap was only from New Zealand, but hey, they were hardly mugs when it comes to sport, and so we waited impatiently for this young international's arrival, gleefully anticipating huge shameful victories over all our local rivals (in school football every game is a massively important local derby against bitter enemies).

When he arrived he was a little smaller and younger than we'd anticipated, but let's face it Garrincha, Juninho and Michael Owen never let that hold them back. Stanko, the exchange student from New Zealand confirmed that yes he was in fact a current 'soccer' international and we immediately forgave him for his height and for getting the name of our round ball sport wrong. His debut was only three days later and of course we won convincingly. Stanko, playing up front where he could do most damage, had quite a quiet game and his role in the victory was more inspirational than actual.

After the match we all descended on the local pub as usual to dissect our play and talk general bollocks until throwing out time. Stanko however couldn't join us and we watched in awe as he was whisked away by Sir Bob Scott, Chairman of Manchester's Olympic bid, to meet Bobby Charlton and the other Directors of Manchester United. Needless to say this revelation had a huge influence on our appraisal of his contribution to the evening's triumph. We recognised that despite the fact that he must be suffering jet lag from his gruelling twenty-five hour flight from Auckland he had shown some impressive touches and clearly could teach us all a few tricks. Some of the older players went quiet and contemplated their own threatened future in the team. Would they be able to keep up with play? Would their inadequacies merely be highlighted by the brilliance of the youngster playing up front? For me the big question was whether I, as fellow striker, would be able to get a last touch on any of his net bound shots and thus beat my last year's grand tally of one goal.

Further interrogation of our new signing revealed that he really had been a guest of Bobby Charlton and had watched United play at the weekend from Charlton's own box. He seemed more impressed by the fact that he spent the entire game sat next to Suzanne Charlton whom he had previously seen reading the weather. The realisation that he had also shared company with a World Cup medal holder, Knight of the Realm and legend of Old Trafford appeared to have made little impression upon him. Perhaps these internationals spend so much time in each others' company that the whole thing becomes a bit passe. Fair enough, if I'd spent the evening in the company of the greatest living geography teacher and Suzanne Charlton I too would be more impressed with the latter.

At school he was quickly put to work training one of the boys' football teams. Given the hierarchical state that exists within schools with the reflected glory that is associated with running the top teams and the incredible sulking involved if a teacher is ever demoted from coaching the First Eleven it was perhaps inevitable that Stanko was assigned to help with my team, the Under-13 'B's. Under his careful tutelage they flourished and it wasn't long before they had all developed new skills. There were few better 'B' teams in the country when it came to the basics of spitting, standing on an opponent's boots at corners and of course, falling to the ground, as if mortally wounded, in the box. This tangible success quickly led to his promotion to the 'A' team (and no I don't mean the one you call if you are in trouble and you need a gilt bedecked, welding, ex-wrestler's help).

The team went from strength to strength. For really important games, or if we expected to lose, he was even allowed to referee the game, and before we knew it we had reached the dizzy heights of the Manchester Schools Cup Final. Even the huge handicap of a neutral referee couldn't stop us now and though we were twice behind, touchline threats of physical violence to key players by our antipodean coach roused our children on to a magnificent win.

There can have been few more shameful sporting sights than the triumphal cheer and pitch invasion from the linesman that greeted our winning goal. As the boys collected their plastic winners' medals we showered them with Pomagne and Ferrero Rocher chocolates. Our lesson to them on how to be magnanimous in victory didn't end there. After mugging the captain and wrestling the Under-13 trophy from his happy hands we headed off into town to celebrate in the time honoured fashion of football professionals (minus the drugs and page three girls, sadly). As we clambered aboard the number Forty-two bus for Piccadilly with the huge glass encased shield between us our appearance was greeted with a huge cheer from all the other passengers. The driver refused to accept payment after hearing that we were the Manchester City Youth team and we had just won this impressive trophy by beating Liverpool 4 -0 in the final.

Eventually we found ourselves, much the worse for wear, lying on the floor of a late night drinking den, beer all down our clothes and curry in our hair. Miraculously we still had the trophy with us and it had hardly picked up a scratch. As consciousness drifted away I became aware of a young female voice whispering in my ear.

'You're Mr. Wheeler aren't you?' I opened my eyes to see a glamorous young girl smiling benevolently at me. Had I died and gone to heaven? Could life really get any better than this?

'You don't recognise me do you?' said this Venus. 'You used to teach me geography years ago. What do you do now?'

With the schoolboys' victory laurels firmly in place we could concentrate on our own performances on the pitch. Frankly Stanko had yet to live up to his billing. He was undeniably fit and fast, though our English sporting traditions of pub and kebab were beginning to slow him down. In conversation it was revealed that not only was he a football international but his sister was a New Zealand netball international, his friend a cricket international, his cousin a New Zealand football regular, currently playing with Leyton Orient, his niece a female rugby international, his uncle did power lifting for New Zealand in the Olympics. His pedigree was bewildering until it gradually dawned on us that in New Zealand (with a population smaller than that of Greater Manchester) everyone is an international.

Eventually, after intensive interrogation, he cracked and revealed that although he was an international, it was only an honorary award. He had never actually played for the 'All Whites' but he had been selected for the New Zealand schoolboy team who don't actually play internationals.

Stanko was here on a mission. He was a guest of Manchester's Olympic bid committee, hence the meetings with Bob Scott, who were keen to impress Stanko because his power-lifting Uncle might have some influence upon the casting of the crucial Vanuatuan vote (or some similar South Pacific giant) in the choice of site for the 2000 Olympics. If Manchester could win some votes from the Southern Hemisphere Olympic Committee members it would considerably strengthen their bid against the rivals of Sydney and Beijing. We set about entertaining Stanko as our part towards Britain's athletic future. No pub was left unvisited, no theme park untried, no effort too great. We took him to discover the beauty of Amsterdam (biggest hit Madam Tussaud's, biggest miss 'Frank Anne's House' which he branded a 'money making scam'); we took him to Dublin to taste the Guinness (opinion 'it's shocking, like gravy'); we took him to see United at the Theatre of Dreams; we took him to see West Ham play Manchester City; we even took him to see Coventry play at Oldham where Kevin Gallacher scored.

Eventually he confessed that the real love of his life was Liverpool FC and what he most wanted to do was to visit Anfield so we even took him there. The greatest moment in his year in England came when he got to see his beloved Reds at Wembley. He had failed to get a ticket for their FA Cup final win but we managed to get a few for the charity shield match against those popular champions Leeds United. This was the first game played after the banning of the back-pass to keeper and it really livened up what might otherwise have been a rather boring season opener. Sadly for

Moving the Goalposts

Manchester's Olympic aspirations the day didn't go well and he left in tears. All too soon it was time for our cultural guest to depart. He was due to fly out on my birthday, the 20th December and before he went he had one final request, that I take him to watch his beloved Liverpool for the final time. So, against my better judgment, I took him to see one last game before his departure. I felt right at home, as Liverpool were playing the Sky Blues at Highfield Road, though quite nervous about the result. Coventry needed a win to ignite a failing season. If Liverpool lost Stanko's last few hours in England would be unbearable and his final memories overwhelmingly negative. The game went completely against form, as we should have guessed it would, and Coventry humiliated his stars before his tear-stung eyes. 5-1, a record City win. I thought we would never stop scoring.

A few months later waiting in Manchester's Castlefield basin, part of the redevelopment of Manchester's inner city in hopeful anticipation of the granting of the Olympics to Britain, we heard that in a three horse race the city's bid had come a very poor third. Notably the crucial Vanuatuan vote had not been cast in favour of the Northern Hemisphere. Personally I have always blamed Borrows (37 [pen],54) Gallacher (61) and Quinn (71,74).

19.

Going nowhere fast

GOING TO WATCH FOOTBALL IN MANCHESTER is an entirely alternate adventure to watching it in Coventry. In Coventry I can turn up at two o'clock, park in my usual place in Hillfields, walk to the ground across a small park and never see a Coventry City shirt or obvious football fan. Frequently I am left wondering whether the game has been abandoned, or rearranged for Sunday to suit Sky TV, or whether I've read the fixture list and newspapers wrong and it was a morning kick off or something. It isn't until I climb the steps out of the park, only ten or so yards from the West Stand that I see anyone else who appears to be going to watch a game of football. In the bad old days when there were less than ten thousand turning up to see the Sky Blues we used to reflect that whereas other teams' fans would watch Match Of The Day in the hope of spotting themselves in the crowd we used to turn on in the expectation of hearing ourselves cough.

A stroll to Maine Road or Old Trafford on a Saturday provides a totally different experience. Fifteen years ago I used to visit each ground on alternate weekends as a cheap substitute to travelling down to Coventry to see my own team. Like all cheap alternatives, it wasn't what I really wanted, but it was marginally better than nothing at all. A methadone supporting experience, you might say. I'd join the huge throng marching to the ground that began some miles from the actual stadium. On arrival I would pay the bloke on the turnstile and that was that, I was in. Now I can't do that at Old Trafford or even Maine Road. The only way I get to see the Sky Blues there is via my work contacts or by supporting the lifestyle of local touts and often the real price to pay has been having to sit among the opposition fans and that detracts somewhat from why I bother watching the team in the first place. The main difference at both the Manchester grounds is the huge number of people. At Coventry we now get over 20,000 turning up but there is never that feeling of being in a huge sea of spectators that you get at the really big clubs, where you get swept along by the human tide all flowing in exactly the same direction. It is a truly inspiring sensation and greatly adds to the sense of occasion and importance of the activity. This isn't mere leisure; it's about a sense of identity and community; of shared purpose and conformity. These are the real advantages of supporting a big club.

I prefer it at Coventry. You may have to wait a bit to see lots of people and they may all arrive at the last minute, but they are all unique and memorable. It's surprising how quickly you can come to recognise and know those other 20,000 people at the ground. Like any human relationships you come to identify and then love people's individual habits and idiosyncrasies. It is a great comfort to see these people who's names remain largely unknown to me but whose routines are destined to collide with my own at such regular intervals. It's lazy mateship, friends without having to make arrangements or remember birthdays, or even really care about how they are.

Crowds are natural things. They are as common in nature as they are in mankind. Things seem to have an innate command or urge that drives them together. Usually this is triggered by some common desire such as a bargain washing machine in the January sales, to see a favourite singer at a concert, to hear an enlightened voice speak at an evangelical meeting or to see some men in polyester shirts kick an inflated plastic sheath into some netting. In the wild, birds and fish commonly flock together for their mutual benefit, be it for feeding or defence. Perhaps the best example is the jellyfish which is of course neither a jelly nor a fish. Despite its distinctive appearance it isn't a single organism at all but a colony of very simple animals clinging together to make a more complex whole. A weird combination of young and old, mature, immature and even the dead, all specialists in different activities - digestion, stinging, inflating, binding, all combining in harmony. At CCFC we can also see specialists in different fields working together to create the atmosphere - the singers, the clappers, the doubters, the miserable old gits, and the boring commentators - all combining in perfect harmony to make up a Coventry crowd in which they have sacrificed their individuality to adopt a common identity.

In the human world crowds tend to take two distinct types. There are those long-lived crowds that have fused together as a single organism and become domesticated by tradition and formalised by ritual all channelling their energies to secure a common goal. Such bodies create distinct boundaries between themselves and the rest of the population and are identifiable as such. This is the type regular football fans form, while historically the Tribes of Israel, the Holy Roman Empire and the Christian Crusades also serve as examples. In contrast there are also short-lived crowds that slowly build to a great crescendo and then die. Such crowds as these can be found during a cup run when a whole town finds itself swept along in the fervour, or it may form to see the deposing of a monarch or company director, or in protest of too rapid a rise in petrol prices. In Manchester, Maine Road has been a frequent focus for such crowds all chanting for Swales' departure and disappearing after achieving their goal. Then gathering again to force Francis Lee out before again dissipating. No doubt it won't be very long before their growth is triggered again.

As our villages first grew into towns and then cities and our cities expanded into conurbations, crowds have become a far more common feature of everyday life. The largest cities house considerably more people than can be found in many small countries and it is inevitable that this has brought increased tension associated with the development of urbanism. As a member of a colony of countless neighbours it is increasingly difficult to make any demonstration of original behaviour or uniqueness. That being said, I don't know anyone else in Manchester who wears Coventry's colours with pride.

In today's society success is increasingly important and people regularly come up with ever new methods to measure our individual and collective successes and failures. These are interesting concepts. Coventry City have survived in the top league for thirty three years against all odds. In that time we have witnessed the relegation of far more successful clubs such as Manchester United, Leeds United and Aston Villa. However these clubs are rightly perceived as far more accomplished than us because they have more than redressed their relegation failures by league championships and cup wins.

In nature success is measured in slightly different terms. The most successful plant is not the one that lifts the prize at the Chelsea flower show that year. That specially created rose or pansy hybrid has no real place in the big scheme of the floral world. Similarly there is no annual distance flying contest for birds, no speed trials for cheetahs, or 'the World's Strongest Elephant' competition. The most successful species in nature are those which have survived the longest. The sharks, bracken and cockroaches which have been around for over two hundred and fifty million years are the winners, while man (less than one million years) and hybrid pansies (between one year and one hundred years maximum) are yet to prove their real success, being the Rushden and Diamonds of the ecosphere. It might be argued that man in his short time has achieved far more than a cockroach or shark can ever dream of. No shark has ever produced a sculpture worth studying, no cockroach has published any meaningful discourse on the nature of existence. All they do is eat and make baby sharks and cockroaches, which isn't an entirely unenviable existence. Also, perhaps more tellingly, sharks' blood is immune to all known cancers and cockroaches are widely believed to be the species best placed to survive a nuclear war, so although the muse has abandoned them and they don't write or sculpt they certainly seem to be pretty well informed.

To labour the point and test your patience still further, the three-leaf clover is an evolutionary success, spreading well and filling any number of habitats with almost perfect replicas of its parents. But a four-leaf clover, the biological impossibility, that freak of nature, is far more interesting. Kevin Keegan is good at commentating on the scoring of a goal, a physics professor can probably explain the dynamics of the act and the trajectory of the ball as energy is transformed from boot to ball and finally to the net. Robbie Keane certainly couldn't but I was far more ready to pay my money and see him and his successors do it than pay the others to tell me about it.

So perhaps we need to review the meaning and value of success. Coventry and sharks' sole priority is to further prolong their already impressive habit for survival. Wimbledon, like Watford and Brighton before them have shone brightly and briefly, the real measure of their successes will depend on a view from hindsight. Watford's glory really didn't add up to much.

Overseas football stars are praised for introducing new flair and wizardry to our football stadiums. The jinks, dribbles, half flicks and over head kicks are all very pretty. However, at Coventry the skill we have come to admire most is longevity. That's why we keep extending Steve Ogrizovic's contract.

20.

A Ron for your money

WHEN I WAS AT SCHOOL IN THE LATE 1970'S one of the subjects I elected to study was 'O' Level economics. In these lessons we learnt all about prices and the free market which seemed to have enormous relevance to football at the time and perhaps has even greater relevance now. It transpired that price and value were not the same thing, that the value of an object or service was perceived rather than actual and thus an object's value differed depending upon who was doing the valuing. This subjectivity was of little interest to the economist as the economist is only concerned with an item's value in exchange, or its sale price. The sale price for the object is theoretically determined by the external forces of Supply and Demand. In its simplest form an item's demand will increase if its price falls and decrease if its price rises. Similarly more of a good will be offered for sale at high prices and less at low. This fairly common sense reasoning results in some equilibrium occurring in the market place which is ultimately reflected in the good's or service's final price.

Such economic theory perfectly fits the experience of football supporters. As demand to watch football increased at the end of the 80's and the game shook off its 'hooligan' image it started courting an new kind of audience. Families and corporations were encouraged to become involved in 'their' local community via the football team and the increased demand resulted in an increased price for the supply of football.

Now I don't want to dwell on the old moan about how we used to be able to watch a World Cup final in our own country, buy a new shirt from Top Man and take Twiggy for a slap up 'Fishy Moore' supper for less than ten shillings, and how nostalgia ain't what it used to be. That would be premature as this is a role I have reserved for later in my life to go alongside how I remember when all this was trees and how money used to have the Queen's face on it, not the Director of the Bundesbank. But what really interested me at the time was a thing called elasticity of demand and supply and how it could justify why footballers all had champagne lifestyles and football spectators didn't.

In the textbooks it explained that footballers were inelastic in supply, that the number of them couldn't stretch, it wasn't flexible. So if Coventry City suddenly needed (or demanded) a few more midfield dynamos it couldn't just nip out and get them because there is a very fixed supply of such a desirable good and that in times of shortage you can't just quickly train up a couple of school kids or get a goalkeeper to retrain and change position. (David Speedie later proved this particularly argument invalid when he took over in goal for a spell). So this puts all the current midfield dynamos in quite an enviable position as they can force up their wages to an inflated rate well above average in the knowledge that there is no chance of outside competition.

Thus Trevor Peake as a specialist right-back got, what at the time, seemed to be huge wages while my economics teacher (who claimed Third class honours from Plymouth Polytechnic) got bugger all. He was easily replaceable as it doesn't take long to train up a Head of Economics. A mere four years for 'O' and 'A' Levels, a three year degree, one year teacher training, one year as a probationary teacher, five years to learn the ropes - a piece of piss.

So, as everybody knew, footballers in the top divisions earned an absolute mint because relatively few people can do what Trevor Peake did every week. The thing that has always puzzled me is how so many players seem to end up flat broke within seconds of them retiring from the game despite having had twenty years on astronomical wages and a final pay packet of a lucrative testimonial year. Where does all the money go? If, as the popular press would like us to believe, they really do spend it all on booze, drugs, fags and shagging they would not be able to get out of bed on a Saturday to play and the Premiership would resemble Sunday league football with all its panting, vomiting and absences, even more than they did in Terry Butcher's Sky Blue era.

If we accept that the wages quoted in the press are the wildest of exaggerations which serve only to give players a better negotiating position and raise their prestige, then only the taxman really knows what they actually earn. Perhaps there lies the reason for their poverty, that they were taxed on their reported rather than their actual income.

Michael Gynn is an interesting example. This CCFC FA Cup winner arrived at Highfield Road from Peterborough and started on two hundred pounds a week. This was fairly modest for the time as Dietmar Brook had been on almost as much in the 1960's and Jim Blyth on considerably more in the 1970's. Micky soon saw his wages rise to four hundred pounds and the Sky Blues overall wage bill had risen to over one million pounds a year.

At the time this was seen as wildly extravagant and football was the job to go into if you wanted to accumulate a huge pile of cash in those pre-National Lottery days. Today we have many Coventry players signed on contracts for a less thrifty twenty-five thousand pounds a week and it will be interesting to see if the current batch of highly paid professionals retire with the same sort of financial difficulties that have forced Michael Gynn to take a postman's job in Coventry, his ex-teammate Greg Downs to join the police force, and Terry Gibson to set up a firm marketing bicycles. It was refreshing to note that Killer Kilcline refused to retire gracefully and is probably still terrorising forwards somewhere in the lower leagues. Meanwhile Trevor Peake, another star of 1987 has returned as youth coach to keep the bailiffs at bay.

If we thought footballers were pretty well off in the past, recent post-Bosman activity has made all previous deals look like small change lost down the back of the Sky Blue sofa and the wage bill for 1996/1997 had increased to eight and a half million pounds with the bulk of that increase coinciding with the Ron Atkinson era.

Ron was a surprising choice as the new Sky Blue manager. It was a surprise that he was offered the job and amazing, given our perilous financial position and his renowned love of spending other peoples' cash, that he accepted. When this larger than life character swanned into Highfield Road he immediately put a couple of thousand on the attendance of each home game.

That perennial strugglers like the Sky Blues could even attract such a big name was heralded as a triumph for Chairman Bryan Richardson. Few fans cared that he was a reject from Aston Villa. Fewer still voiced disapproval of a self-proclaimed boyhood Villa fan taking controls of the Sky Blues. Instead the buzz was that Big Ron always won things. More specifically he always won cups and that is all any realistic Coventry fan dare aspire to. So we turned up, bought the Big Ron's Barmy Army T-Shirt and waited for the inevitable cup triumph, secretly hoping that it would be a second victorious campaign in the F.A. Cup rather than a first success in that lesser cup competition, the one with a fizzy drink title.

But all too soon the orange tan of the once great man began to fade. He spent sixteen million pounds on a squad that only avoided relegation on the last day of the season and then only on goal difference. To fans reared on last day scares the use of so much money to achieve so little seemed faintly scandalous. The difference between that relegation scare and the many previous flirtations with the drop was that we had been led to expect more.

Nobody expects much when your top players are recruited from lower divisions, the youth team or other top club's reserve squads. That is exactly what made the F.A. cup triumph of 1987 so important. It wasn't just that Coventry City could not afford to buy any of the Tottenham players, the club didn't even have the resources to pay such valuable players their wages had they arrived on a free transfer. This was the sort of history that supporters of our unfashionable Midland club grew up with. It wasn't really the sort of history that had room for a character with the monicker 'Big'. The only big thing in the history of Coventry City is Jimmy Hill's chin and even that left us for the glamour and bright lights of Fulham.

In the end Ron had to go and find someone else's funds to invest, but the great media manipulator was even denied the opportunity to stage-manage his own departure. News was leaked, possibly through a director, to the Mirror newspaper. Big Ron was not happy. In a display of purposeful aggression that had been sadly lacking from his team he pointed the finger at Geoffrey Robinson, the Labour M.P. whose funds helped buy club captain Gary McAllister and have allegedly also helped some leading politicians pay their mortgage.

'It was leaked by a member of the board,' Ron fumed. 'I shan't name the person, but put it this way, I shall be voting Tory at the next election.' And we had always assumed he was a member of the Socialist Workers Party.

Moving the Goalposts

As for Big Ron's history; he won successive promotions at Cambridge, impressed at West Bromwich and won the F.A. Cup, but never the league, with Man Utd. With Sheffield Wednesday he won promotion and the League Cup but in the end few friends. At Aston Villa he won the League Cup in 1994 but was sacked because of the teams' poor league form. After Coventry he temporarily returned to Sheffield Wednesday.

At Coventry he presided over fourteen wins in sixty-eight league games and early cup exits in all attempts. As he passed over the mantle to his assistant he left the club firmly embedded in the relegation zone. But he left the club in a far better position than he had found it and had sowed the seed that would later germinate so productively because one of the names lured to our unfashionable location was his replacement, the fierce Scot Gordon Strachan. Wee Gordon soon bolstered up the squad he inherited with a bit more steel and a lot more effort. Those who didn't like hard work were sidelined and other, less famous, new faces drafted in. Although his first season ended with the slimmest of Premier survivals, his first full year was far more impressive as City spent most of the time well inside the top half of the table. With Dion Dublin winning the golden boot, being nominated for PFA player of the year and earning our first England cap since Cyrille Regis few could have hoped for a better season. Gordon bought (and crucially sold) widely and wisely in a manner more associated with previous Coventry gaffers. The bargain basements of Scandinavia were plundered in Viking fashion and some real gems unearthed. Roland Nilsson brought a maturity, class and confidence to the defence that had long been absent. Magnus Hedman proved to be a worthy successor to the peerless Oggy. George Boateng was snapped up from Feyenoord for small change, scored twice in our first ever league win at Villa Park, and then was sold to them for a huge profit. With European, African and South American players arriving (and some leaving for a large profit) Coventry City were managing to swim with the sharks while keeping their heads above water. After many years of close shaves Gordon Strachan managed to negotiate the club into a safer position. Not threatening the big clubs but not likely to get pulled under by the other strugglers.

It all appears far rosier than when one Jimmy Hill first took over the reins at this failing midlands club.

21.

I can manage

JIMMY HILL BECAME THE YOUNG MANAGER of Coventry City
Football Club in December 1961, just after City had hit rock bottom following an F.A. Cup defeat by King's Lynn of the Southern League. Jimmy
insisted on complete control when he took over and few could have suspected he would use the power so originally and successfully. This new
broom swept through the old cobwebs at Highfield road and changed nearly everything. He abandoned the team strip in favour of Manchester City's
colours and nicknamed the team the Sky Blues. He took the traditional
matchday programme, that had the look and all the interest of a hymn
sheet, and revamped it into a glossy, readable magazine with bright pictures
of his young stars. This wasn't merely window dressing. He made the club
a more attractive venue for Coventry's citizens to visit and, crucially,
attempted to make them feel part of what he dubbed 'The Sky Blue
Revolution'. He was years ahead of his time and the club have reaped the
dividends since. Effectively he transformed an unsuccessful Third Division
team into a top league club with the infrastructure in place to keep them
there for over thirty years.

Highfield Road was developed from an antique ruin into one of the
most modern stadiums in the country, the first all-seater, with training facilities at Ryton better than anything else available at the time. Hill built a team
that contained some enduring names. Hudson was the fans' favourite,
though two defenders, George Curtis and John Sillett were ultimately have
a greater influence, and become national stars, in the long run.

On April twenty fifth 1964 Coventry played Colchester United needing a victory to ensure promotion out of Division Three. A crowd of

123

36,901 saw City win 1-0 to be crowned Third Division Champions and the climb had begun. By April 1967 the Sky Blues had secured promotion to the First Division and 51,000 witnessed a home victory over Wolves that virtually secured the Second Division championship. After guiding the Sky Blues to the top flight, as the fans sang the Sky Blue song that he had written, Jimmy Hill resigned to enter television punditry. Though the Sky Blue Messiah did finally make a 'second coming' almost a decade later as Managing Director, his novel approach failed to have the same impact second time around. The club lost money on investments in the fledgling NASL and its own leisure complex, and eventually had to sell the Ryton Training Centre.

Jimmy's successor in 1967, Noel Cantwell, took Coventry into the promised land of European cup football. The Sky Blues' only season in Europe started with a convincing 4-1 home win over Takia Plodiv in the first round of the European Fairs Cup. A further 2-0 away win allowed some confidence to develop though this was sadly short-lived. In the next round Coventry found themselves under a German bombardment almost as severe as that of November 1940 as a Bayern Munich team that contained half the West German national team hammered us 6-1 in the away leg. A 2-1 victory back in Coventry allowed us to restore a little dignity to what has remained our sole European excursion. We thought that we were into the UEFA cup in 1978 but a late Roger Osbourne goal in the FA Cup Final meant that the place was lost. The events at Heysel prevented City taking part in the 1987/8 European Cup-winners cup so that, for the time being, is that.

After Cantwell, Bob Dennison acted as caretaker manager (and managed to avoid relegation) until the appointment of the first of two very successful double-acts, Joe Mercer and Gordon Milne. The larger than life Mercer served as a perfect foil to the more conservative Milne. Milne eventually took over complete control and managed to build and then sell three teams, but his sides were always hampered by the lack of funds. Next came Dave Sexton, a manager of proven pedigree with Manchester United. He developed a youthful team that included Danny Thomas, Garry Gillespie and Mark Hately. Early success had the Sky Blue Army scenting trophies, but our traditional post-Christmas slide resulted in Sexton's departure on the morning of the final match of the season in 1983. Sexton was undoubtedly a fine coach and whilst at Coventry led the England Under-21 side to victory in the European championship. He was popular with the players and it needed a big character to win back their, and the supporters', faith. The next management appointment was going to be crucial.

The job was given to Bobby Gould, a popular ex-Sky Blue player and a Coventrian through and through. Unfortunately many of the squad he inherited had come to the end of their contracts and wanted to move elsewhere and so Gould was forced to rebuild the team. In this he was inspirational and has come to epitomise what the fans at Coventry expect from their manager. He bought twenty-five players in eighteen months and the bulk of them were bargains from the lower leagues. Peake, Gibson, Pearce, Bennett, Adams, Kilcline and Ogrizovic were all virtually unknown, while Regis was widely considered to be well past his sell by date. Together they formed the basis of a squad that went on to win the FA Cup, while Pearce and Adams left at a large profit. As luck would have it Bobby Gould's buys did not flower quickly enough to save him and too close a flirtation with the relegation zone saw him replaced by Don Mackay.

The team continued to struggle. Eight games without a win and the selling of Terry Gibson forced Mackay's resignation and Coventry were on the look for another manager. George Curtis and John Sillett took over with three games left. They oversaw two wins and thus the Sky Blues narrowly avoided relegation. By the end of the following season they had won the cup. Things couldn't get any better.

The success-fuelled expectations eventually expedited Sillett's departure and there then followed a trickle of less effective 'Big Names'. Terry Butcher was a player of widespread repute. A heroic former England skipper with a taste for a battle. The kind of scrapper you might expect to find harmony with the Coventry psyche. Sadly his indiscipline and a remarkably short-lived arthritis affliction meant the player-manager played little, sold fan favourites Speedie and Regis and as a result his departure was not greatly mourned. Don Howe and Phil Neal both had a go at the job but found managing Coventry a bit more daunting than coaching England. Eventually Bobby Gould returned again for a short spell but financial hardship and the threat of having to sell his best players forced an early resignation which made the appointment of the next manager seem rather strange.

Somehow between the departure of Gould and the arrival of

Atkinson the Sky Blues discovered previously undreamt of wealth. Whether the Chairman discovered oil under the main stand, or gained income from investment advice from the millionaire M.P. Geoffrey Robinson, a CCFC Director, may never be known, but suddenly Coventry City was a buying club and Ron was soon doing what he is best known for, spending money. Some buys proved initially very successful, such as Whelan and Burrows, others were less impressive and Jess, Evtushok, Lamptey, Isaias, etc never showed any hint that they might be worth the millions spent on them.

Nevertheless the Ron Atkinson and Gordon Strachan double act, an athletic and more entertaining version of Little and Large, coincided with the club's most stable financial and league position for a considerable time. Under their leadership a solid team has been collected that should not look out of place in the all new Mega-Stadium that the Chairman has set out to develop.

When the Head of Games at the school I teach at decided to entrust his Under-13 football team to my unproven coaching skills he could at least console himself that there was no danger of me doing a Big Ron. School's teams are sadly not allowed to operate like their counterparts in the real world. There are no transfer fees, bungs, loans or fines of a week's wages to enliven a boring season, and there is no relegation threat nor Chairman's vote of confidence to add nerves to a poor one. There is little in the traditional role of manager for a teacher to do. The job is basically one of picking a team, telling them their positions and then trying to explain what went wrong if they lose, or trying not to look too smug when they win. Given the insular position school team coaches occupy it is quite easy to drift into a dream world and become a farcical creature, a hybrid form of part David Pleat, a bit of Ron Atkinson and the silken tongue of Graeme Taylor. The pre-match team talk takes on a mystical property and what with the half time tactical changes, cajoling/bollocking and post match analysis it is easy to get caught up in the fantasy.

I suppose it is just about conceivable that real football managers could fall prey to such illusions of grandeur. Can we really be expected to take seriously anyone who insists on fellow adults addressing him as 'The Gaffer' or 'Guv'nor'? The pretentiousness of it is comical. It is the manner one might more readily associate with a Victorian mill owner rather than a senior supervisor of a multi-million pound industry. It is hard to imagine a Doctor or bank manager asking all his staff to call him or her 'Gaffer'? It would be funny if it was meant in parody, but you have to suspect the intention is rather different. The really sad thing is that all other adults will immediately emulate such behaviour given the merest sniff of a chance.

Many school coaches soon adopt the manager's jacket and chief scout's flat cap. They pick up a northern or a dour Scot's accent and become uncharacteristically reticent when bedecked in their Saturday morning costume. The only sillier site on the school playing field or park touchline is that of the over-zealous parent who spends the entire match giving individual coaching, abuse or massages to the offspring who carries within his or her frame all their own failed aspirations. Sometimes the teacher and dad inevitably come to blows as the teacher says 'Play wide' and the dad says 'Take the centre of the park'; the teacher says 'Hold the line' and the dad says 'Push forward' the teacher says 'Shut up, you are confusing him' and the dad says 'You're not using him right'. Eventually as two almighty egos clash the teacher says 'It's a team game see the big picture', dad says 'My lad is the only one who can play a bit'. It all comes to a head when finally the teacher informs the dad that his child is substituted and the frustrated dad hits him. The dad gets touchline ban and the whole procedure starts again the following week with all the same lads, minus the original dad who has now been replaced by some Uncle, Mum, brother, or Gran. It's no wonder footballers so frequently place themselves in a position where their actions provoke an accusation of them acting like dissenting prima donnas. After all for many of the children the sad reality is that the only time they get any male parental attention is when they are on the football pitch and then their guiding role model is busy abusing the referee from the touchline. It isn't a great example to be set.

Such ridiculous behavior is not restricted to school matches, or even just to humans. My experience and understanding of the animal kingdom is very limited as I am an urban species. I'm far happier wandering around Earlsdon or Rusholme than in the fields around Stoneleigh or in the wilderness of the Peak District. However despite this ignorance of the natural world it does seem to me that in the animal kingdom it is predominantly the male that feels compelled to put on displays in the desire to be noticed. The brightly coloured mallard duck makes his female companion seem very drab by comparison. Male peacocks are famous for their feathers and lions for their shaggy manes. Stags grow antlers and walruses develop tusks for display rather than combat.

It has been suggested that football is for man-cubs who refuse to grow up. An acceptable unifier and meeting place for the growing 'Lad culture'. As man has evolved from hunter into office clerk the need to be able to fell a marauding woolly mammoth has declined, but the urge has still remained. In the Neolithic period mankind largely changed from being a species of hunters into one of gatherers and cultivators. Unfortunately there is very little joy to be had in bragging about the size of the carrot you have just harvested for your tea and so we males have had to seek an alternative. The real focus for our show off displays are potential mates (by that I mean breeders rather than people to drink beer with). Thus men have evolved elaborate display behaviours that make the posturing of a proud peacock seem downright halfhearted. The big, fast sports car may be a replacement for the hunter's steed but in these days of perpetual traffic jams it is really little more than an expensive sofa. In the male psyche, however, it becomes the tool that will enable him to be first to the kill. The first to hunt out new feeding and breeding territories. But our sexual displays don't stop there. Everything we do is in the hope of being noticed by a potential conquest. When pulling on a brand new pair of shoes, or the latest CCFC away shirt for wandering down to the newsagents, or when standing in the seating area in the West Terrace attempting to start a chant that will unite all the Beta males behind us we are acting in this time fashioned role. Men belch and fart with the maximum force they can muster, often risking a hernia or haemorrhoidal burns in the process, because they believe it will gain attention and respect. It cries out 'I have fed well and am ready to procreate so please form an orderly queue and wait your turn'. Incredibly, despite the Millennia over which we have perfected these subtle mannerisms they seem to actually have the opposite affect on their intended victims. Which just goes to show it doesn't matter how hard you try, there is no pleasing some people.

That isn't to say women are averse to their own display behaviour, after all, I've seen girls doing things to attract attention in 'Irish 2000' and 'Champers' that would make Peter Stringfellow blush, but it does seem less of an urgent need than men exhibit.

Moving the Goalposts

Some women have adopted and adapted the male displays and can be seen on the terraces chanting abuse and farting along with their male compatriots. Much of the female display seems to have a more logical aim than the male boorishness. Lipstick and make-up give the impression of good health while a Wonderbra emphasises the nurturing capacities of the breasts. Tight jeans or micro-skirts emphasise the child bearing hips and high heels give the impression of greater height and health. It seems women can adapt prehistoric behaviour more appropriately for modern day use. Those years spent watching men's pathetic posturing has made the female of the species realise how ridiculous the worst excesses of such activity look and consequently girls seem less enthusiastic about fully immersing themselves in such foolishness. So for the time being it falls to the men to show the next generation of society how to behave like a complete knob.

HALF-TIME

TO OUR GREAT SURPRISE Fat Jill wasn't fat any more.
Though Jill was her christened name, Martin and I had always called her Marilyn because of the enormous jeans she wore. Every time she left we would sing in our best Elton John falsetto 'goodbye 'normous jeans..'. Jill was a bit rummer than her girth might give you cause to believe. She wore stockings and suspenders under her jeans 'just in case'. To be honest we didn't really like her hanging around us because people might think one of us was having some sort of physical intimacy with her. We shared her company because we needed a third person to help pay the rent, but that was as far as the relationship went. I suppose that that isn't entirely true. Fat Jill performed another crucial defining role. She ensured Martin and I never fell out with each other because with Fat Jill around there was always someone else to blame or abuse. She was a vital butt to our crueller urges and such was her loneliness that she allowed us to treat her like shit. It felt great having someone who seems relatively happy to accept such a position and having experienced the situation I can fully understand how it took so long to abolish slavery. You know what you are doing is wrong but it isn't illegal and it does make your own life so much easier. At the end of the year we tired of Jill and told her to fuck off elsewhere and bother someone else, which wasn't very nice considering the huge number of menial and demeaning tasks she had done on our behalf.
Jill didn't help herself. She was fat, it was true, but plenty of fat people manage to retain their self esteem and dignity. Jill was also sweaty and clumsy, an unappealing combination and though she claimed to have strawberry blond hair most people agreed it was really tangerine. Her face was a picture. She bore an uncanny resemblance to Degas' 'the Absinthe drinker'. The first time I saw that painting in the Musee D'Orsay in Paris I almost choked on my winegums such was the resemblance. The loose flabby jowl and bulldog features were hardly the considered classic image of beauty. We used to joke that the only way to get her out of the bath was to turn the taps on. To be honest I think that if I hadn't been around Martin would have tapped off with her because he was a right lazy bastard like that, always taking the easy route. Once I caught him snogging

her in a night club and was compelled to remind him of that proverb that says shagging fat girls is like riding a moped as both feel great until your mates find out. He took my warning and refused to fall prey to Jill's doubtful but accessible charms.

Then a year later we saw her again and she looked great. Just like in all the American romantic films where the persecuted bookish heroine removes her glasses and lets her hair down to reveal that, just like we'd all suspected, she had been beautiful all along. I fear Jill's transformation had not been quite so sudden. She was totally unrecognisable. Not just because of her downsizing and the busy swarm of blokes trying to feed off her. The huge shedding of her unwelcome load had revealed a totally different physiognomy. Even her voice sounded different, gentler, less guttural and throaty. I could tell Martin was blaming me for not letting him get off with her when he'd had the chance. This was no longer a moped, more a Harley Davidson and it hadn't even been road tested when he'd first got his hands on it. Now its value had increased well out of his scope and he held the regret common to all those who have spotted a fantastic investment opportunity after the price has peaked.

After a brief chat Jill returned to her entourage of admirers and left us to our own contemplations. She was grinning as she walked away, the bitch. I preferred her when she had been ugly and unpopular. Now our roles had been reversed.

By this time Martin's short relocation up in Manchester was almost over. He'd moved up here in 1989 and we three had formed an unholy trinity of house mates in Stretford when I came back after spending purgatory in Leicester and Colchester. Now he had got a job back in Coventry and was more than happy to return. His departure made me feel all aloof. I had managed to shrug off the shackles of my home town while his fledgling attempt to escape the nest had failed and he was back under the old protective wing. My relocation a mere ninety minutes away up the M6 symbolised that I had discovered true independence and had gone off to explore the world and all its mysteries. I was carving out a new life for myself in the wilderness. My postal address implied Northern Soul and I walked with a swagger that I hoped suggested I cohabited in an Algerian commune rather than merely rented a shitty Withington bedsit. My attitude was typical of those arrogant offspring who have left their home to discover that they can survive on junk food and public transport. In my mind I criticised Coventry for its Coventryness, its lack of vitality, its smallness, for not being Manchester, but really it was clear that I still loved it. Not that I would ever admit as much. My Victorianesque protestant background would place admitting you loved anything on a level akin to confessing to homosexual feelings towards the Pope - both were acceptable enough in themselves but it would take a lot of guts to admit it out loud.

131

Moving the Goalposts

But I loved Coventry with its car factories (now deceased) its statue of Lady Godiva (in which you can't see her tits for her hair) with its Midlands beer and the spiritual home of the Sky Blues, it was a great place. Its lack of change and small rules such as no drinking in public areas, or playing ball games on the grass, or farting in the library; the way it was all so neatly self contained with its pedestrianised shopping centre surrounded and bounded by the ring road which prevented excessive growth or change. Not at all like Manchester which didn't seem to know where its centre was as it moved from Piccadilly to Market Street and on to Deansgate depending on the latest developer's whims. But now things had changed. Jill was thin and had made a better life for herself without us. Martin was setting up a permanent base. He was buying a house which implied far more than just security of tenure. He was putting down his own roots and like those plants that put out runners rather than dispersing seeds to the wild winds his roots were still in direct touch with his nursery beds. Martin had changed and the clues had been there all along. The shaving, the deepening voice, the clean clothes and regular diurnal activity. Martin and Jill had secretly grown up without warning me about what was going on. It was as if they had both, separately, discovered some great secret and neither of them was prepared to share it with me. So I was condemned like the tribes of Israel to endless wandering in the wilderness, left alone to contemplate the sheer nastiness that lay at the heart of my soul. But Martin wasn't completely free. His new world was clearly not as perfect as he had hoped and I had feared. He was like Antaeus the giant, son of Poseidon, who gained his strength from the earth and who was finally slain by Hercules who held him off the ground, thus depriving him of the source of his energy and so his strength drained away. To me Martin had become an inverse Antaeus. Stripped of vital life force by the confines of the office he had enslaved himself within, surrounded by concrete and plastic, watching the computer leach the colour out of his cheeks on the third floor of Cathedral Lanes. Hence his desperate weekend rush to the countryside on a mountain bike, to recharge his batteries. The fifty weeks a year spent anticipating a fortnight in Corfu when finally he could nourish his roots and dream of the vestal virgin that got away.

Chatting to Brian the snailman about Martin's predicament I hoped for some revelatory insight. Unfortunately Brian's view was that we all choose our own paths and for him this was certainly true as there was no mistaking the dramatic fork in the road he had stumbled down during his wander through life. Jill, Brian and Martin had all made deliberate moves to change their lives and mold them in a direction they knew would bring them greater happiness. Me, I seemed to be drifting like some flotsam on the twice-daily tide. In, out, in, out, and at weekends, shake it all about. In a desperate attempt

Moving the Goalposts

to light a firework up my own arse I agreed to spend a night with Brian on the streets of Manchester. We sat in a doorway as day turned to dusk and the deepest thought that entered my tiny head was the pathetic realisation of just how weak my bladder is. The cold concrete floor was sucking the life-force out of me and was giving me piles despite the fact that I had gathered up a huge mass of newspapers to cushion my delicate rear. My fingers were going numb and I was waiting for what seemed an inevitable assault from some pissed up revellers.

Brian's revealed that his trick to keeping inner warmth and tranquility was to think about far away places that you dreamed of visiting and then imagine travelling to them. What a bit of luck, I informed him, what with me being a Sagittarian and all. His gaze pierced my thick skull and spoke to me. 'What the fuck are you going on about?' So I explained to him that Sagittarians such as myself are in fact born under a wandering star and are filled with wanderlust, so he asked where my wanderlust had taken me on this shrinking globe of universal access and cheap flights to all points on the compass and I told him France and Spain and Greece and Guernsey, and he pissed himself and my twin globes shrivelled up even smaller and I tried explaining that wanderlust was a metaphysical rather than a physical act but he could see right through my skin and into the real me and he could see I had no guts and no spine and I hadn't gone anywhere because I was too lazy and too scared and too dependent on my family and friends and he informed me in no uncertain terms that I was a bloody disgrace to my star sign and as I pondered his rebuke I noticed happily that he was building a fire at last.

I'm not a complete wimp. I did stay out, living rough, on the streets, free as a bird, all that night. No slinking off early for me. I stared at the night stars trying to pick out Orion, the only system I might vaguely recognise, but the only pattern I could make out was not a man with a sword and belt, nor even a Bear or a Plough, but just two fingers showing exactly what the solar system thought of me. Suddenly I was gripped by a deep thought. 'I want to be home, in the warmth, forever'.

Thanks for listening. I feel much better now.

22.

Our Souls

SAINT AUGUSTINE WROTE OF 'de Civitate dei', the city of the soul, built on the ruins of an older sadder world, a forerunner to Coventry's own rise from the post-war ashes. St. Augustine, like Aristotle before him, saw the city as a living force, more than just an aggregation of living spaces and a flocculation of people, far more than mere residency, but forming a crucial role as a focus for a community, the focus of birthright and patriotism.

Man demonstrates his ambition through his city and it is possible to excavate its layers like a geologist sorting through sedimentary strata and investigating the fossil record. The evidence of past riches and poverties are there to be discovered and explained.

Once Homo Sapiens became a sedentary creature his immediate needs were for food, drink and shelter. Without water we can survive for a few days, without food we can survive for weeks, but without shelter we will very rapidly succumb to the elements and so the impulse to seek protective shelter is a primary need. William's first act upon the conquering of King Harold's forces at Hastings was to build the Tower of London to defend himself (well maybe not literally the first, he probably had a celebratory ale and went to the lavatory, but you know what I mean). Manchester occupies a defensive site between the rivers Irk and Irwell; Colchester lies at the highest navigable point of the river Colne using the water and forest as a natural barricade; Coventry's early settlers occupied a cliff overlooking the valley of the River Sherbourne. All three sites reflect the impulse to seek a safe protective haven.

Cities reflect the needs of their occupiers, be they native born or migrant, and over time the human geography becomes a more important focus driving the growth or death of a settlement than the original physical factors. Man is an economic opportunist and will settle wherever there appears to be the means to support him and provide him with shelter and his other essential demands. In times of prosperity he will be joined by new waves of economic migrants and in times of recession he may have to get on his bike and find work elsewhere. So Coventry has grown in waves fuelled by the textile and engineering industries and the city still carries some of the scars left by her previous occupants. The Mediaeval textile trade earned particular fame for the blue dye used in local cloth with the Coventry Blue earning a national reputation for it's outstanding quality. The city's pioneering spirit resulted in the construction of the first bicycle and the first car produced on a commercial basis. It was the first English city to make Dunlop pneumatic tyres and the industry that developed from these seeds drew more and more migrants as Coventry grew faster than any other city in the country. A population of under 70,000 had swelled to almost 350,000 in only seventy years. Newlyweds looked to Coventry to provide for their fledgling family and the average age of the population fell. But bust follows boom and the busy city of the sixties and early seventies suffered more than most from deindustrialisation in the 1980's as manufacturing competitors sprung up in south east Asia and elsewhere and the British car industry shrivelled. The town had to look to new stimuli for growth and its features changed again as services replaced manufacturing as the leading employer.

Coventry's defining landmark is the three spires and a climb to the top of Saint Michael's spire, at the foot of the old Cathedral, still provides the best view of the city. From the benefit of this vista you can take in just what and where Coventry is all about. The first instinct upon climbing the one hundred and eighty steps is to gaze as far into the distance as possible, to try and make out the limits or boundaries of the city. In our world of ever expanding, poorly defined, conurbations such boundaries have become blurred and largely arbitrary. It isn't possible to see where Coventry ends and Kenilworth, or Nuneaton or Birmingham begins. That Coventry is a part of a larger West Midlands urban sprawl becomes obvious. It is only when we reduce the range of our vision that any real patterns emerge. From the viewing platform on St. Michael's all the city's distinct zones are revealed. To the north lies Foleshill with its prominent mosques and minarets decorating the urban environment that stretches as far as the eye can see. There are industrial chimneys instead of trees and at the edge of the horizon you can make out the giant form of Keresley colliery. To the west, looking beyond the city centre's famous precinct Meriden water tower can be picked out. To the south lies Kenilworth, a dormitory town for the city, which appears like a brick and tarmac island, surrounded by a sea of green. The city's growth seems to have been limited in this direction. It has spread slower and less completely over this southern landscape which contains a fourth, modern spire, larger than the ancient three, the huge chimney of Whitley refuse incinerator. To the east the eye is caught by the flash of light on glass as the sun reflects off the windscreens of hundreds of new cars waiting for transportation from the Ryton assembly plant. Beyond Ryton lie the midland mountains, Burton Dasset hills.

Eventually the eye is drawn back into the centre and we can begin to pick out the patterns that are invisible at street level. Viewing a city from its tallest monument is far more useful than any map for providing an immediate impression of the urban morphology. In Barcelona you can climb the hill at Tibidabo which reveals just how incredibly regimented and organised the city's pattern is. A huge area of the heart of that place is made up of regular squares which are a stark contrast to the piecemeal infilling we see looking down on Coventry. Similarly in Paris the view from the top of the Arc de Triumph gives real pattern and design to what appears at pedestrian level to be total chaos. From this elevated position you can witness the big picture. Napoleon's plan becomes clear as all the wide avenues combine like ley-lines on this his central focus for the city. Gazing down onto Coventry's roads no such pattern emerges as the surrounding ring road seems to have been built to keep the traffic out or at least at arm's length, rather then welcoming it in.

Staring into the abyss at the roads which pulse like arteries through the corporate form of the city there seems no clear rhyme or reason. The traffic's stop start flow, like blood through tarmacadam veins, is really the vital force that sustains the city. How strange that a city which grew from the desire to own private means of transport should be the first to redesign itself, excluding these cars from its own centre. Thus Coventry's precinct set a trend that so many others have had to follow. Coventry's cars made towns more accessible and helped the populations expand out of the core.

Moving the Goalposts

How ironic that they then have choked the centres they helped grow.

Up here taking in the view it is difficult to see the wood for the trees, in a manner of speaking. It is hard to pick out many individuals from the homogeneous form below, but if you know where to look they are there. At the foot of the tower lies the soul of Coventry, the two cathedrals, the Guild Hall, the Council house and the law courts. The roofless old cathedral is swarming with tourists inspecting the relicts left behind after the visit by some more destructive company half a century ago. Attached to this old ruin is the new cathedral saprophytically feeding off its older relative. The mediaeval Guild Hall of St. Mary's and the Council house survived the firebombing and they look curious remnants in the new surroundings. Their appearance is less out of place than many of the ephemeral 1950's developments which eventually sprung up around them, several of which have already been replaced and those that remain look as inappropriate as a psychedelic tie at a funeral. Everywhere you gaze there is gentrification, demolition or redevelopment. The city planners never stop, like soldier ants, spurred on perhaps by the belief that one day they will get it right.

The recent processes of urbanisation, suburbanistaion, infilling and comprehensive redevelopment schemes have forced our towns to burst through their boundaries. They too are on the move, migrating like their no longer sedentary residents. Seeking out greener and quieter locations, destroying in the process, what they are hunting for.

But if we have shaped our towns, they too have shaped us. Our places of birth suggest personality traits within us. Scousers are funny, Geordies passionate, Glaswegians like the odd drink whilst everyone knows what the staple diet of the inhabitants of Cheddar and Melton Mowbray is. So what do outsiders think of the people of Coventry? A recently published Australian tourist guide book toured the U.K and came to the conclusion that English people speak unintelligible dialects and don't wash. It claimed that you could tell almost exactly where you are in Britain by the strength of the tea. The stronger the taste in your cup, the further north you had strayed. They recommended that Australians intent on visiting Britain should pack a waterproof jacket, a medical kit, a neck pouch, and thongs for shared bathrooms. Amazingly it described Coventry as the worst place their researchers visited, a place to be avoided, 'a dismal city of car parks, ring roads and windswept shopping precincts'. This is the city that was forced to remove signs which described itself as lying 'at the heart of Shakespeare country'. The 'Rough Guide' for Britain is even more damning, it doesn't even give us a mention. Not worthy of even a solitary line.

In spite of such criticism tourists still flock to see Coventry's sites for themselves. The whole West Midlands has changed from the Black Country that earned its name from its choking fumes and glowing foundries to a huge heritage park for the entertainment of foreign and domestic visitors. Thus the Cadbury factory at Bournville has become 'Cadburyworld' providing a diverting day out for the family as heritage tourism finds fertile soil in the region. At Coalbrookedale and Ironbridge families can now tour the sanitised sites of former industrial production with all traces of any danger, poverty, deprivation or child abuse carefully forgotten.

Some visitors take advantage of Coventry's central location and proximity to Birmingham airport to use the city as a base for investigating regional attractions and cultural icons such as Warwick castle, Stratford upon Avon and Alton Towers. Thus Coventry has become a tourist town and has witnessed a growth in its service sector. This economic diversification provided me with an unexpected opportunity to act as an unofficial ambassador for my home town. In the summer holiday of 1988, as a buffer between learning to be a teacher at Leicester and being paid to be one in Colchester, I got a job in the city teaching French students to speak English. That a company should be prepared to pay someone with so little grasp of French and an open admission of a total inability to learn languages was a reasonable reflection on how unattractive the job is to most people.

The set up was fairly informal. In the mornings there would be language lessons conducted entirely in English and in the afternoon the students were taken to visit some suitably impressive national monument such as the Museum of motor transport or the Gilbert rugby ball factory. The lessons were a revelation. The girls flirted and smoked, the boys spat and smoked while the younger students just smoked. In an effort to cut down on my passive smoking I decided to arrange a few local outdoor field trips. The classroom lessons were being taught in the Coventry Polytechnic buildings which lay in fortuitously close proximity to the shops, cathedral and various other distractions suitable for eating up plenty of my teaching time.

Moving the Goalposts

Every day I would take the students on some walking tour and they were expected to fill in a very simple quiz sheet as they processed through the town centre. The first to complete it would win a small prize of ten Benson's or a new lighter. In one test they were asked to find the price of a first class stamp with the result that forty-five French teenagers all rushed into the main post office, ignored the snake of waiting pensioners and made a beeline for the counter assistant who bemusedly had to repeat the cost of a stamp forty-five times to people who didn't want to buy one. It must have been a relief to get back to the pensioners and their cheery complaints about how they can remember when a twenty pence stamp only cost ten pence.

In response to another question 'What is the headline in today's newspaper?' there was considerable surprise when they discovered that the main story was that Elvis Presley had been found living on the moon. They were staggered and could hardly draw breath on their Gitannes. When they saw that the other main story was that a Mexican chief of police's son had been turned into an olive by aliens and his father had accidentally swallowed the evidence, they were in a state of shock. It had to be true as it was on the front page of a national newspaper. Clearly they don't have anything quite like the Daily Sport at home. In fact they were very naive to such satire. They believed me when I told them that they mustn't use the word gullible as it had been taken out of the English dictionary and many of them thought that irony was how President Reagan used to introduce himself.

Sadly these daily excursions had to be abandoned after a public complaint about two of the French visitors simulating a sex act in the cathedral ruins. Fortunately these improvised tours lasted long enough to provide me with a valuable tourist's eye view of Coventry. What the students liked best were the quirky things such as the old one pence coins inlaid in the floor of the new cathedral. They liked the huge tapestry of Christ but refused to believe it was larger than their own bit of cloth in Bayeux. They liked the engraved glass windows and the wooden thorns that surround the choir's pulpits and look like a tangled mess of coat hangers. They enjoyed visiting the ruins of Kenilworth castle in which they could run wild and play but were bored in the formal and restrictive surroundings of Warwick castle. They loved Alton Towers and hated the Herbert Art Gallery. The Museum of Motor History was okay, but only because the land speed record holding 'Thrust 2' was on display, the general consensus was that ten pin bowling at The Forum was better. The swimming baths were great and the weather fine, the shops good, particularly the indoor market where they could buy Doctor Martin's at a fraction of the cost of home. Sadly these attractions didn't compensate for the lack of evening distractions. Most of them weren't old enough to buy an alcoholic drink in Britain. There were no clubs for teenagers, no beaches to hang out in at night, no coffee shops or casual restaurants in which to while away the evenings smoking and laughing. Instead they had to stay at home with the families who were hosting them and watch baffling game shows and quizzes on the television. By the end of the fortnight most of them were desperate to go back home for a holiday.

23.

Arseholes

The Great nations have always acted like gangsters,
and the small nations like prostitutes.'
Stanley Kubrick, US Film Director, The Guardian 5 June 1963.

I AM ILL IN MANCHESTER. My head is banging to some distant beat, my limbs hurt and my face is swollen. I don't know what has happened to me but it seems reasonable to assume I have been beaten up. I went out last night for a couple of quiet drinks and then one or two loud ones. We had a curry (the beer and balti stains on my T-shirt are evidence of this). I walked home and, after some delay, I arrived here sorer, poorer and nursing more than a just a hangover.

Manchester is a good place to be ill. As the dark clouds pass overhead casting dreary shadows on my bedroom window it is hard not to believe being tucked up in bed is the best place to be. When as a child in Coventry I was recuperating from any of the huge list of childhood ailments that we all apparently have to suffer on the way to adulthood I used to press my nose up against the lounge window and curse the world that I should be imprisoned indoors when there was all that outdoors just waiting to be played in. Pleading with my mother every ten minutes to be allowed to kick a ball around the garden proved futile and as frustrating for her as for me.

This really is a good place to be ill. Just down the road from my sickbed are four hospitals of national or international reputation. There is the large, modern Wythenshawe hospital that serves much of the south of the city; a bit nearer lies St. Mary's where my son and daughter were both born and adjacent to that hospital there is the ancient looking Manchester Royal Infirmary, an important teaching hospital and regular film set for the more

141

dramatic episodes of Coronation Street; even nearer to my bed is the world famous Christie hospital where ground breaking research into cancer is undertaken. Whilst wallowing in my own self-pity I can also reflect that within ear shot there is the Eye Hospital, Manchester University Dental School, the University Medical School, the Institute for Sickle Cell Thalassaemia, and numerous other buildings hosting departments studying diseases that I know too little about to properly fear. This really is a comforting place to be ill. There seem to be a lot of people around here who know what they are doing when it comes to germs and such stuff.

My memories of hospitals in Coventry are more painful. I still carry the scars. The last time I was in hospital as a patient was when I was thirteen. I have been lucky. At the time I was visiting Gulson Road hospital as an outpatient to have some cyst or growth removed from my back where it had begun to grow with a rapidity usually associated with an alien plague in Dr. Who or some other science-fiction masterpiece. I lay on my back, stripped of all my clothes and all my teenage dignity, with my arse exposed to the elements for the inspection of all the nurses, orderlies, tea ladies, passing students, fly-on-the-wall documentary makers, lost travellers and anyone else with time on their hands. Everyone had a good look, everyone except the doctor that is. The nurses comforted me with the news that he was still out to lunch, but shouldn't be too late as the pub was just around the corner. When he finally appeared the nurses joked about his dietary choice and I could smell the wine on his breath. I was tempted to do a runner, but prevented by the realisation that to run naked through a hospital in the hope of escape was the act of a raving lunatic.

'You won't feel a thing.' The doctor lied as he pushed the scalpel into me after pausing to wipe away all the dust that had accumulated during my wait. But I could feel everything. I could have given a running commentary on just how he was carving me up as my bare backside lay exposed adding humiliation to my pain.

'These stitches won't show', he added. They burst open the following week leaving me with a lesion that is impressive enough to allow me to convince the feeble minded that it is 'the result of a rat bite I suffered when playing down Canley Ford as a child.

Eventually I was allowed to cover up my backside and get dressed back into my school uniform. The blood stain never washed out of my white shirt. Then my dad arrived and picked me up and took me home. He had my weekly 2000 AD comic with him. He bought me a copy every Wednesday as soon as it appeared in the shops. Like the scars I still have it.

A few weeks later, as a recuperation treat, I was taken to one of the nearby zoos or game parks. I can't remember whether it was Whipsnade or Twycross or Woburn Abbey. That isn't the detail that has been burned into my memory of that day. During the long summer holidays we liked to do the usual trawl of regional tourist sites. I was too old to enjoy such a trip and too young to really hate it, so I wandered around with a face that I hoped expressed my sullen indifference, but probably really suggested that I was simple. It was a hot and stuffy day and I remember that yet again I was dressed like a nonce, even by my own appalling standards of garb. The excursion is only memorable for its dullness as we wandered round cage and enclosure after cage and enclosure containing a collection of the most forlorn and dishevelled looking animals to be found anywhere outside a Russian Circus. Camels with alopecia were followed by limping giraffes. Fierce predators lay passively as their keepers emptied trays of offcuts into their pens. It was a terminally depressing scene in which spectator and entertainer were equally bored and united in their wish that they had been left in peace at home.

That I have remembered this sojourn for the rest of my life is because of the fantastic show put on by the monkeys. These were some unimpressive breed of primate, certainly not comical, tea-swilling chimps nor entrepreneurial baboons, just some indistinguishable generic brand of tree-swinger. As we rounded a corner and came upon their pen they were audience-less, just sitting innocently on the concrete floor or perched upon the pneumatic tyres so thoughtfully provided to recreate their natural ecosystem and environment. The conveyor belt of visitors seemed to have broken down at this stage and there was no group in front of us, though we were gradually being caught up by other visitors following in our wake. We stopped and read the small plaque explaining where these animals lived in the wild and how many there were left in the whole world. We peered through the wire netting to see if there were any babies we could all coo at or if there was anything remotely interesting to focus upon, secretly all sharing the same hope that they wouldn't embarrass us by suddenly masturbating or shagging each other, little realising that even worse was soon

143

to follow.

Then I noticed some banana coloured excrement on the wire fence. In fact there was quite a lot of it. How had it got there? Surely they didn't scrape their arses on the fence to remove irritating dangly bits of primate poo. Gradually quite a crowd was gathering and one or two other people had spotted the excrement on the fence. When I noticed the yellow monkey crap on the hedge next to me, far beyond the perimeter fence I began to get nervous. There is a moment in most American action movies where you can tell that all hell is just about to cut loose, crucial seconds before the film's dull witted protagonists do. For the first and only time in my life I found myself in such a position and to my dismay discovered that I was powerless to escape from the carnage that the simians were about to unleash. My legs were leaden and my mouth went bone dry preventing me from issuing a warning shout to the rest of the crowd. The next few seconds are etched on my memory in slow motion like film clips from a war archive. In a perfectly coordinated team effort the monkeys shat into their hands and began lobbing it at us. When all the immediate ammunition was spent they began anal-digging for reserves. The scene on the human occupied side of the fence was of absolute horror and panic. It was fantastic. We couldn't scatter fast enough. All discipline and stiff upper lip disappeared. There is no place for a 'women and children first' mentality when the shit is quite literally hitting the wildlife fans. When the monkeys finally called a cease-fire and surveyed their handiwork it was clear they had conquered man far more convincingly than in any of the Planet of the Apes films. If the wildlife park had had the sense to market this display as an attraction it would draw larger crowds than Blackpool Pleasure beach and they would be internationally famous. After all, as they say in the North, where there's muck there's brass.

Mind you, where there is brass there is also usually a fair amount of muck too. Lucre seems to produce filth as a by-product. The rich towns of South America provide a stark image of this, with their sky scrapers and obvious wealth in the town centre, dwarfed by the surrounding symbiotic shanty town feeding off the enormous amount of waste that all towns produce, both physical and human. Back home it is also possible to find such contrasts if not on quite the same scale. Towns are living organisms and as such can be sick or healthy.

Moving the Goalposts

Edmund Chadwick's 'Report on the sanitary condition of the labouring population of Great Britain', published in 1842, revealed that the life expectancy of a professional worker in rural Rutland was fifty-eight but in Manchester he could only expect to live to the age of thirty-eight. Those less fortunate, namely the tradesmen and skilled labourers, who lived closer to the city's industrial heart were only likely to reach the ripe young age of seventeen before their life was over. The corresponding life expectancy for these groups in Rutland was thirty-eight. Clearly you had to live fast if at all in Manchester. Add a few years of terminal or debilitating sickness and it hardly seemed possible that anyone managed to bear children in such a terrible environment. It seems incredible that town's like Manchester managed to survive and thrive with such a sickly workforce.

To really diagnose the health of the town we need to look at the bricks and mortar and in so doing it is evident that Manchester was anything but a delicate child. The buildings of Manchester have far outlived and outgrown those of Oakham and they blossomed far more brightly. The merchants who thrived in Victorian Manchester have been described as merchant Princes and like all royalty they wished to own a palace and leave behind some lasting monument to remind those who were still to come what their predecessors had achieved. The great warehouses, many of them designed by Edward Walters, were castles of solid stature adorned with Italian facades. Walters' most famous construction, the Free Trade Hall, is seen as the finest jewel of the 'pallazzo' style with which he furnished so many of the city's warehouses. Other architects used classical designs, as seen in The Bank of England in King Street, designed by Charles Robert Cockerell. The pallazo and classic styles were followed by the Gothic Revival that resulted in Alfred Waterhouse's design for the jail at Strangeways and the Refuge Assurance building on Oxford Road, now the Palace Hotel. To this list we can add the Royal Exchange, the Central library and the hundreds of impressive structures that are dispersed throughout the city that hearken back to the phenomenal wealth and the growth that was nurtured in the town when cotton was king.

It is doubtful whether the architectural marvels that were springing up offered much comfort to those residents living in waterlogged cellars in the slums of 'Little Ireland' between what is now the Oxford Road railway station and the U.M.I.S.T. campus. It has been said that the fastest way out of Manchester is through a bottle of gin and though Mancunians took what pleasure they could from their immediate environment many of them were not content to merely accept the status quo. Manchester has a long and hard-earned reputation for being a hotbed of rebellion and sedition. In the Civil War the town's five thousand residents were on the side of Parliament and were against the King. Yet after experiencing Cromwell's oppressive regime Mancunians changed sides and pragmatically became supporters of the Stuart cause.

As the town grew so did its reputation for political agitation and rebellion. Food riots have a persistent and important place in the history of British social unrest. As the large towns grew they found themselves completely divorced from the food producing rural economy yet entirely dependent on it for food supplies. As the town's nourishment now came from all over the country rather than just the immediate rural fringe there was little that the local authority could do to control the price and quality of the food on sale in towns. When in 1957 the wheat on sale in Manchester was found to be adulterated with ingredients as diverse and unsavoury as horse dung and acorns people took to the streets to protest. Women and children were key components in such demonstrations. A report in 1800 reads 'All public disturbances commence with the clamour of women and the folly of boys'. After the 1812 Food Riots Hannah Smith was hung for stopping potato and butter street vendors and distributing their wares. Manchester's unruliness was well known. For decades the town was occupied by London troops as its population was seen to be dangerously subversive and out of control. Activism was also affecting the workplace. Luddite attacks on modern production methods in the textile industry kept steam driven looms and new advances in mechanical machines out of the town until Peter Drinkwater installed one in his mill in 1789. When Robert Grimshaw of Gorton had his weaving mill at Knott Mill burned to the ground there were no more machines installed until 1806.

Political tradition continued to grow with more food riots and Luddite attacks but the most famous event was the Peterloo massacre on 16th August 1819. Accounts differ on whether this was a massacre of women and children by an over enthusiastic army or a riot that had to be subdued because the threat to life and limb was ever escalating. What is certain is that at least eleven people were killed after meeting at St. Peters Field in Manchester to protest at the conditions they had to live in. When a meeting of Tory Loyalists in the Exchange Hall was transformed into an anti-government riot in 1812 we had the first sign of a class based conflict. Gangs of poor Mancunians went out and attacked any visibly more affluent denizens that they could find. Robin Hood had abandoned the forest and moved into town.

Manchester had become a large town but was still being governed as a feudal village, with no effective policing nor political representation for its people. When Manchester's New Police replaced the old watchmen the town had its first taste of zero-tolerance policing. Street meetings were prohibited and broken up, informal beer shops were shut down.

It is perhaps surprising, given the level of social injustice, the appalling squalor, the hunger and abject poverty that there wasn't a more bloody expression of discontent, similar to the French Revolution. That it never occurred cannot be due to a lack of organisation at grass root level. After all this is where the Co-operative movement, Chartism and Trade Unions all began. Some have suggested that the lack of violence is due to the growth of Methodism in the region at the time of greatest poverty. Others have pointed out that the bosses were not landed aristocracy but fellow working men who had done well for themselves. They were not a privileged elite but an emerging middle-class who had risen from the ranks because of their own enterprise. Most of all there seems to have been a tolerance by the working men who realised that their own livelihoods were dependent upon those of their bosses, even if their own share of the cake was wafer thin. If an improved quality of life wasn't going to come from cheaper and better quality food it would have to be gained through higher wages. So the next political route was to create trade unions to replace the mediaeval craft guilds. Trade Unions offered a nonviolent means of expressing discontent and inequality. From 1758 there had been in Manchester an Union of Operators and in 1868 the first ever Trades Union Congress was held, appropriately enough, in Manchester.

Civil unrest was subsequently largely directed towards perceived trade barriers and most notably the Corn Laws, opposition to which fostered the People's Charter and the Chartists, who are often regarded as the first working class political organisation in Europe. Richard Cobden and John Bright, key advocates of Free Trade, were agitators against the Corn

Laws and both were returned as members of the Commons after being put up as candidates by the Anti-Corn Law League. Bright's statue stares purposefully at the Manchester Town Hall, pointing the way to the nearby shops in St. Anne's Square where a statue of Cobden takes over the guide duties and his outstretched arm directs the traveller onwards towards the largest Marks and Spencer in the world. Their activism led to the development of a political theory that was given the name 'The Manchester School'. They were the public face of the rapidly emerging middle class radicals. While the meek may eventually inherit the Earth, it wasn't quite their time yet.

However the middle and the working class agitators weren't working towards exactly the same goals, and it was ultimately the free marketeers that gained most from this period. For as the economy began to boom again at the end of the 1840's bosses could afford to offer better conditions of work and were even moved to set up the first recognised weekend break, from Saturday lunchtime until Monday morning - the Manchester weekend. With increased wealth there came greater respectability as the middle classes won control over a working class placated by increased free-time, better wages and more opportunity to spend it. New products and habits developed. Bovril sellers offered their wares and Vimto was invented in the town in 1908 by Noel Nicholls of Granby Road and marketed as an invigorating tonic. Even the Temperance bars now had an exciting product to sell. By the end of the 19th century affluence had increased and spread widely enough for huge retail enterprises to open to the public, most notably Kendal-Milnes and Lewis's. The recreational activity called 'shopping' had arrived and the town centre would never be the same again.

If Manchester was a precocious child, born in a hurry and developed in quick, sharp spurts then Coventry is the elderly relative that observes such newcomers with a knowing, seen it all before, tolerance. Coventry has a longer, more stable, history though it too has experienced several growth stages since it first formed. Sadly much of this history has been less kindly preserved partly because of the bombs that fell in the 1940's and partly because of some of the wilder whims of planners and developers since then. Its oldest remains have all been corralled together in Spon End, presumably to protect the few that remain, providing safety in numbers. The rest of the city became an urban experiment, pedestrianised and sanitised, a concrete creation that retains a charm which often amazes many first time visitors, lured by the new Cathedral and pleasantly surprised by its environs. Around the ruined mediaeval core a new city has grown up and though old and new in such proximity can occasionally jar (such as in the old and new Council chambers) the result became a blue print for many other towns that needed redevelopment.

After 1945 employment prospects in Coventry became uncertain. Many employers had vastly increased their output and capacity during the war but few felt able to maintain that level and the necessary overtime payments with the spectre of a future peacetime recession ahead. Coventry however went from Blitz town to boom town and soon gained a reputation as a high-wage engineering centre of excellence, partly because of an agreement struck between Sir John Black of Standard and the Coventry Engineering Unions in 1948. In Coventry's engineering works a gang system had evolved where a team of workers led by a 'ganger' or steward would take responsibility for their own output. This system evolved first at Bagington in the aircraft industry where each aircraft produced at A.W.A. had a team working on it for a considerable time. This provided an environment in which each team of workers could foster a real sense of proprietorship for their finished product. The ganger was often a shop-steward who would take charge of the whole team, assign work details and give daily instructions. He would report to a foreman whose own responsibility was mainly as a technical advisor. This system proved itself a success at Bagington and then passed to the Standard works at Canley when they began to manufacture the Mosquito airframes for the Royal Air Force. Black wanted to treat all his workers at Canley as one gang and those at Banner Lane as another. The gang members were paid a basic wage and all members of the gang were paid an incentive bonus dependent upon how many cars or tractors were produced in a month. The system appeared to benefit both workers and management as trading profits were healthy and this mutual feel good factor continued until a fall in demand after 1955 which eventually resulted in the strikes and redundancies that were to become a feature of Midlands motor industry in the 1970's. Consequently Coventry faced its greatest threat since the firebombs of the 1940's. The only option was to evolve and diversify or to face gradual decline. The city that had enjoyed such a period of rapid growth and prosperity realised that if jobs continued to disappear in its major employment sector then there would be little else to keep people and they would move on to the next boom town like a band of strolling minstrels or fruit-pickers following the harvest.

Migrants are the nutrients for a city. Without them it will shrink and fade. But if a city creates opportunities that attract transient labour it will grow and expand. Towns reflect the origins of the migrants they have lured, be it in street or district names, local accents or even the skills and trades its new arrivals have brought with them. The mixture of backgrounds and cultures make our towns melting pots in which some groups assimilate and disperse among their hosts while other chose to form a ghetto for self-support.

Perhaps the best account of the influence of migrant groups on an urban area was written by Burgess based upon his study of Chicago in the inter-war period. He mapped out the Chicago regions, which was quite a brave act considering the nature of some of the areas, and he discovered a pattern of distinct, almost circular zones had evolved, and within these zones there were distinguishable clusters of different groups of people. 1930's Chicago was an interesting place to live and work in. The era of prohibition had stretched police resources so thin that the distinct ethnic and social enclaves often formed their own communities and method of rule enforcement. The most famous example would be Al Capone's Italian immigrants.

Burgess discovered a distinct German cluster, a Chinatown, a 'Little Sicily' a 'Black belt' and other distinct social groupings such as a 'Twilight zone' around the city centre that was comprised of slum properties awaiting demolition and large warehouses and declining industrial units. Also in this belt there could be found a large 'red light' district, though his writings reveal very few details about the depth of his research into that service industry. Close by lay a sector Burgess called 'Hobohemia', which was inhabited mainly by itinerant men, salesmen, travellers and tramps. Around this central core lay subsequent rings of progressively more affluent housing and social groups, right out to the periphery of the city where the richest in society made their home, away from the filth and bustle of the congested core.

Burgess' model has subsequently been used as the starting point and guide map for the study of all western cities and most seem to follow a remarkably similar pattern. Not all contain an equivalent of Al Capone and his cohorts, but any absences are usually filled by some other distinct social, cultural or ethnic collection. Burgess was really an ecologist rather than a town planner and he was the first to compare the growth of urban areas to the growth of an ecosystem. He saw a healthy town as one that grew from successive waves of 'invaders' of a new species of which the most successfully adapted would flourish and those unsuited for the environment would perish and become fertiliser to feed the stronger species. Thus poor and rich, and different ethnic and social groups were all intricately linked, and as the town began to offer more attractions it would grow with successive migrant waves.

Such a picture is also true of our own towns and cities. Coventry's mediaeval core grew into its main shopping precinct which was surrounded by a zone containing the poorest quality housing and old industrial premises. The most affluent groups make full use of their own private means of transport to live in leafy suburbs such as the dormitory town of Kenilworth. Manchester too has a large twilight ring which includes districts as disparate as Castlefield, Beswick and Hulme. We can easily identify distinct ethnic groups in Broughton Park, Rusholme and Moss Side. These groups are now well established, but the newest migrant has traditionally ended up in the harshest and most impoverished parts of the city. New arrivals usually can only find and afford to reside in the least desirable parts of the city, the areas recently vacated by those who have been around long enough to consolidate their position and move out into a more favourable location.

When a town grows as quickly as Manchester did in the eighteenth century the conditions that had to be borne by its poorest citizens were often intolerable and life-threatening. Faced with harsh jobs, harsh living conditions and a short life-expectancy it is little surprise that they took whatever pleasures presented themselves. Friedrich Engels is the most quoted commentator of the poor state of existence that the working classes in Manchester had to survive in, but before Engels another foreign visitor had been shocked by the experience of travelling through the city. He was a Frenchman called Leon Faucher who was moved by what he saw to write an account called 'Manchester in 1844'. While Engels felt hopelessness at the conditions of the urban environment that people had to endure, Faucher was shocked by the behaviour of the people who lived in such squalor. He describes a people who have evolved within their inhumane environment to a state other than he feels acceptable in a civilised society.

'The factory girls are strangers to modesty. Their language is gross and often obscene: and when they do not marry early, they form illicit connections which degrade them still more than premature marriage. It is a common occurrence to meet in the intervals of labour, in the back streets, couples of males and females which the caprice of the moment has brought together.'

It is good to see some old traditions are still being maintained.

In 1843 Manchester possessed nine hundred and twenty beer retailers, six hundred and twenty four public houses and thirty one inns. Faucher quotes an observer who saw one hundred and twelve men and one hundred and sixty three women enter a single tavern in only forty minutes. He reflects that the craving for alcohol from women was worse than that of the men. Of course the worst of this debauchery occurred at weekends.

The 1840's saw Manchester's degradation into an industrial quagmire. The River Irwell, a key feature in the original development of the settlement, in which salmon had once flourished had become stagnant, vile smelling - an open sewer covered with tar, and the Medlock was no better. Yet it was the confluence of these two rivers that provided the Roman General Agricola with an easily defended site with its own natural moat and thus influenced him to set up the first permanent camp here. These rivers are the arteries that bring life into a town and take away waste and dirt to leave the town in a sanitary condition. They were also crucial to the site's growth as they provided means for transport and their head waters fuelled the early days of mechanised industry. Their Pennine water was essential for textile cleaning and in fabric dyeing. Most crucially they satiated the towns thirst. Now the urban river is little more than a channel for carcinogens. As nobody owned the rivers there was no economic incentive to keep them healthy. Instead they provided a cheap and easy opportunity for the huge number of industries located on their banks to discharge their waste, to let nature pick up the cleaning bill. Any fines were minor and it was hardly as if people were going to complain about the smell and the view, the industrial smog from all the factory chimneys made that unlikely. People couldn't see or smell anything.

Under the old feudal system of government the Police Commissioners were responsible for organising refuse disposal and the provision of paving, both of which proved beyond their means. Industry was crucial to the town's wealth and to its occupants for employment. Nobody wanted to support a policy that might harm job opportunities. Change came slowly by evolution rather than bloody revolution. When regulation was finally deemed necessary it was hampered by those with a vested interest in maintaining the status quo. Only after the Second World War did Manchester take any steps to eliminate the infamous industrial smoke that had for so long covered all its buildings in a distinctive black coat that made them look as though they had been carefully carved from pure coal. It wasn't until 1st May 1958 that central Manchester was declared a smokeless zone within which only smoke free fuels could be burnt. This was long after Coventry had shown the way by becoming the first city in the country with a smokeless zone.

Slowly Britain's industrial cities were detoxifying themselves, but Manchester had been a chain smoker for over two centuries and found it difficult to do without. As the factories closed many sites remained derelict for decades and where they had been the clean air revealed large pools of labour waiting without purpose on street corners for new employment that wasn't coming. The people left searching for money and status discovered that it wasn't to be found in the traditional manner.

Large idle pools of workers left unemployed and in poverty are cancers on a healthy city that will spread and cause further decline. Faced with little new investment and growing foreign competition for traditional heavy industries like Lancashire's cotton, Liverpool's shipbuilding and the North's coal fields, these towns needed to find a new raison d'etre. As fledgling firms increasingly looked for greenfield sites on the clean, open spaces next to the flexible transport networks outside of the gridlocked towns, those people left behind in the decaying inner cities were fast becoming an underclass, ill served by employers or services. Schools, libraries and other important public services became underfunded as there was little revenue to be generated from empty warehouses and mills. A cycle of poverty began as the new suburbs left the inner cities behind and began sucking money, capital and people out of the city centres to the new fresh clean and accessible

153

outskirts. This was urbanisation in reverse as people headed back to the villages and towns that had seen their populations disappear to the big local towns some century before and it threatened to create a 'donut affect' which would leave our urban heartlands without economic or social support. With people and manufacturing industries abandoning the towns it wasn't long before retailers saw which way the wind was blowing and followed suit. 'Out of town' meant big, clean and new in the physical form of superstores and new housing estates away from the numbers and noise of city life. Technological change made cities less important as e-commerce, telephone banking, e-mail and direct debits meant people no longer had to travel into town to buy some new shoes, to pay their life assurance or to work. Fax and phone have enabled people to work at home returning to a version of domestic, cottage industry that had preceded the development of towns. And if you didn't have to go into town to work, why bother going at all? The new supermarkets were all out of town, it was almost impossible to do your weekly shop in the city centre, so why go in? Towns began to economically shrink. After food retailers, other services moved out. Cinemas discovered the benefits of out of town site which could offer free parking, multiple screens on cheap land all on one level. After cinemas, jobs and shops there were only administration and entertainment functions left and they too were under attack from new forms of pub and club and consumers prepared to go into the countryside to make their own parties happen.

Just as reported in the Coventry Evening Telegraph in 1997 the city couldn't even supply enough evening trade to keep a single American fast food bar open. The city was like an old man who drifted off to sleep in the early evening and had no time or enthusiasm for nocturnal entertainments. If this was to continue our towns would all become inverted, people and business being further and further repelled by the centre that had previously been such an irresistible draw. It seems that towns are resilient. Rumours of their imminent demise have proven to be premature. Just as Coventry had to rebuild itself from the glowing embers other towns have shown similar tenacity when under commercial threat and demonstrated that they add up to far more than merely the sum of their individual parts. Citizens weren't about to desert their home towns. People returned to the central business districts of our urban centres because that's where the action was and that's where it will always be.

To walk through Manchester at night is to step in the footprints of those who have gone before. To gaze skywards when pissed up in Piccadilly or wasted in Whitworth Street is to become aware that one is in the presence of giants. This is an exciting town. It continues to evolve and amaze. It used to be said that 'what Manchester thinks today, the world thinks tomorrow'. That may be a reference to the industrial innovations that were developed around the town but in club-land and music terms it is still as true today.

As towns and cities developed, feeding off the rural land around them, sucking in economic and social migrants, all latter-day Dick Whittingtons searching for the streets that they had heard were paved with gold, they have earned a reputation for being less peaceful and calm than the countryside. If rural Britain is portrayed as an idyll populated by rustic simpletons and dominated by their lords and masters, towns are believed to be far less benign places for the unwary, operating as refuges for those who desire vice or hope to benefit from it. Gangland and gangsters have long been part of the urban tradition. Maybe not in the way portrayed in 'The Untouchables' or by Jimmy Cagney, or even by our own home grown Krays, but criminal hierarchies have always existed, from local bullies to the more professional earning an unhealthy income from enforcing their own brand of control in areas often perceived to have been abandoned by traditional police enforcement.

The word 'thug' has for centuries been used to describe those sections of society whose behaviour is deemed antisocial by the moral majority. The term is most commonly used in its plural form as the average thug rarely operates alone. A solo thug is a nutter, a group of thugs a gang. Their strength, like the body politic, comes from their numbers. Their size attracts wannabes too cowardly to operate under their own initiative or too dumb to operate without clear leadership or role models to imitate. The word thug is derivative from the name of one of the most dangerous bands of murderers and thieves the world has ever hosted, an Indian hoodlum brigand known as the 'Thuggees', itself derived from the Hindustani word 'Thag' meaning 'cheat' or 'rascal'. The group is said to be responsible, from their origination in the 1550's, with the murder of more than two million people, the majority of whom were wealthy travellers. The Thuggees operated in gangs, often disguised in similar clothes to their intended victims. To remain in the gang each member had to kill at least once a year, and as one of their guiding principles was to never shed blood, strangulation was the preferred method of dispatch. To justify themselves they killed in the name of a higher order, as sacrifices to Kali, the goddess of destruction. Over time they became less disciplined about their practices and adopted the use of knives and clubs. Eventually they became too much of a nuisance. Public opinion insisted that something as done to control these outlaws and from 1829 to 1848 the ruling British suppressed them with mass arrests and speedy executions so that by 1882 the last known Thuggee was believed to have been hanged.

To judge by the newspaper headlines in the 1970's and 1980's it would appear that the group had recently been reincarnated and had returned with the sole aim of destroying the moral fabric of the society that readers of the Daily Mail and Express believed that they themselves had created. This time their activities weren't in the far flung colonies but actually took place within or in the near vicinity of English football stadiums. No doubt if polled the readers of such organs would have happily recommended that modern thugs should face the same speedy dispatch that their namesakes endured.

In the 1970's and 1980's it was clear to every reader of the popular press that football as a sport was only operating as a cover for people who really wanted to commit acts of grievous bodily harm upon each other. It was argued that nobody really went to watch the game, they went to take place in well organised and highly ritualised violence. During this period I was aware of the risk of attack that going to watch CCFC was likely to put me in, but the reality of the situation was that, like most people, I rarely saw any trouble at all. The real trouble took place away from football grounds and the only 'aggro' I ever witnessed was a bit of 'rushing' in the West End and the occasional chase across Gosford Green, and I vaguely remember some Manchester City fans tearing up some seats and throwing them into the netting that separated home and away supporters. These were little more than skirmishes. Since then I have seen much worse behaviour in school playgrounds and far worse scenes were taking place at the time in local night clubs where there were regular bloody, glassed faces in the Pink Parrot and a murder outside the Robin Hood club. These weren't isolated incidents as alcohol fuelled affrays were part of the average weekend experience. Pubs at throwing out time and nightclubs have always been likely venues for violent clashes, and that's if you manage to get past the doormen. All this was to take a sinister turn in the 1990's when doormen themselves became more closely involved. As alcohol became less important to the rave generation ownership of a club referred less to the licensed victualler whose name was written above the entrance and more to those who controlled the doors and thus the dealing that took place within.

By the early 1990's club owners in many major cities had lost control of the drug that their customers were buying. Lager became replaced as the narcotic of choice by the new kid on the block - ecstasy. Alcohol sales fell and pub and club owners were hardly recompensed by the increased sales of designer water. It became increasingly important for dealers to control the door at nightclubs to prevent rival businessmen getting inside. Thus violence came off the dance floor and into the doorway as rival gangs slugged it out for control of each venue.

As Ecstasy took over as the fashionable club drug many cities were not entirely dissimilar to Al Capone's Chicago of the 1930's, with E being the prohibited drug illicitly offered to a growing and enthusiastically consuming market. In Manchester the most public face of the new battles taking place at night was the ongoing struggle for control of The Hacienda, but many other clubs faced the same conflicts. The techniques for persuading a club owner that they needed your doormen were wide ranging, from sending in local kids or young gang members to start fights to more direct means such as stabbing and shooting the current door staff to intimidate and replace them.

This movement by dealers to take indirect control of clubs is just what any group of management consultants would have recommended. They were really only using the market place most efficiently and as any economist would tell you the easiest way to maximise your profit is to operate as a monopoly and then integrate your operations vertically to take control of the producers and, most importantly, the retail outlets. Thus all the Ecstasy dealers were doing was exactly the same strategy Bass and Boddington's had adopted when they moved from being merely brewers into chains that also controlled the pubs and the hops suppliers.

Obviously the average club goer wasn't really bothered who ran the door, there was hardly the brand loyalty enjoyed by Kelloggs or Tesco's, though it may only be a matter of time before the dealers issue loyalty cards and offer airmiles. The only time the consumer became aware of the trouble was when it spread beyond the door and onto the dance floor. This was very bad for business and so most people rarely witnessed the uglier example of the conflicts.

This violence was tolerated because the clubbers wanted and expected to be able to get their non-prescription drugs at a reasonable standard and price in the clubs. If it hadn't been available they would have moved elsewhere. The media has been surprisingly slow to brand the huge numbers of recreational drug users as scum and the scourge of society. They have adopted a far more liberal tone than was used to brand passive football spectators a decade before. Such liberalism is also obvious in reports on modern football violence. Pitch invasions and fights in the crowd are condemned, but the real vitriol is heaped on players who misbehave on the pitch. The witch-hunters seem to recognise the fashionable status of Rave and now Premiership Euro-football and can't justify abusing their own readers in print.

Cities are shaped by their violent anti-socialists as much as they are by their angels. Most of their growth is a function of the aggressive act rather than the passive. Coventry has been an important player in the armaments business, from Alvis to Rolls Royce and beyond. Manchester's greatest structural developments since the war have been the result of bombing attacks. The Arndale Centre and the Market Street shopping arcade that was built in the 70's could only take form because of the damage caused to the area by the Luftwaffe in the 1940's. That the area damaged was not munition factories around Trafford Park, as intended, but slum housing around the Cathedral, was fortuitous and provided Manchester with the opportunity to clear and rebuild its centre. Similarly the IRA bomb attack behind the Arndale Centre in the 1990's gave the city planners the opportunity to clear away much of the ugliness that had sprung up around the centre and develop the new, more attractive environment. Coventry too is a modern city on a mediaeval site, because so much of the past was cleared away in the air raids of 1942. That we could then build the first precinct in England and the largest circular indoor market was only possible because of the clearance caused by all the destruction. Cities are fashioned slowly by evolution and quickly by revolutions. Thus the development of motor manufacture gave Coventry impetus for growth, while the slow decline of that industry in the region allowed new opportunities to evolve.

Manchester's image may have taken a battering as it was transformed from 'Madchester' to 'Gunchester' with gangs replacing the shiny happy people in clubs and causing many of them to avoid visiting the centre of the city at all at night. However, salvation was to arrive in an unexpected form, for after Gunchester came 'Gaychester' as the media picked up on the story of the rise of the 'Pink pound' in the Manchester economy and found that the new subject was so much more photogenic and far keener to pose for the cameras than the gangsters. With the gentrification of the centre of town and derelict warehouses being redeveloped as luxury canal side flats, Canal Street became the heart of a prosperous 'Gay Village' of international fame. There had been a thriving underground homosexual scene in the city for decades, in some cases quite literally underground as meeting places were basements and clubs around the arches along Whitworth Street such as 'Archways', but the linear development around Mantos on Canal Street ((C) anal (S) treet as it was rechristened by wags defacing its road signs) became the new focus for a minority that were proud to be out and seen.

The importance of the pink pound in Manchester's redevelopment shouldn't be underestimated. At the risk of stereotyping huge numbers of unique individuals, Manchester's inner city and twilight zone have flourished in recent years because of the affluence of two 'invader species', the student and the gay. As Manchester's four universities have grown in the last twenty years bringing in countless thousands of new academic refugees they have given the local economy a financial shot in the arm, especially those sections linked to leisure and youth culture. The old terrace houses that used to stretch along Oxford Road were bulldozed and replaced by an academic wedge filled with halls of residence and expanded University facilities. When former Manchester University graduate Tom Bloxham first bought some derelict property in Oldham Street in 1987 to sell second hand records and pop posters he little realised that this 'Affleck's Palace' would become a focus for regenerating the whole of the Northern Quarter. When he set up Urban Splash with architect Jonathan Falkington in 1993 he had formed an award winning renovator of Manchester's derelict industrial past. By converting industrial buildings into loft apartments and leisure facilities Urban Splash has led the way in filling a void and has greatly strengthened the city's economy and improved its environment. Just as influential are the large pools of disposable income ready for conspicuous consumption available in the bulging wallets of considerable numbers of predominantly single men and women with professional jobs, no children, ample leisure time and a willingness to spend lavishly upon lifestyle accessories. This emergent group of predominantly gay men and women who work in, and want to rest and play in, the heart of the city has financed the profusion of new bars and coincided with the development of Yuppie-style flats and apartments in the rejuvenated industrial belts surrounding the town centre. As one homophobe reflected 'Gangsters have been replaced by arse-bandits', but his observation was ill-judged. Bandits prey upon travellers, robbing them and sometimes taking their life, not really an appropriate term for a group of migrants who have brought wealth and given life back.

24.

Waving - not drowning

'Fancy a tea, Ern?'
Morecambe and Wise.

COVENTRY IS THE CITY IN ENGLAND that lies furthest from any
recognisable stretch of coastline and Manchester is hardly a northern version of Cornwall. One of my few regrets about living in these two cities is
their distance from the salty brine. While Coventry's nearest retreat is the
dubious charms of Weston, Manchester has more of a choice. There is a
fair bit of sea within a couple of hours drive and the options include enjoying a green sunset over the chemical works at Ellesmere Port, or joining a
pensioners outing to Llandudno (which is Welsh for 'The land that time
forgot'). For a more traditional trip to the seaside the real alternatives are a
day out in Morecambe or its big brother Blackpool.

When I first visited Morecambe in 1989 it was a typical English seaside resort, cold, wet and incredibly miserable. The sea was busy reclaiming
a dangerously derelict pier and a walk along the featureless promenade was
about as rewarding as a day spent wandering the beach searching for treasure with a metal detector. A sign painted on the wall next to the Midland
Hotel, which was generally recognised as one of the finest examples of Art
Deco architecture, perfectly summed up the mood of the place. It simply
read, '2 pint jugs of tea 50p'. This inscription was far more eloquent than
any social indicator statistics at revealing exactly the sort of clientele
Morecambe was used to hosting. Who can drink two pints of tea? Fifty
pence!! Hey big spender.

I loved the place, it was even more miserable than Clacton in a
storm.

So who are the other visitors? Historically the resort catered for the huge conurbations of Clydeside, West Yorkshire and, to a lesser extent, Manchester/Liverpool. Now, according to the weather beaten locals in the sea front pubs, the only outsiders were D.S.S. Scousers who'd decided to take up residence in the under-occupied B and B's, and pensioners who were coming back for their fiftieth visit in as many years. The real geographical question was who was going to pass away first, the visitors or the resort.

Financially Morecambe was not skimming off the cream of the tourist dollar. Figures for 1987 revealed that the average visitor spent only five pounds and eleven pence a day while the comparable figure for nearby Blackpool was ten pounds and down south in Brighton sixteen quid.

Though Morecambe lies in a catchment area that contains around ten million people living within a two hour drive, it is in a region with many alternative tourist attractions such as the Lake District, Peak District, Derbyshire Dales and North Wales. The cities of Manchester, Liverpool and Chester are all better placed to use the competing resorts such as Blackpool, Llandudno or Southport.

Morecambe may draw comfort from the fact that visitor trips to the seaside aren't necessarily a short term search for hedonism. In the Eighteenth Century bathers took to the briny waters as a violent therapeutic immersion in which fragile gentle ladies would be forcibly immersed by burly 'Dippers' until they were blue in the lips and barely conscious. The British gentlefolk seemed prepared to suffer such life threatening indignity for the alleged benefits of seawater. Until the 'discovery' of the warmer Mediterranean waters turned bathing into a frivolous rather than improving activity the dips were for nervous as well as physical malaise. If brutal bathing makes a comeback, in what is, after all, a fashion industry, Morecambe is ideally placed to serve the masochist masses once more.

Morecambe Bay first began to attract visitors over a century ago. With the coming of the railway the place boomed and rivalled Blackpool as a Mecca for the mill workers and miners of Lancashire, Yorkshire and Glasgow. That it became known as 'Bradford by the sea' is a reflection of the origin of many of its earliest visitors. Even on holiday the visitors' work ethic was so strong that the first generation of them to have regular holidays called themselves holiday 'makers'. As their numbers grew, so did the town. Like its successors on the Costa del Sol, Morecambe was built quickly and on the cheap. Instead of high-rise towers and theme pubs there were privet hedges and bay-windowed terraces. Just as the first visitors to Spain found themselves in an alien landscape, Morecambe had little in common with the mill towns of its visitors. No factory sirens or whistles and, until the construction of two nuclear power stations at nearby Heysham in the 1980's, no polluting chimneys.

Morecambe flourished and innovated; it produced the first lettered rock and BINGO was christened there. In the 1930's it housed the biggest stuffed whale in captivity and tried, without success, to make the Empire's biggest Christmas pudding. One hundred thousand people witnessed the first night of the lights in 1949, more than attended the Festival of Britain two years later.

However by 1963, when both The Beatles and The Rolling Stones played live in the town, tourism had already passed its peak. Within ten years the decline was physical and visible. In the 1970's Colin Crompton, a renowned wit and raconteur, earned local fame for describing Morecambe as the Costa Geriactrica.

The season shortened and the old theatres decayed until they all collapsed, financially or structurally, victims of the growth of motorways and alternative attractions. Majorca drew ever closer and when the middle classes emerged as the new masses, they sought out new honey-pots. When the last cinema shut in 1983 there was nowhere in Morecambe for visitors to go. The town boarded up. Still cheap but no longer cheerful. The old industrial towns no longer sent their workers, instead they now sent their unemployed, supported by the D.S.S. and adverts in Blackburn and Liverpool.

By the 1990's Morecambe seemed to have run out of time and friends. The neighbouring town of Lancaster had successfully redeveloped its own central shopping area to such an extent that it attracted Morecambe's residents to shop there. Morecambe appeared to be on its last legs.

The appearance and quality of the environment are said to be among the most important factors in forming visitors impressions of a holiday destination, yet despite its Victorian origins Morecambe contains few listed buildings. The town had become visibly unappealing. Its once famous buildings, the station, the Midland Hotel, The Winter Garden and The Central Pier had fallen into such disrepair they were believed to be liabilities rather than assets. The 1984 Planning Report acknowledged 'The physical signs of the resort's decline are undoubtedly Morecambe's greatest weakness'. But as any holidaymaker will acknowledge, the darkest clouds are just before the dawn and Morecambe has brought itself back from the brink.

Faced with the stark realities of its situation the town planners and civic leaders were forced to decide which road to take to encourage economic growth and regeneration. The decision was made to make a feature of what was believed to be the town's greatest asset. The bay that was so unappealing to human bathers was an important site for migrating birds, thus the 'Tern Project' was born. Named after the small fork-tailed cousin of the more numerous Gulls, this project gave the redevelopment of the town a clear theme. As the urban landscape was gentrified a series of municipal art works were built at pivotal sites to give an overall impression of the importance of bird-life in the area.

As the new century approached the effectiveness of the strategy could be assessed and there was much to be proud of. The overall physical redevelopment of the sea front was regarded as a success and the resort's decline had been halted with a growth in day trip visitors who had come to view the bird-life. However the best was yet to come. With the completion of the 'Tern' art works a proposal to build one more statue on the promenade was roundly approved. This time it was to be of a mammalian migrant, one of the area's most famous sons who had left the town to make his fortune, namely John Eric Bartholomew whose parents had met at a dance in the Winter Garden and who was later to incorporate the town of his birth in his stage name as Eric Morecambe. On July 23rd 1999 Her Majesty the Queen unveiled the statue of Eric that had been created by sculptor Graham Ibesson.

The impact was as unexpected as it was welcome. Visitors have flocked in such numbers that it put the migrating birds to shame. The statue has become a modern shrine to those who loved the good, clean, fresh, harmless fun that was Eric and Ernie's trademark, - the same simple values that had made Morecambe the holiday destination of choice for so many working class northern families. Around the statue are various Eric and Ernie soundbites such as 'What do you think of it so far?'- 'Rubbish!' and perhaps most appropriately 'Bring Me Sunshine'.

Moving the Goalposts

Coventry City must be hoping for a similar redevelopment windfall. Why else would a club with an average gate of twenty one thousand announce their decision to build the most expensive stadium ever constructed by an English football club? The plans may have been delayed somewhat, partly by delays in the approval of planning permission and because of a problem relocating a family that had resided in the shadow of the gas towers since World War Two and were rightly a bit hesitant about tearing up the roots of the family home.

Sky Blue supporters always get especially excited at the prospect of an away day at the coast. Given the regular lack of seaside towns in the Premier League (unless you include Southampton) we usually have to sit in eager anticipation of an away cup draw against the likes of Southend or Dover Athletic. Historically we have had relatively few fixtures against beach-side teams. If we are given a sniff of sea-spray it has nearly always been in the form of a match at Norwich. Not that the Norfolk town has been a site of too much joy in our stuttering cup runs. We visited them in the FA Cup in 1983, '93 and '95 and lost each time. In recent years we have also hired a charabanc for trips to Scarborough in 1995 and Bournemouth in 88 which was somewhat more triumphant than the trip to Sutton later in the season. In 1988, as cup holders, we were blessed with a third round FA Cup draw to the English Riviera to play Torquay before going out in the next round at home to Watford.

Before this there was the fixture against Brighton on the 1980-81 League Cup run that saw us reach our first ever semi-final, only to fall to West Ham over two thrilling legs. It just shows how important an early recuperative trip to the briny sea can be.

So it was with huge joy that I received the news that the 1997 Coca-Cola Cup Second round draw had paired us with Blackpool. Excellent. Blackpool, everyone's favourite day out if the Raymond Review bar is closed for redecoration. Blackpool, England's cultural icon. The home of rock, the tower, false tits and 'Kiss me quick' hats. If you can't enjoy yourself at Blackpool then you are already dead. All you need is a full wallet and empty bowels for a ride on the Pepsi Max Big One or the World's least safe looking roller-coaster.

So didn't we have a lovely time the day we went to Blackpool? Well, to be honest, no. It was completely crap from start to finish. The weather was shocking. I managed to park within spitting distance of the ground, though this was no great achievement as the wind was so fierce I could spit nearly two miles across the barren acres of car-park. A storm was howling off the Irish sea stinging the eyes and chilling the soul. The possibility of staying in the car for the four hours before kick off seemed by far the most attractive proposition, but then that isn't the sort of spirit that made Britain great. If Scott had decided to stay snuggled up in the warm with a nice book and a mug of steaming cocoa, he would have survived his Antarctic adventure and not earned eternal schoolboy fame by perishing in the frozen wastes. If Sir Edmund Hilary had decided that the peak of Everest seemed a bit tricky, that great Mountain would have remained unconquered. To which I have to conclude, so what? What possible benefit has accrued mankind from Sir Edmund Hilary allowing himself to be carried up Mount Everest by a group of Sherpas whose own fame never extended beyond having an ugly freight van named after them?

I looked over at the stadium. It seemed about as sturdy as a tent erected by particularly clumsy girl guides. The corrugated steel sides resembled a flimsy Japanese kite more than a football stadium. It probably wouldn't survive until kick-off. Surely the sensible thing to do was to start the engine (before it got flooded with rainwater) and head back home. I could always hide in the pub at the bottom of my street and watch the match news appear on Sky. I could then claim to have seen the game and nobody need be any the wiser. But if the Blackpool ground did get swept out to sea, it would be impossible for me to maintain such a lie. The prospect of such a loss of face was sufficient a spur for me to prise open the car door and clamber outside. Having come straight from work I was dressed in a manner entirely suitable for teaching disinterested teenagers in a centrally heated classroom, and entirely unsuited to venturing into a gale and torrential rainstorm. I was soaked before I got out of the car park. Now I knew why they sell buckets and spades all year round, it's to bale out your car.

I headed for the Golden Mile. It was golden in the same way that clouds have silver lining, or Cockneys are diamond geezers. It was as gold as a dog turd. Some inner programming embedded within all of us that are born so far from the seaside forced me onwards. I must reach the beach, I must see the sea. I battled on. The sea-front was completely deserted. Even the Lifeboat office was closed and had a 'Bugger Off' sign hanging in its window. There was just me and a bloke chained to the sea-wall railings, who was offering deckchairs for hire at the reduced rate of 50p because, as he said, 'business has been pretty slow today.'

I was convinced that I had already contracted pneumonia and decided to seek shelter in a pub before frostbite robbed me of those appendages that local brass monkeys hadn't already made off with. The nearest pub, 'The Sunbeam', was packed with a silent huddled throng. The patrons all wore Sky Blue replica shirts and the long suffering weary expression one usually sees on news reports from refugee camps. A temporary sickbay had been erected by the toilets and a young nurse from 'Medicins Sans Frontiers' was applying Vaseline to wind-chapped and bleeding faces. I stayed for a couple of hours. It seemed like years.

There was just time before kick-off for a traditional Blackpool meal. I ordered cod and chips from the Chippy by the ground, then opened the newspaper and watched the wind blow the whole lot out to sea again. My cod was back with his family. Surely that is where I ought to be. At last the stadium was open. The prospect of shelter warmed me inside. I paid and was in. I climbed the steps up to the raised terrace which gave a great view of the pitch. Or it would have if it had been covered. But this raised vista was unsheltered and exposed to the full strength of the onshore gusts. All the spectators on it were blinded by the rain driven horizontally into our eyes. Word got out that some Coventry fans had seats under shelter in the adjacent stand. To get there all we had to do was run across the pitch. We waited for the ball to get blown up the other side of the pitch and then groups scaled the advertising hoardings and ran across to join our relatively dry comrades. There were ten stewards trying to stop each break away. About five City fans were caught and ejected during each charge. This ongoing battle was far more exciting than the football. I decided that discretion was the better part of valour and stayed on the uncovered terrace. Suddenly through the haze we saw Kyle Lightbourne in front of the far goal with the ball at his feet. He shot. It was a goal. Wasn't it? We all cheered. 1-0 to us. We witnessed no more goals and assumed Coventry had earned a valuable away win in the first leg. There were some mutterings of surprise when we heard the tannoy announce that the final score was 1-0 to Blackpool. Kyle must have missed after all, and Blackpool must have scored during one of the many moments that the rain had made us collectively blind. Bloody hell.

We poured back to our cars and buses. I was sodden to the skin. I thought that if I tried to drive home like this I would die. There was only one option. I stripped off naked in the car and turned the heating on full. My car is an 'E' registration Peugeot so when the heating is on full it gives off about the same heat as a mouse on a treadmill. I drove home but the steam coming off the pile of wet clothes on the backseat had created a small cloud in the car. I could hardly see the road. The terrible realisation dawned upon me that I was likely to crash. My wife would be informed that her husband was found naked and alone in a steamed up car on the M6. What would she make of this?

I heard later that Kyle Lightbourne missed his open goal because one of the Blackpool fans shot him in the eye with a laser pen. If this is true it was the only bright spark seen all night.

If Blackpool is the flagship resort of the English tourist board then it is no wonder that nearly everybody goes to the Costa Brava these days with only pensioners trekking faithfully back to Blackpool, Morecambe and Lytham St.Annes. It is far better to be hot on the continent than wet with the incontinent. I'm glad we live so far away from the coastline. It's safer like this.

25.

Who are yah?

THIS MAY SURPRISE SOME PEOPLE but like all other academic subjects, geography occasional redefines itself and takes a fresh look at what it
wants to be. Public opinion seems to take the view that geography is basically just a pub quiz subject (What's the capital of Outer Mongolia? What
is the currency of Albania? How many words do the Lapps have for snow?)
mixed with a bit of map reading, and of course there is a great deal of truth
in such a view. However, for geography to remain manageable, with its
ambitious focus of all things Earth related, it has to narrow its view and
concentrate on one or two key ideas rather than attempting to explain
absolutely everything about the planet. Naturally, over time, various groups
of people have had vastly different ideas about what the most important
areas of study should be and every now and them the focus of the key topics shifts. Sometimes this has proven very successful, notably after
Columbus' voyage didn't fall off the globe, but instead hit a new continent,
or more recently the discovery that volcanoes make very pretty photo
opportunities. When I was studying the subject during the early 1980's the
latest fad was, unfortunately, what has come to be known as the 'quantita-
tive revolution'. Geography at the time chose to prove itself as a science,
fuelled no doubt by Margaret Thatcher (a chemist) insisting that all things
scientific were great and deserving of extra funding while matters of the
Arts were lightweight, the soap opera and chat shows of academia and as
such should scrabble amongst the leftovers for crumbs of funding. So
geography took a more scientific approach in its studies and attempted to
measure everything it had previously been happy merely to describe. The
subject became swamped with numbers as statistics replaced maps as the

main tool of the geographer. Books of foreign places with exotic people and names were replaced by books of numbers about the percentage of stone roundness in various river beds. Out went the slides of staggering scenery and in came logarithmic graph paper and statistical analysis.

Although this new view of what geographers ought to do was popular with our leaders and with educational policy advisers, teachers were more resistant to change. As the new boy in my school department I became press ganged into teaching this statistics course while the others continued to tell their stories about Pygmies and the Inuit and life as a Bushman of the Kalahari, much as before. In my newly imposed role as statistical analysis expert it quickly became apparent to me that statistics are absolute bollocks. You take a lot of unrelated numbers, massage, cajole and perhaps even change one or two until you find some otherwise meaningless pattern and then state that there might be a 99.9 % chance that this indicates that the relationship didn't occur by chance, that it reflects a process. Huge triumphant cheering and we all move on to the next test. The overwhelming feeling very quickly becomes so what? Who gives a shit? What does it matter? The brighter students pick this up in the first couple of lessons and quickly discover through their own calculations that you can prove just about whatever you like. They can point to clear statistical relationships between the number of storks in a town and the birth rate. They can show that where there are more hospitals there is a higher death rate and conclude that hospitals are bad for the health. But perhaps the most revealing statistic is that one in eight car crashes involves a drunk driver; therefore seven out of eight car crashes were by sober drivers so we can conclude it is far safer to drive drunk than sober.

Let me assure you that I am no trainspotting anorak wearer, but even I must grudgingly admit that some statistics do interest me (insert your own Benny Hill joke here), namely those that relate to football. If the probability of an act occurring depends on the frequency of all possible outcomes, then the chances of a game being won are 1 in 3 as the possibilities are win, lose or draw. The exception to this rule is for cup games when one of the two teams must win and thus the chance of success is one in two. For a Premier league team to win the FA Cup it has to win six games (i.e. 6 x 1 in 2). So you would expect to reach the final every thirty two years and win it every sixty four years. So Coventry City's win in 1987 could be regarded as premature because we had only been in the top league for twenty years.

However, another way of looking at it is that every team entering has an equal chance, so as the cup is nearly always won by a top league team and the league contains twenty clubs the odds are one in twenty and we should reach the final every ten years or so. Alternatively, according to statistics at least, every club stands exactly the same chance of winning. So all clubs who enter the competition at the third round have an equal chance, while those in the previous or preliminary rounds have less chance, not because they are crap and have no internationals in their team, but because they have to play more games to win and thus the statistics are stacked against them. As with all statistical analyses we are left with two completely opposite conclusions. Either Coventry City are over-achievers by winning one major trophy during their three decades in the top flight, or they are massive underachievers, winning only one major trophy in well over a century of trying. It's open to debate as to which is the more realistic conclusion.

Recently football has followed Geography's path into the adoration of statistics and what used to be an interesting sideline to impress your mates with in the post match pub analysis has become far more sinister with such developments as pass-completion rates and Carling Opta statistics tables which prove that players we all judged as crap are in fact fantastic but just look crap. You can no longer say Williams' distribution was poor. You now have to back it up and say 'Williams' completion rate was a disappointing 25% down on his seasonal average'. 'We could have had a hatful' becomes 'we totalled twelve shots, eight were on target and forced a save, of which five were from under six metres.'

It isn't quite as relaxed as I would like. An even worse evolution is the constant TV replays which forbid any colourful elaboration and exaggeration. It's no good telling your mate in the pub after a game about a shot from the half way line that winded the keeper, if he can watch it later that night and analyse it himself with Alan Hansen or Andy Gray measuring the exact speed and distance.

Looking through my copy of 'COVENTRY- the complete history of the club' by Neville Foulger, the former chief sports writer of the Coventry Evening Telegraph, (which, incidentally, contains an excellent collection of pre-mullet dodgy hair-do's, of which the flame red tight curl Afro sported by Ian Wallace remains the most intimidating) there are at the back the complete league tables for CCFC from season 1919/1920 until 1978/1979 and very interesting reading it makes too. As well as charting the club's unique travels through seven different leagues it also highlights the many low lights in our history. The years and decades spent struggling in the lowest reaches of the football league hierarchy are only slightly lightened by the realisation that such luminaries as Manchester United were often down there with us. How we both have grown. These tables only give the briefest of glimpses of how frustrating it must have been to be a City supporter all those seasons ago. For example, few could have realised that the relegation in 1925 would be followed by eleven years spent in the variously titled bottom division. Or that the promising season of 1950/51, which must have fuelled expectations of a far better future, would be followed by a narrow relegation and twelve more years at the root end of English football. The real tragedy of what it meant to follow Coventry City over those many decades is played out in the pages of league tables all headed '3rd Division, 3rd Division (North), 3rd Division (South) and 4th Division'. People mock the Sky Blues for their willingness to celebrate what amounts to little more than survival. Given Coventry's history both on and off the pitch it is no wonder that living to fight another day is heralded as such an achievement. The names in these ancient league tables read like the names carved on a cenotaph or on the plaques to be found at the foot of the trees in the Memorial Park, remembering those who have fallen before us. Aberdare Athletic, Bradford Park Avenue, Clapton Orient, Accrington Stanley, Nelson, Aldershot....

A close inspection of the post-Jimmy Hill tables reveals just how close we have so often come to sinking back down again. So many last day miracle results that kept us up at someone else's expense. What chance would we have had of bouncing back up again? Coventry would probably have done a Stoke or a Luton or a West Brom or a Wolves or a Norwich, the list goes on and on. Since the development of the Premier League the fall has become much further. A grim warning of how terrible it might be is depicted by Sir Jacob Epstein's bronze statue of St. Michael standing above the first of the fallen which adorns the entrance to the new Cathedral, a fall from grace may indeed be irredeemable.

Clearly it is more important than ever before that a club the size of

Moving the Goalposts

CCFC manages to retain its status in the short term and builds upon its relatively meagre support in the long term. If we are to compete effectively even just with the bottom third of the Premier League we need to be able to match them for finance and facilities. So when I first heard that Highfield Road was possibly going to be abandoned in favour of a new stadium that would be the envy of the rest of the country and would host future international matches and possibly the 2006 World Cup, I grudgingly found myself in favour of the idea. In favour despite the fact that it will mean giving up all the comforts that I now take for granted such as my regular parking place, just a four minute walk from the West Terrace entrance, my regular drive via well learned short-cuts, that allows me a speedy exit and avoids all the traffic jams at 5.05p.m. It will be even more difficult to give up watching the regular procession of familiar faces and habits I witness on a matchday. We are all going to have to develop new routines and comforts now. To be honest I don't think everyone is up to such a change and I half expect that there will be a small, residual group of people left wandering the streets of Hillfields every other Saturday in a state of extreme confusion, long after everyone else has decamped over to the Foleshill gasworks.

I liken the new stadium to staying in a top class hotel. Everything is nicer, posher and more pampering than at home, but it's not as comfy because we haven't worn it in and shaped it to fit the nuances of our daily life. Consequently it's impossible to relax and stretch out in the manner of one who is lord of all he surveys even if that happens to be a third floor bedsit in Stretford.

Much as I have come to hate the bulk of what the Premier League stands for - viewers rather than spectators, stadium piped-music rather than self-generated atmosphere, media pandering over non-stories about non-characters, etc. I don't really much fancy the alternative as 'enjoyed' by a friend who religiously follows Hereford United, and all the despondency that that inevitably involves. So even a card carrying Luddite like me is left with little alternative other than to welcome with open arms and misty eyes Bryan Richardson's vision of the future and hope that it is, at the very least no worse than the recent past.

26.

Mind Your Language

'An Englishman's way of speaking absolutely classifies him
The moment he talks he makes some other Englishman despise him.'
My Fair Lady.

'I WILL NOT TOLERATE PEOPLE using language in front of me', said my English teacher oblivious to his own poetic irony.

I was being told off again, as happened most days at school. This time my crime was describing Wales as 'crap'. A viewpoint that apparently didn't go down well with my Welsh school teacher and he demanded that I repeat this abusive heresy. I assured him that he had misheard me and I had merely said Wales were 'crabs' – i.e. that as a nation they were going sideways, rather than forward. The point was being made in relation to a forthcoming rugby international and I had mistakenly assumed that we were having an off-the-record teacher/pupil bonding session. Clearly I had overestimated him and my weekend was spent writing out four hundred lines. Fear of litigation prevents me from naming and shaming this educational impostor. It is suffice to say his nickname was 'Dildo' and my good mate and confidant 'Gobber' reckoned that once, on a school trip to Paris, he caught him playing with himself in his bedroom. A curious reversal of the traditional pupil and teacher roles.

Funnily enough only twenty five years later I found myself in a similar position, only this time I was the authority figure. A young pupil said a word considerably more shocking than 'crap' and then immediately bit his tongue at his unfortunate slip up. There was a short silence between us while we both considered what we were supposed to do in such a situation. He cracked first. 'You wouldn't punish someone for accidentally swearing would you?' he asked. I couldn't resist it. 'Would I bollocks,' I replied.

174

Moving the Goalposts

With the English language being so versatile it is a little bit depressing just how easily I succumb to using the coarsest phrases it has to offer and the pleasure I get from an ill timed oath or repugnant and inappropriate ejaculation. I have always got an unreasonable amount of joy from swearing and misusing the mother tongue. There is almost certainly some glaringly obvious Freudian explanation for this. No doubt I had some bad breast-feeding experiences that left me desperate to cause pain via my mouth. It's just that our language is so flexible, a veritable verbal plasticine, and we are so used to hearing it misused that the oral exception is now the rule more often than not. We mix up all the colours of speech until they are a weird swirling psychedelic mess without rhyme and reason, that is so jumbled up it can never be sorted out into the neat coloured strips again.

Fortunately I'm not alone, otherwise I would have already been isolated, diagnosed as suffering from Tourette's disorder and offered daily medication to stop me from upsetting the rest of society. As it happens, everyone round here speaks just as badly as me. In fact if the Reverend Spooner was to do a bit of his predictable stand up routine around here nobody would laugh because there would be no joke. His deliberate abuses of language look crude and forced compared with the daily assaults inflicted so casually in the Somerfield checkout queue.

Montesquieu, writing in the 1730's declared 'I have seen the country in the world which is most worthy of our curiosity - I mean England'. His expressed curiosity was in response to episodes of bizarre behaviour he had witnessed whilst travelling in the country. The English have long been identified as a nation of maverick personalities with a peculiar taste for social violence whilst demanding that such affrays conform to the communal sense of fair play. Even back in Montesquieu's day we were generally regarded as a mystery. Only the English preferred running errands to walking them, rushed about all day and in the time they had saved took further recreational walks for pleasure. We have an insatiable desire to read salacious scandals as we digest our breakfast and yet seek our own privacy behind the locked doors of our house, hidden from view by our privet hedges. We speak in clipped tones, always careful to disguise our thoughts behind our words, Talleyrand's 'une taciturnite toute anglaise'. Despite the warning afforded by our international reputation visitors to this sceptred Isle are still usually bemused when they come face to face and tongue to

175

tongue with a native English speaker. They are already well aware of the average Briton's aversion to the idea of learning a foreign language. The eighteenth century British classicist Richard Porson once said, 'life is too short to learn German'. What comes as a surprise to the foreign arrival is that we appear not to have bothered to learn English either. The language spoken in the fields and towns of Britain is a vastly different beast to the English taught in schools overseas and classrooms at home. Worse still is to follow for the scholars of our tongue who travel to this country to observe English as spoken by the locals only to discover after painstaking months of studying the native speakers around them that the 'real' English they have acquired is accurate only for the immediate environs and is completely different to the grammar and vocabulary used twenty odd miles up the road. As if to fool potential invaders every town, village and hamlet appears to have developed its own language. Never mind that the Lapps have fifteen different words for the colour of snow, we've got fifteen thousand different words for the male genitals and several million euphemisms for 'going to the toilet'. The ultimate impression must be that the English are so poor at foreign languages because we haven't mastered our own yet.

As if to muddy the waters still further, our language varies temporally as well as spatially. Even within the same house it is possible to find three or four different versions being spoken such as 'infant', 'adult', 'old fogey', 'teen male' and 'teen female'. Different generations of a single family struggle to understand each other's uniquely evolved vocabulary. While most oldsters speak in a mumbling monotone of non sequiturs and incoherent rambles, most teenagers try to converse in what they imagine to be the common street talk found in the rougher areas of one of the Chicago 'projects' or the vernacular commonly used by the meanest gang in 'Hell's kitchen'. They believe they are communicating via an intimidating use of 'Gangsta-rap', but the sad reality is that from our own children's mouths these oaths are about as menacing as the similarly imported 'Have a nice day' delivered by a teenage wage-slave serving in a Starbuck's coffee store in Clitheroe. It is the mimicry of a particularly bright parrot or particularly dim simpleton.

From the early days of broadcasting the 'plum in the gob' tones of the B.B.C. provided the world with a sound they assumed was the voice of the English people. How cruelly and completely they have been deceived.

Moving the Goalposts

The way we use our words and decorate it with accents provides countless wonderful traps to incapacitate the educated, enthusiastic visitor and to shatter their confidence. Even if they eventually begin to master the accent, (as Peter Schmeichel and Jan Molby managed) then there are always the distinct regional dialects left around to further disguise a conversant's true meaning.

The more sensitive soul may actually become aware that the guest to his country is in fact struggling to follow plain English. In such a case the most common response is to modify the words into a form considered simple enough even to be comprehended by a Johnny Foreigner. 'Me no speakee the lingo, you speakee the lingo, savvy?' Just to add an additional pitfall in case there was any risk of being understood.

Where English is taught as a foreign language the traditional accent to be learned is 'R.P.' or received pronunciation. The term 'received' is used in its nineteenth century sense of 'as accepted in the best society'. Although British society has gone through enormous and radical changes in the last couple of centuries, one small section of our populace has remained frozen, like a mammoth trapped in glacial ice, namely those in the upper most reaches of the social ladder. They can be recognised by their education, income, profession, title and, most obviously, by their school tie. These are the people to whom R.P. English is the native tongue, as still taught in the few remaining old Public Schools. The R.P. speakers can disguise the geography of their actual origin by subsuming any natural twangs within the words they utter, thus proving themselves ubiquitous rather than localised. A study by Trudgill in 1979 estimated that only three percent of English people speak in the R.P. manner, yet it remains the version of our language that is taught because it is perceived as the best. This is despite the fact that the BBC have long since abandoned such haughty tones in favour of more distinct regional brogues, seeming to prefer accents from the extreme periphery of these lands.

Although our language aids us it can also betray us. An explicit example was revealed by an experiment that was conducted in South Wales where a University lecturer was introduced to two separate groups of sixteen to eighteen year olds. He proceeded to give both of the groups exactly the same speech, with the only difference being that each time he varied the accent. One he delivered in R.P. and the other was delivered in a

Birmingham accent. After he had finished the lecture both audiences of schoolchildren were then asked to evaluate him and their response was that those who had heard him speak in the Birmingham accent gave him a significantly lower rating in intelligence than the other group. This probably comes as little surprise to most non-Brummies, and all who have seen presenters of 'Midlands Today' amazingly lose their local intonation when the prospect of a job on national TV became available.

Regardless of where they come from footballers have a distinct language of their own, just like pirates used to. 'Pirates only speaks in the present tenses does pirates', while footballers frequently show a preference for the multiple negative, inappropriate plurals, the simple unadulterated cliche or even a mixture of all three. 'No club never spent no moneys, Brian'. Given the amount of air-time devoted to interviews of footballers by former or current footballers and then post match analysis by ancient footballers, it may not be much longer before such bizarre and bland offerings as regularly distributed via satellite tellevision all over the world under the disguise of expert analysis on Match of the Day, become the new B.B.C. 'Received Pronunciation.'

With such a tiny percentage of the country's population speaking the official dialect in the approved accent, overseas visitors really shouldn't bother even trying to understand us. Nor should they assume that we British have it any easier when travelling through our own homeland. When I was a child my family used to regularly visit a strange and bewildering country where men lay in the gutters; where it always rained; where the buildings and the sky were a depressing grey colour and where the locals grunted like the missing link so sought after by anthropologists. These regular holiday trips to see our Scottish relatives were as welcome as an appointment slip from the dentist, or the news from school that today was the day when the school nurse would perform her annual inspection of our testicular development. A mere five hour drive and we would find ourselves in a place where our daily norms and routines were banished and we had to assimilate the behaviour of an alien culture.

I remember that one year when I must have been feeling particularly bold I actually ventured out alone to the corner shop to buy some chocolate and a comic. It turned out that 'Look and Learn' was all the shop had that remotely fitted such a title and such was my desperation for any meagre form of escapism and frivolity as a release from the harsh reality of the holiday that I was prepared to blow all my pocket money on such over priced and woefully inferior goods. However, when I took my intended purchases to the till and asked the beard behind the counter how much I owed him, his reply was just a noise with no clearly discernible words in it, not even foreign ones. It was just like any number of childhood nightmares. You want something, you can't find it and then for no reason at all some mythological beast appears. I can't recall how this story ended as like 99% of that holiday I have managed to repress the memory deep within the least retractable parts of my subconscious. The one other incident that I do remember reveals that I wasn't alone in my ignorance of the foreign tongue of our near neighbours and relatives. When we strayed beyond our base in Argyle Street in Glasgow we were submerged into a world of bizarre place names and locals who still had Culloden on their minds. On one trip to feed the midges at Loch Lomond we got sufficiently lost to have to resort to seeking directions from an old man wandering down the lane. As we listened in communal confusion to his response from the safety of our locked car, through a two inch gap in the minimally opened window, I helpfully offered my considered opinion from the back seat, 'I think he's trying to speak'.

It may be just a coincidence but many regions seem to have have developed an accent that reflects the characteristics of the local people. The Somerset accent makes its speaker sound as though he or she is completely inebriated regardless of the time of day and that county is famous for consuming gallons of the roughest cider around, stuff even passed over in favour of warm meth.s by those gents who lie slumped outside Yates' Blob shop conversing with paving slabs. Similarly, Scot's men and women always sound fiery and on the brink of committing a violent assault. The clipped Essex tones make the speaker sound as if he couldn't give a shit about anyone else, the rural Leicester accent is akin to the noise one expects to hear uttered by a Victorian dullard and the giggling Guernsey tone is disarmingly charming and welcoming. As I say, this is all probably just a coincidence.

Language and accent is a reflection of the ancestry of the occupants of an area. Liverpool and Manchester dialects have been influenced by the huge numbers of immigrant settlers that have arrived in those cities over the last century, particularly those from Southern Ireland. Just as in Patrick

179

Moving the Goalposts

Suskind's excellent book 'Perfume', about a man with no personal scent who was shunned by society because of his deficiency, as a Coventrian I am often rejected because of my lack of accent (though I am prepared to consider the possibility that there may also be other more individual reasons). A common misconception amongst non-Midlanders is that people from Coventry speak with a Brummie accent. That is about as accurate and, may I add as offensive, as saying all Mancunians speak with a Scouse accent or all Scots speak with an Irish accent. We Coventrians in fact have no natural accent of our own. If we ever did it seems to have been bred out of us by the continual recycling and movement of the migrant workforce into and out of the city. When the rapid growth of engineering and other associated industries caused a similarly quick expansion of the city, the result was that the new population lacked the homogeneity of other towns and urban areas. The vast influx of workers from every corner of the country and the Commonwealth have resulted in softening the worst regional accents of Coventry's citizens in favour of a more neutral non-accent. Unfortunately this marks us apart from all other areas and as such we are abused by southerners for our northern bray and by northerners for our southern Jessie lilt. Still at least we aren't cursed with that echoey discord that issues from the mouth of our Birmingham neighbours. Not unless we are suffering from a particularly disabling case of influenza, that is.

27.

Moving On

MOVING HOME IS UNIVERSALLY AGREED to be one of life's less pleasant experiences. Everyone hates it, even estate agents, although getting a thousand pounds for doing bugger all no doubt softens the blow somewhat. Animals hate moving house as much as we do. For example, I have just evicted a colony of wasps from their squat in my attic and boy were they pissed off. As I sat at home dabbing ointment on my stings and casually fending off curious inquiries, 'It's elephantitis actually, and apparently very contagious', I learnt that you aren't meant to deal with these impressively constructed paper domiciles yourself, that it's really a job for qualified council pest controllers. Some hope. Where I live sweeping the street is beyond the local authorities' resources so I doubt they have a crack SWAT team on standby to exterminate these little buggers. And it's not just wasps. When I finally got home from 'Accident and Emergency' I took revenge on the insect world by quickly dispatching a couple of boiling kettle loads down an offending ants nest and they looked pretty fed up about the destruction of their property too. Yeah well next time keep your thieving mandibles off my bloody doughnuts, you bastards.

Moving back to matters Homo Sapiens, I can recount that in a freak moment of life planning that was without precedent and has yet to be repeated, a few years ago my wife and I agreed on a three year plan that stated we would (a) move house, (b) see wild elephants in Africa and (c) have a child, preferably in that order. It felt good to be controlling one's destiny and formalising it into a plan and though it shames me to admit it I must confess that of the three, (b) was my immediate priority. I had always harboured a dream of visiting the scene of so many of Tarzan's adventures and Africa had seemed from my childhood the most exciting place on Earth. More recently Coventry City had unearthed a rare gem when on tour to Bulawayo, namely Peter Ndlovu, so we agreed to go to Zimbabwe in the footsteps of Livingston, Stanley and, less famously, John Sillett. That was the easy bit of the triangular tradeoff. All we did was pick up a brochure, select a time and place, quote MasterCard details and that was that. The travel agent did their job and we received our tickets, itinerary etc, much as expected. If only the estate agents operated on such logical lines.

People are keen to tell you, whenever they get whiff of an impending move, that moving house is the third most stressful life experience after the death of a loved one and marriage. They are wrong. According to a psychology text book I found myself reading in the library one wet afternoon, moving house doesn't even feature in the top twenty stressful experiences (you mean there are over twenty worse things, Christ, are you trying to depress me?). The loss of your job is actually third in this list, but that isn't really the point. What matters is that it feels like it is the third most stressful thing. Moving home, like the third item on our to-do list, is rarely painless.

Most people over the age of sixteen have their own house-moving nightmare to tell. The older the person is, the greater the likelihood is that they will have experienced a significant and difficult move, probably involving a chain of buyers and sellers and multiple solicitors, building societies, estate agents and general hangers-on and so the horror story begins to grow into one of 'The Exorcist' proportions. But everyone else who has ever moved had it piss easy compared with us. Now I don't want to dwell on this as I still find it very distressing to talk about but we had all the usual problems. Namely two years on the market with no viewers, mainly because every time we visited the estate agent to see how things were progressing we discovered that they had no details of our property on display or even accessible on file to show any potential customers. Only a prospective house buyer with precognitive powers stood any chance of learning that our house was up for sale. Then, after our own leg work had attracted a buyer we were gazumped during the slowest moving housing market this century. Then our buyer went on holiday the week we were due to complete - for two months!!! We were all packed up but had to send the removal vans back empty, inform the rest of the chain, try and get the phone reconnected, plead with the gas and electricity suppliers to ignore their final readings, and so on. Far worse was to follow. Rather than relive those painful memories I will just suggest that it is a universally agreed truism that moving home is never easy. If people had any sense or real choice we would all stay put, passing down our properties from generation to generation, making sure we only have one or two children to prevent the need for sub-dividing the house. But if I thought that moving home was to be my major trauma of the decade I was in for another shock.

I remember vividly my son's birth. As the doctor attached the vanteuse suction pump and pulled my unborn child's head with all the force of the Isle of Wight's champion tug-of-war team all I could think was that the little chap's head was bound to come off. If any one pulled my head that hard I'm sure it would tear completely off from my shoulders trailing most of my spinal column in its wake, and babies are supposed to have delicate skulls. The suction built up and the doctor pulled harder and harder. Now he had his foot up, pushing against the end of the bed for extra leverage. The sweat was pouring off him and dripping into the blood that was everywhere. My wife looked like the victim of a shark attack or land mine. Still he pulled. Suddenly there was a huge popping noise like the biggest cork in the world being pulled from a gigantic bottle of wine. The doctor flew back against the maternity room wall. There was no sign of the baby in his hands. My worst fears appeared realised as I tried to remain calm with the man who had apparently decapitated my firstborn. It was OK he reassured me. No damage done. The suction cap had just come off. We would try again. 'Why don't you just smash its skull with a hammer if that makes it easier you murdering bastard', was the response I fought to keep back. The struggle continued. Reluctant baby against tiring doctor and mother. Nothing happened for ages. The doctor called for an orderly and a huge bloke walked in. Please don't start joining in was my silent wish. Even James Herriot showed more dignity to the calves he was delivering. But the orderly wasn't yet required for tugging duty. He was needed to swab up the pools of gore that were spilling on the floor. Then, just as we were all forgetting what this ordeal was in aid of, the doctor did some dazzling hand movements, like a magician pulling a rabbit from a hat. Suddenly, out of thin air he made an object appear which he then proceeded to throw onto my wife's stomach like a tuna fisherman landing his catch. My first thought as I gazed in awe at the world's newest citizen was ' bloody hell, my wife's been unfaithful with a purple person.'

According to his birth certificate my son Oliver was born a Mancunian in Whitworth Park (not the actual park, although I have witnessed a number of attempted conceptions upon its open, grassy plains). The same district of Manchester where his Mum and Dad lived when they were students. If he supports Coventry City when he grows up, will he be merely an inverse glory hunter, a sort of misery seeker? Our house is closer to Maine Road than any other football stadium. In fact it is only a leisurely ten-minute stroll away, so perhaps he will become a Kappa Slappa, a Manchester City fan. If so at least I can take some comfort from the fact that he will inherit the sporting despair that I have enjoyed for so long. I will also be able to regale him with the tale that in the year of his birth I saw his City relegated and was at their final home game when a bizarre own goal, possibly the most impressive I have ever witnessed, by City captain Jamie Pollock, destined them to the dreaded drop to the Second Division (the old Third) for the first time in their increasingly inglorious history. That was on Saturday twenty-fifth April 1998. At least I had the comfort to watch with a neutral's indifference from one of Dennis Tueart's 'Millennial Suite' hospitality seats and the dismal proceedings were tempered by an excellent meal and free alcohol, all won for a one pound raffle ticket and no, before you ask the second prize wasn't four tickets.

I was making a bit of a habit of seeing Manchester City relegated. This was the first time I'd seen them in a competitive fixture other than those involving the Sky Blues, since their relegation by Luton in 1982. Still before I gloat it is only fair to reflect that Manchester City came up from the depths of the league far quicker than Coventry City managed it all those decades ago. By the time my lad is old enough to go to matches City will have gone from Maine Road, choosing to relocate over in Beswick in the Manchester Commonwealth Games Stadium at Eastlands. Manchester City have decided to turn their back on the obvious local support around Burnage, Moss Side, Rusholme, Withington and Fallowfield, and leave behind the Victorian surroundings of Maine Road in favour of a stadium built for Athletics on what has been one of Manchester's most obviously derelict and deprived areas. Since coal mining stopped in that part of the region Beswick has struggled, losing jobs and inhabitants, fleeing as economic refugees to other, more favoured locations. By the end of the 1990's the only people who remained were pensioners trapped in their homes and Daily Mail reporters looking to do another story on Redvers Street, the 'worst street in England' for crime and dereliction.

To the outsider it might seem a curious decision for Manchester City to take. They are the team who pride themselves on the local nature of most of their support relative to the spectators at Old Trafford who increasingly travel to their home matches by aeroplane. Now they have chosen to give up their ancestral home and move into someone else's recently vacated pad on a piece of formerly toxic waste ground. Still, that's progress for you. And Manchester City aren't alone in wishing to move their home after many happy years in one place.

28.

Stadium 2000

IN NOVEMBER 1997 BRYAN RICHARDSON, the Sky Blues Chairman, proudly announced his dream for the City. The whole scene was reminiscent of a cheesy old Bond Movie. There was Bryan, in his office, or perhaps it was his underground bunker, talking of his plans for global domination, or at the very least, being the best team in the West Midlands. This vision was based on some futuristic, technological model that had all the telltale gimmicks that we have come to associate with evil dictators who intend to blackmail the Earth's leaders into total subservience. It had the shiny silver towers, the glass surrounds, a roof that opened to reveal the arsenal hidden within and there was the usual talk of tens of millions of pounds being involved. There were even going to be explosions in old disused gasworks and the whole Bond script seemed just about in place. All that was missing was the rocket-firing car, a couple of lithe future wives of George Best decorated in bikinis, a cat on Richardson's lap and then the famous theme tune could begin. It was just a little bit disappointing that this blueprint for the future turned out to be both exciting and realistic. He revealed plans for a new sixty million pound super stadium that would be far more than just a ground for the local football team. His vision was for a multi-use facility capable of hosting concerts and a variety of sporting events. Based on Vitesse Arnhem's new stadium it was to be part of England's bid for the 2006 World Cup.

The site for this new dream was the abandoned Foleshill gasworks. Foleshill, or in Ancient English Folkeshill (or Folc's hill), literally means 'The hill of the people', and probably gained its original name because it was some sort of meeting place. Could this be a good omen? A sign that

186

the new site would bring people together. Would the ancient site have some natural pulling power in the manner of Songlines or ley-lines that would draw huge support into the new ground? As the pitch would be retractable the stadium could be used for a huge variety of speciality leisure events and it would trigger economic growth through the four thousand jobs to be created building and running the complex and through the fostering of subsidiary industries around this growth pole. The original plans stated a site with parking for six hundred cars and three hundred coaches, a new railway link and station, a capacity of forty to forty-five thousand with adjustable advertising screens for blanking out unsold areas. The total cost was broken down into a figure of forty two million pounds for the stadium shell and a further eighteen million pounds to equip it. An old industrial wasteland would be detoxified and transformed into a visual treat with its terra cotta tiled facade and imposing spires. The project's designer, Geoff Mann, labelled it a cathedral for the twenty-first century. It would be more than just a sports venue. The scheme includes the provision of two superstores of almost one hundred thousand square feet each and a district centre with ten more large units. Other leisure facilities will also be created including restaurants, clubs, fitness centres and hotels.

Not everyone was ready to embrace the idea of a new out of town development. There are those who suggest out of town shopping centres can cause the economic and physical decline of towns and cities. The development of Davenport Green and the five hundred million pound Trafford Park shopping village, a huge temple in which to worship Mammon, which rose on a site near Manchester, was believed to be responsible for the death of hundreds of small businesses in twenty two towns across the North West region. In 1999 The Association of Town Centre Management commissioned a report to discover what the effects of the Trafford Centre were likely to be on the surrounding neighbourhood settlements. They discovered that old market towns such as Altrincham and Stockport would lose an estimated twenty seven percent of all their shoppers within three years of the opening of the shopping village. The report concluded that if towns were to survive such competition from out of town sites then they would have to encourage a lively evening economy by promoting leisure within their own centres. This might be done through the development of a cafe-bar culture and by improving pedestrian and parking areas. On the more positive side it was noted that should towns rise to this challenge, the threat posed by out of town centres could well provide a catalyst for regeneration and redevelopment of some underused central sites.

Some people fear that creating a new development on the fringe of the city is like giving a patient a heart bypass and leaving the heart outside the body. The new development thrives but the city that spawned it is doomed to slow decay. Part of Coventry City's new plan was to develop the eighty eight acre site at Foleshill with retail units and housing in tandem with the stadium, particularly providing single person accommodation and starter homes. The site is intended to be a magnet for first time buyers. With a proposed quarter of a million square feet of shopping outlets on site the new residents are not going to have to travel far to do their shopping, despite the choice of transport routes at their disposal, both into Coventry and beyond by rail, road or even bike.

One area that will definitely notice the change when a new Arena opens is Hillfields with its shabby Father Christmas mural that for decades claimed that 'Santa always shops in Hillfields'. If that claim were true our Christmas stockings would probably have been filled with ironmongery from the district's main retailer and drugs and crack pipes bought, without guarantee, from less formal traders of that district. Hillfields has already started preparing for life after football when the club that has lived there for a century finally moves away. Santa's smiling face has been demolished as have most of the old businesses and shops that lay adjacent to it. The road has been cleared and replaced with clean and bright brick buildings which are there to serve the expanding Coventry University as it spreads across this part of the city. An area once burdened with an unfavourable reputation for vice and violence has been given a facelift in preparation for the next stage of its history. Highfield Road was sold to developers as long ago as 1999 and it too is to be used for accommodation and retail uses. The actual site owned by CCFC was considerably more than the one hectare stadium because the club also controlled much of the surrounding land and its use. These ten sky blue acres will soon be buried beneath new shops and houses. The only memorial of the heartache and occasional joy that was shared by City crowds for over a century will be a small grass play area and perhaps a monument on what was the former centre circle. Although this is hardly likely ever to develop into a site capable of attracting international tourist hordes it will no doubt be occasionally visited by an aging bunch of nostalgists all hearkening back to the glory days. Those times when Tommy Hutchinson would bamboozle defenders as he skipped down the flanks and when halftime entertainment meant 'Johnny Reggae' being played on a record player over the announcer's Tannoy rather than trying not to stare too obviously at jailbait dancers gyrating provocatively whilst adorned in inappropriate American cheerleader costumes. Despite any lingering misgivings harboured by Sky Blue supporters the club itself seems happy enough to turn its back on the premises and surroundings that have served the team and the City well enough for one hundred and one years.

I bloody love birthdays, especially my own. Perhaps it's the presents, or the celebratory partying which has progressed, along with the number of candles on my cake, from ice cream and jelly to beer and fags and eventually back again as I've aged. Or maybe it's the fact that the postman brings more than just bills on that day. Whatever the reason for my own excitement about such annual celebrations it is clear to me that not all people feel the same way. Some folks seem to think each new birthday is a step closer to the grave and consequently they resent this annual reminder of their own mortality. For them they would gladly forego the presents if they could be allowed to remain officially the same age year after year. Not for them the joy of ever increasing digits and the prospect of an annual delivery of slippers, Bassets liquorice allsorts and dodgy aftershave. Some birthdays are, of course, bigger than others. Very few people go wild over their twenty third but most do on their eighteenth, twenty-first and sixty-fifth. Certain numbers have more meaning than others and deserve a bigger party. As with wedding anniversaries and Pokemon cards each numeral is charged with its own special meaning and power.

I recently discovered that even my house has a birthday, and though we won't hold a party for it every twelve months, this year it does deserve one as it has reached the one hundredth anniversary of its construction. Incredibly in a city that has experienced many periods of growth and clearance this house has survived a whole century. What changes it must have seen, real highs and lows, some of which I know about (according to one surveyor's report that we were given a very limited glimpse of before we exchanged contracts the whole side of the house collapsed fifteen years ago) most of which I don't. And though I've only lived in it for five years, well you've got to celebrate haven't you, I mean one hundred years is a huge event. Isn't it?

Well no, apparently if you are Coventry City FC it isn't. When Highfield Road celebrated its centenary in the year 2000 the club were very quiet about that particular milestone in Sky Blue history. The only memorabilia I spotted was one enamel badge on sale in the club shop. It's hardly a telegraph from the queen. The Highfield Road stadium has been a central feature in Hillfields for a century, from way back when the Queen Vic. was a dour monarch dressed in black rather than a fictional East-end pub and hostilities in South Africa concerned the Boer war rather than regular cricket defeats.

Today's financial big boys - Manchester United and Arsenal - were small fry way back then, playing as Newton Heath and Woolwich Arsenal in the old Second Division. Coventry City were floundering around the bottom of the Birmingham and District League while giants such as Glossop North End were promoted into the First Division as the Derbyshire town became the smallest settlement to have a team in the top league, although they were already all but down again by Christmas, winning only four of their thirty-four matches. It might bring a smile to note that one of their few wins came against Aston Villa on the sixteenth of December with a goal from Davidson, their two hundred and sixty pound signing from Third Lanark.

On the twenty-fourth of January that year a battle took place on a hill in South Africa called Spion Kop and this gave its name to Coventry's old Eastern terrace (I think Liverpool may also have used it). Coventry City had recently changed their name from Singers FC and this was to be a momentous year for the club as they moved from Stoke Road to a new base in Highfield Road. Their first season here was truly abysmal as Coventry finished last in the Birmingham League and had to apply for reelection. Finances were in a terrible mess, there were contractual disputes and a real risk that the club would be shut down. The following season was even worse with a disastrous 14-0 defeat at the hands of Aston Villa reserves of all people. Once again we finished bottom and had to apply for reelection. To add further to the catalogue of woe we also suffered our heaviest FA Cup defeat, 11-2 against Berwick Rangers which all goes to illustrate how far we have come during our stay here.

Moving the Goalposts

Just like today, a century ago referees were never happier than when making the headlines. The Glossop Chronicle wrote of the referee after their 4-1 defeat by Derby in 1900 'The question of when a penalty shall be given and when a man is offside seem to have no presence in his brain.' Penalties had only recently been introduced and Jimmy Crabtree became the Gareth Southgate of his day when he became the first England player to take - and miss - a spot-kick. As England won the game against Ireland 13-2 it was hardly as costly as Southgate's gaffe.

The F.A. Chairman Charles Clegg remained opposed to professional footballers and rallied against the corrupting influence of money in football, adding that he considered the buying and selling of players as 'most objectionable' and 'unsportsmanlike'. Dubbed 'the Napoleon of Football' he wanted a maximum transfer fee of ten pounds but players were already trading for three hundred pounds so his was a lone voice in the wilderness.

One hundred years later Clegg will be turning in his grave. His beloved FA Cup is sponsored, media companies own stakes in many top clubs, players can earn in excess of one million pounds a year, the most exciting players in the league are Moroccans, Italians and Eastern Europeans and the club he was devoted to, Sheffield Wednesday, are well on course to follow Glossop's dramatic demise, having taken the first step by relegation from the top flight.

That so little fuss was made over Highfield Road's landmark centenary birthday might be because the club didn't want too much publicity over the present home when they are investing so much time, money and P.R. over the move to the Foleshill gasworks site. The last thing they needed was for the civically proud Coventry public to get all misty eyed about how fantastic the old place was and how much we will all miss it. I personally doubt that most people will be terribly sad to leave. The move makes commercial sense and if you want to see CCFC in the Premier League then commercial sense has to be the ruling God. There is no place for nostalgia in the modern sporting calendar as Manchester United proved when they elected to shun their defence of the crappy old FA Cup for a prestigious tournament whose name eludes me that took place some six thousand or more kilometres away, and as our own FA demonstrated when they decided that Wembley must be levelled and rebuilt - destroying the twin towers - thus eliminating the only possible reason for keeping that inaccessible location as the site of our national stadium.

Just as Sunderland had to abandon the Roker Roar to keep up with the big boys, and Derby had to give up the home advantage of playing in the bog of the baseball ground, so the Sky Blues will be moving to an all singing, all dancing (albeit only Tina Turner, according to promotional literature), sparkling new super stadium where the sun always shines, and if it doesn't we'll close the roof, and where the pitch can be put out to graze so we don't end up with the rutted mess that former City teams had to endure. So Highfield Road didn't get a big centennial birthday party, instead the celebration it got to host was its own funeral.

Others have seen it all before. Those who have followed the fortunes of the Sky Blues since the Jimmy Hill era have witnessed many strange innovations and plans. Not all were total successes and, happily, not all came to fruition. Derek Robbins' attempt to put squash courts under the Spion Kop was fortunately thwarted, though it does provoke a question about how much market research was done before the proposal. Having a quick game of squash is hardly part of most football fans pre-match ritual. Similarly the decision to become the first all-seater stadium also proved unpopular.

Some of the doubts being expressed are a reaction to the problems already experienced at other developments. Stoke City's move to the brand new Britannia stadium heralded their worst seasons for decades and a plummet into the Second Division. Sunderland's Stadium of Light may be a beautiful stadium but it will never recreate the Roker roar despite the huge attendances. Derby's new stadium at Pride Park provides such a good playing surface that they have given up their old advantage that came from being the only species that loved wallowing in mud as much as hippos. Middlesborough's new stadium was peripheral to the town and its wasteland location was hardly the stuff of football romance. Bolton's Reebok offered much better facilities than Burnden, with no impaired view and good catering, but the price was a loss of access and no free parking. The new stadium is not within walking distance and to park your car adds five pounds to the cost of your ticket. On top of that the exit was hampered as all thirty thousand spectators tried to depart on one slip road to the M6. There are clearly banana skins that need avoiding on the path to the new stadium.

Moving the Goalposts

On July 9th 1998, Coventry City Council's planning committee gave the go-ahead for three of the most significant redevelopment projects in the city since the post-war rebuilding. Plans were accepted to transform the old Coventry Colliery at Keresley into an industrial and housing estate. There was also approval for a one hundred and ninety million pound super hospital to be built at Walsgrave or in the city centre and thirdly the Sky Blues' Arena 2000 was given the green light. By now the new stadium's cost was being quoted as one hundred and thirty five million pounds. It had leapt by seventy five million pounds in six months and continued to rise. A taste of things to come. The council seemed confident that the three plans would get Coventry buzzing again.

There are other lessons to be learnt. When the French built the new national stadium on an old industrial site at St. Denis in Paris there was fulsome praise for the original design. Many observers likened its sleek lines to that of a U.F.O., but like outer-space the ground has no atmosphere. A reminder of the tag line for the film 'Alien' - which read 'In space nobody can hear you scream'. The huge gap between the stands and the roof allow sound to escape beyond the stratosphere rather than echo and multiply. The 1998 World Cup final was even quieter than its predecessor in the United States despite the presence of the home side in the final. Part of the blame for this was the ticketing policy which forced the vast majority of the tickets into the hands of corporate entertainers via the intermediary touts. FIFA effectively endorsed the growing trend of alienating traditional support in favour of picking up some more lucrative transient spectators. Long term this may prove costly if supporters turn away from the game, but given the two billion worldwide television spectators this is unlikely. There will always be those who want to see games. A return to the post-Heysel empty stadiums and footballs loss of popularity is unlikely. Football clubs serve a new audience now who expect better catering, parking, seats and comfort, who will not tolerate being rained on, and who watch the game in suits rather than polyester replica shirts. They may not be a majority in numbers but they hold the financial whip hand. Corporate sponsorship has come a huge way from Jimmy Hill's fledgling attempts to get CCFC renamed Coventry Talbot and to wear 'big - T' shirts to overcome a ban on advertising. With McDonald's family stands and a healthily growing number of female fans the tired old cliche of football being the working man's sport can be buried, which is just as well in a society where the working class have been superseded by a share and property owning expanded middle-class. A society where more people have stock-brokers than belong to a trade union and more speculate on the market value of stocks via the internet than put on a bet with Ladbrokes. A new population demands a new type of recreation, and it does not expect the bloke next to them to piss in their Paul Smith designed pocket.

Football clubs can no longer be run like enthusiastic amateur bowls clubs. There is too much at stake financially and those who stand still to review the situation will quickly find themselves left behind with no real chance of ever catching up again. It takes brave decisions based on financial acumen and fair bit of guesswork and kidology. So Coventry City, a team that only fifteen years go was regularly getting crowds of around ten thousand, is now moving to a stadium that will hold as many as forty-eight thousand spectators. To many this seems a little ambitious. Even whilst in the Premier League we have played in front of some empty seats at home when our capacity at Highfield road is a mere twenty-three thousand. Why double the capacity if we can't even manage to consistently fill the current level? Again it seems the Bryan Richardson has the answers. The new stadium is not just for football and so it needs to be flexible enough to cater for audiences much larger than its week in week out average. Also, experience suggests that the move will coincide with a large increase in our average attendances. When Ajax moved from their nineteen thousand seater stadium to the new Amsterdam Arena they attracted gates of forty-eight thousand despite no success on the pitch. Similarly the Vitesse Arnhem stadium upon which the original Arena 2000 plan was based saw their own crowds triple to twenty-four thousand when they relocated to the new ground. Closer to home when Sunderland and Middlesboro' moved they may have turned their back on tradition but they have both been rewarded with far higher support.

Estate agents are renowned for the opinion that the three most important factors to consider when moving to a new home are 'location, location and location'. The Sky Blues seem to have taken this simple idea to heart. The improved transport situation that will be available at Coventry's new Arena provides the club with a far greater potential market as it will be more accessible to a larger number of West Midlands residents.

Considerably more people will lie within half-an-hour's travelling time of the Foleshill site than are within thirty minutes commute of Highfield Road. The proximity of junction three of the M6, the closeness of Birmingham international airport some fifteen minutes away and the construction of a new rail link to the West Coast line should shorten the transport time for people on the fringes of Coventry and increase the physical range of our 'local' support as new spectators are expected to be lured in by the ease and comfort of visiting the stadium. With its four prominent spires it is easy to understand why it has been described as a cathedral for the new century in the city with the slogan 'Coventry Inspires'.

If Coventry City Football Club want to play competitively in the top flight, with a realistic chance of eventually winning more silverware, then we have to level the playing field, or even tilt it in our favour. In an interview on Talk-Radio in May 2000 Bryan Richardson estimated that any club needs a turnover of around fifty million pounds to realistically compete in the Premier League. At the time our turnover was around twenty million pounds. The clear implication is that without the move, the Sky Blues would find their natural level at around mid-table in the Nationwide First Division. The move to a new site offers the possibility of raising the stakes without risking the type of financial pitfall that so nearly put Crystal Palace out of business. The new Arena is funded from a variety of sources, with the most significant contributors being the adjacent retail and leisure developments and cash from sponsors. The club is to become a tenant of the Arena in order to insulate itself from the construction costs so that it should never find itself in a position where it has to sell a player in order to buy more bricks or tiles. If the new stadium does not attract a full house there are plans to fill the empty spaces with banks of hologramatically generated advertisements which will effectively blanket off empty areas so as not to destroy the atmosphere. The club says that it is confident that it can fill the stands with supporters despite the competition in the region from so many other teams with strong local support. What is in Coventry's favour is that the area is thriving economically, with new businesses moving in attracted by the skilled labour force and the two Universities which provide a regular supply of graduates with some local ties. Perhaps more significantly the previous boom generation of the 1960's and 1970's have at last begun to put down roots here. Coventry is no longer a transition camp full of temporary economic migrants with emotional loyalties to some other town or region. The city's population now has far more of a sense of being Coventrian and this is reflected in the steadily increasing numbers who choose to watch the Sky Blues on a regular basis. The club shop now shifts some fifty thousand replica shirts when previously the figure was around six thousand. If they can persuade all these people that own the shirts to wear them with pride in the new stadium then it won't be long before the club has to consider ways to increase the capacity beyond the forty-five thousand seats that will be available.

FINAL WHISTLE

THE REMOVAL MEN HAVE GONE and we are left alone in our new house. The first house I have ever owned. Except I won't actually own it for another twenty five years, and will only own it then if it turns out that I haven't been mis-sold an endowment mortgage for the flat we have just moved out of. Twenty five years of worry ahead about meeting the monthly payment, of not losing my job, of that warning that any failure to meet repayments will result in the lender seizing the property and flogging it off cheap to someone else whilst putting me on a credit black list which is effectively like putting the mark of Cain upon me or labelling me a plague carrier. And that is after we manage to unpack all the boxes we've loaded into the new place.

An awful sense of impotence and not being able to cope hangs in the air. There are so many jobs that need doing. Wallpaper is hanging off the ceilings or lies ripped on the floor. The carpets are on their last legs, the boiler makes horrible noises and fills the bath with yellowy water and fragments of wasps from God only knows where. The cellar is damp and clearly a future liability rather than immediate asset. There is even worse news from the surveyor who has told us that because there is evidence indicating that one of the walls had previously collapsed and been rebuilt we'd best consider having all the other walls underpinned. And he didn't mean the garden walls. As for the garden, only napalm and Agent Orange would make an impression. So we sit on the stairs with our head in our hands gulping in the atmosphere of our new home taking in the scent that tells us 'a dog has lived here for the last ten years'.

We decide to make a list of all the good things about moving here. It's bigger (more cleaning). It's got a garden (more gardening). It's got an extra bedroom so we can have guests round to stay, (but it is in terrible state and will need urgent decorating). It's got a big kitchen which will allow more than one person in at a time (no complaints here). Best of all it is detached so we won't be kept awake all night listening to the flat below's maudlin Lionel Ritchie and Simply Red albums which tell us that our neighbour has another failed relationship to contemplate into the small hours (but detached means we are responsible for all three of the garden fences which look like they are going to blow

Moving the Goalposts

down in the first storm of winter). All I can see stretching into the horizon is a list of jobs longer than Dorothy's yellow brick road. Mild panic has been overtaken by a full-scale anxiety attack but I can't let myself succumb to it because we aren't even registered for a doctor around here.

In the attic there is a treasure chest. Honestly. Just like in all those Boy's Own adventure books. It's encrusted with the dust of a century, though bizarrely inside it contains a decent collection of early 1970's L.P.'s, if there is any such thing as a decent collection of 70's music. That's another terrible thing about moving. You nearly always leave stuff behind, by accident, by intent or because you can't shift it. I've already forgotten exactly how the kitchen of the flat looked when viewed through the serving hatch. How long will it be before I start forgetting other absolutely crucial memories from my past.

Will this building ever feel like home?

It's an emotive subject. I remember a terrible moment that happened a couple of years after I first move up to Manchester. My dad and I were chatting on the phone about something or nothing, probably discussing how much more money I wanted to borrow off him, and in the end we agreed to sort out the details, as he put it, 'When you come home'. Then there was an embarrassed pause and he added. 'I mean our home.' i.e. he was recognising that I too had a home and he wasn't meaning to dismiss it. My parents have only hinted at how it felt for them when I went away to University. The first of their children to leave a very close family unit. They knew then, even though I didn't, that it was a big break. It wasn't to be a temporary dislocation, a long holiday. They knew that I was going for good and all our routines and daily conversations and things we did for each other were forever gone. Don't bother setting me a place for dinner folks, I'm hitting the road.

A similar, but worse situation happened after I'd been gone for two years. I was back in Coventry during the holidays and at some point I casually let out 'When I go back home...' and I knew that I had said something terrible. I'd classified that vomit stained, urine stinking, breeze block student cell in Manchester as my home. I had accidentally rejected the nest that they had struggled to build to protect and nurture me. The arrogant phrase hung there in the air above us. We all looked up as if to see the speech bubble floating there and read whether I had really said those insensitive words. Because home isn't a casual or throwaway term, despite my attempt to devalue it with that sentence. The word home contains no ambiguity and regardless of what international jet setting stars may believe a person can't have homes all over the place, they can only have houses. There is only one real home. People can't invest all that emotion and heartache in a whole catalogue of postal and zip codes.

Moving the Goalposts

I get into the car and take a ride back to the other side of Rusholme to sneak a look at the flat we have virtually given away to someone who doesn't deserve to live there. Negative equity on that place. It is incredible. We have effectively paid someone else to take it off our hands. I wish my dad could have sorted all this man stuff out for me and let me watch TV or play with my toys instead. Why can't things just stay the same?

* * * * * * *

A year later and its like we've always been here. Hardly miss the old place at all. Got the new house decorated. There's still the odd wasp in the bath but we've long since stopped worrying about little things like that. The garden looks like a garden, albeit like one of the student gardens that fill most of our street, a bit like a cross between a traditional wild country garden and a pub beer garden. It's not quite what Alan Titchmarsh would consider finished. There's no decking or Japanese bamboo, or even a water feature, except when we get particularly heavy rain, then there's quite an impressive , if ephemeral water feature. But there is space to sit out on the three sunny evenings we get every year around here, so we can do the Aussie barbecue thing like they do in real suburbia. Little by little it has become more our place as we stamp our own mark upon it. I still miss the other place, but I don't go and stare at it any more. Emotionally I'm back down to two homes again. One up here and one where I was brought up and where my Mum and Dad live and still look after boxes of childhood stuff I couldn't ever bear to throw away but, have never missed enough to allow to clutter up my own house up here. Things like beer glasses collected from around the world; Warlord comics from the 1970's and Wizards and Hotspurs from the 1960's; my old school blazer from when I was ten years old and my first ever rugby shirt. As I said, a real treasure trove that would leave future generations culturally impoverished should it ever be thrown away.

It's not as though my continual hoarding of what really is little more than household waste is abnormal. I have many friends whose idea of tidying up their personal effects is to put them into a fresh carrier bag and shove it under the bed with all the other carrier bags. Martin is the most organised of all my friends. He hangs his carrier bags up in his wardrobe, in chronological order and though he is the calmest man I know even he is pushed too far and goes absolutely ape with his wife if she ever moves one of these carriers just so she can hang some clothes up. There are worse than us. I know people who have so much crap that they fill their garden with it and call it a collection. I would never go that far. And a lad I know has got a Manchester City seat in his house. One of those tip up ones. It's totally useless. He's never going to be allowed to fix it to a wall.

199

Moving the Goalposts

I also once read about a bloke who bought a whole strip of wooden seats the last time Highfield Road was tarted up. That is taking things too far. But when Highfield Road is closed for good I hope that they sell off all the old stuff to souvenir hunters because we need a bench in the garden and I'm sure that a short strip of terrace seats would look far nicer than one of those white plastic B&Q ensembles. Nothing too long, that would look silly. Just a family size row. Or even better I could buy four short strips, one each from the West Terrace, Main Stand, East Terrace and M&B Stand and I could arrange them into quite a brilliant garden feature around a strip of real Highfield Road grass. That would look a treat. After all, I'm always being encouraged to show more interest in the garden. Well I'm fired up with enthusiasm now. I wonder if they are taking orders yet?

29.

An Obituary

I WAS READING THE OBITUARIES the other day, trying to cheer myself up during a quiet lunch break, when I was suddenly struck by the realisation that everybody who has ever died was, apparently, a really decent, good-humoured and widely respected person. This surprised me as nearly everyone I know would probably admit that they are criticised by far more people than they gain praise from. Goodness only knows what was said in Hitler's or Dr. Crippen's obituaries, probably something like, 'Devoted to his mother. A keen artist and a dog lover right up until his death' for the former and 'renowned medic, always prepared to take his work home with him' for the latter.

It seems incredible that everyone good and respected in the world should have died, leaving only the imperfect, bad-humoured and barely tolerable behind. What a curious circumstance. It's unfeasible that this can merely be a coincidence, there must be some sort of cover up involved. Somehow Satan's cohorts have gradually succeeded in their mission of populating the planet with the spiteful, the ambitious, the self-seeking, the two-faced, the weak in spirit and the followers of evil, through a process of selectively culling the pure and the good. Scientists need no longer waste billions of research dollars seeking a miracle cure for every known and undiscovered disease as clearly the secret of eternal life is simply to be a complete and utter shit who is despised by everyone. I await my Nobel prize for medicine with eager anticipation and will use the money that I am awarded preparing for my many centuries of retirement.

So if I had to pen an obituary for Highfield Road I would no doubt find myself remembering how great were the days spent on the Spion Kop, frozen and soaked, trying to regain some feeling in my toes and fingers as I watched an aimless (literally) goal-less draw or even worse, a humiliating defeat. The whole of Highfield Road will soon be shrouded in a halo of happy memories.

As today is the last home game at Highfield Road in what was expected to be its penultimate season I have decided to walk to the ground. This time next year the game will be a sell out, whether it is a relegation six pointer that means the difference between survival or slump, or whether, like today, it is really a bit meaningless. This season we can't be relegated and we can't reach the stratospheric levels of a place in Europe. In fact win, lose or draw we can't do better or worse than our current position of four-teenth. Respectable if disappointing. An excellent season at home has been tempered by a truly dismal away record. But today we are at home and to savour what will be the last visit of the year I'm walking to the ground. I want to make the most of it because soon this journey will be taken away from me. Then I will have to buy a car park season ticket, or a West Midlands travel pass and take the train, or leave my car in a Park and Ride scheme. I will no longer be in control, I will have to plan my day out far more carefully and I will have to spend more money. Such is the nature of progress.

There are a number of different routes I could take from Earlsdon to Hillfields and as it is a nice day and because it is an important day, a day for reflection, I have decided to take the odd detour to pass by some of the more familiar sights on the way. I set off and head past the Memorial Park whose circumference I used to run around in various efforts to get fit or at least to be able to tighten another notch in my belt. Beyond the park I pass two of the schools I have spent various lengths of time wishing I was out-doors looking in. Well today I am outside and despite what people always told me I don't yearn back to my school days with a longing. Parts of them were good and parts were bad but generally I would have rather stayed at home and played in the woods, or gone for a ride on my bike, or played on my skateboard, or read a book, or watched crap on the television. Given a choice I would have preferred to stay at home. Now that I am round and grey and cynical I can consider myself to be an adult. Having spent all but five years of my life within school walls, I feel appropriately placed to dis-cuss the role of schools in child and adult development and find instead that I don't have any opinions at all on the subject. Bits are good, bits are bad and some bits, most bits, are average.

I take a turn into Spencer Park just before I reach Coventry railway station, so that I can take a stroll across Anarchy Bridge. This used to be a great bridge, though it has been tarted up now. It had the best graffiti I have ever found anywhere, and I realise that makes me sound as though I have spent years of painstaking research by hanging around in public conveniences but I can assure you that the shadowy figure over by the paper towel dispenser wasn't me. My favourite messages were the bizarre 'Beware of the Snords'; the surreal, 'I used to think Smirnoff was a type of Vodka before I forgot the rest of the joke'; the political 'animals are innocent, eat the rich'; the sensitive 'Love Laughs At Locksmiths' to which a post-script had been added, 'So does Slippery Jim de-Griz'; and the communally entertaining, the best of which was the set of Pink Panther footprints that appeared one night and crossed the whole length of the bridge, eventually climbing a wall at the far side and jumping across onto one of the roofs in the British Rail sidings. It was a beautiful piece of work, carried out with painstaking care. There were no paint slops, or uneven strides, just carefully laid pink footprints, and the prints that marked the landing point on the adjacent roof were magnificent. This artist could teach Disney a thing or two about pacing and proportion.

The only trouble with this vast display of creativity is that you often forget to watch where you are stepping and as this bridge links a park with an urban desert devoid of grass it is a major dog highway so the floor often resembles Chris Ofili's Turner Prize winning artwork as unfortunate pedestrians have spread various shades of brown colour across the pathway on the soles of their feet.

All too soon the bridge comes to an end. Regret that the show is over is tinged with relief that I haven't been mugged. Not that this is much of a risk these days, now the bridge has been improved and cleaned up and is part of another new retail park built on the old railway yards. The bridge marks a boundary between urban and suburban. On one side there are parks, trees and urban wildlife, on the other there is tarmac, brick and steel. This is how I like my nature. Unobtrusive and well managed, genetically modified wildlife. The great outdoors has always looked better from inside a pub or a car or presented on widescreen in technicolour. The looks are deceptive. Out in the wild birds and animals are in control. Back in the town this order is reversed and a bird that would happily crap on you from thirty feet up in the air is far less cocky when presented in a game pate along with a wild berry coulis. The best way to pacify a charging bull is to serve him up in a peppercorn sauce. He looks and smells tons better too. I don't even like cut flowers in the house. Scented stocks and beautiful lilies bring me out in hayfever, make my nose glow and sinuses drip. Even domesticated animals cause more trouble than they are worth, making their owners and their homes smell and covering the streets with pungent excrement that seems a magnet for children and deep treaded training shoes. Nature is better in the countryside where ramblers can gang up and march all over it before comparing their Goretex and the latest Arctic fleeces, and where farmers can protect it by ripping out hedges and spraying chemicals all over it to make the greens greener and the browns browner and their Landrovers bigger and shinier. When it boils down to it I guess I am a human geographer rather than a physical one. I love the coast, but prefer it to have a nice taverna or restaurant and a decent promenade with interesting shops, rather than just rocks, crabs and sand.

Stepping off the bridge we are immediately into the Specials' 'Concrete Jungle'. It's all underpasses and ring-roads, with more tunnels than Cu Chi running off left and right, all curving so you can't see where they come out. Turn right and you are heading back to the station, turn left and you are heading towards the famous Starley Road, with its slogan 'We Saved it'. This may well be the most famous and now most sought after, road in the city. Back in the late 70's it was on the condemned list. Its properties had fallen into disrepair because of a lack of investment which was in turn due to a proposed road scheme that never appeared. It got so bad that even the homeless families put there by the city council began to complain. The Council's response to such criticism was a threat to demolish what was perceived as a blight and an eyesore too close to the heart of the city. In December 1977 along with the traditional Christmas cards the postman delivered eviction orders and the residents faced displacement to the outer fringes of Coventry. The tenants responded by forming a housing cooperative and fostering a new community spirit. A government loan signalled a change in the local council's intentions and the street with its huge 'Save It!' mural had succeeded. Today its former derelict houses have become transformed into a well-maintained cul de sac of solid Edwardian terraces that contain flats and even four and five bedroom houses. The co-operative is sufficiently well managed to be able to have recently replaced all the windows with double-glazing and to have a slush fund that allows them to take elderly residents out for Christmas dinner and give them each a ten pound note.

Progressing into the central shopping precinct, I find myself in a car free zone in the city constructed to house car builders. I cut through the centre of the town between its rival shopping centres and down past the spires, beyond the swimming pool and sports centre that apparently looks like an elephant to its designer and like a huge inverted skip to everyone else and before you know it we are approaching Hillfields. It is hardly recognisable now. New roads front new shops and new residents live in the student accommodation. New animals stock the urban farm and the district has lost most of its former menace. As I cross through the small playground and pass the Special Brew and White Lightening swillers I am already within view of the Highfield Road ground but have yet to spot any other spectators. It's more than an hour before kick off and even the police haven't arrived yet. In another thirty minutes they will start blocking off the Thackhall street entrance to prevent road traffic and a crowd will begin to form outside the closed turnstiles and around the Sky Blue Tavern. Familiar faces appear and short conversations are indulged. The talk is dominated by rumours of dressing room disputes and information about who is going to be sold over the summer. Some of these eventually come true, most are sham.

Surveying the immediate surroundings outside the ground, many of the houses appear empty but are clearly lived in. Empty houses rarely stay that well maintained for very long. These properties are well looked after. Perhaps their residents go out every Saturday to avoid the disruption. Or perhaps they barricade themselves inside in front of the television and wait for the uninvited visitors to go away again. A couple of houses opposite the West Terrace are always incredibly busy with people coming and going and an open door policy. Children wander about, make friends then fall out with each other and seek refuge behind the various front doors. This scene seems out of place. Part of a community that doesn't exist anymore outside television soap operas. A place where people can push open their neighbour's door, cry a greeting and wander in unannounced. When I am in Manchester if someone comes to my door I immediately go upstairs and look through the bedroom curtains to see who it is. We don't get visitors in Fallowfield. We get hawkers, vendors and salesmen, but never visitors unless we have planned it a week in advance. On extremely rare occasions a neighbouring student will ring our door bell in desperation, seeking a fuse, or a spanner, or a litre of petrol for their car, but usually our bell is little more than door jewellery. Yet here around Highfield Road people wander into each others house with confidence and presumably receive a welcome. Well in a year or so all this will be theirs and theirs alone. There won't be any more disruption from day-trippers then. I wonder if they will hold a street party to celebrate their liberation, like Starley Road did?

Some groups of spectators arrive together but many come and leave alone. Martin stopped coming over a decade ago and though I sometimes spot and chat to old friends I am really a solo spectator. My wife came to a couple of games but never really enjoyed it. I once spotted the pair of us on 'Match of the Day'. I was standing celebrating the award of a corner while she was sitting sheltering from the persistent rain by holding the matchday programme over her head. I have to admit that I have seen her looking happier. I never again tried to persuade her that she would enjoy an afternoon out in the rain at the football.

Once inside the ground it doesn't matter whether you have arrived in a double-decker bus full of your closest friends or whether you walked in alone. It's not like a nightclub or a party where a person standing in splendid isolation marks themselves out as a 'Billy No-mates'. The game starts and finishes. The result was favourable but, this time, irrelevant. People leave, most of them happy, the visiting Sheffield Wednesday fans less so. A few people have left already, the 'dashers' who always miss the last five minutes of the match, preferring to miss a goal than run the risk of getting caught in any traffic. Most supporters have stayed behind to say farewell for a few months to the players, realising that a number of them may never return in Sky Blue. Some rumours will turn out to be true. Steve Ogrizovic is given an ovation. Not for his performance on the day, which was good, but for his performances over the previous six hundred league matches. This year he is retiring. Next year, or perhaps the year after, it will the Highfield Road stadium's turn. All the players leave the pitch. Some are in more of a hurry than others to get a shower. All the spectators leave the ground. Some of them in more of a hurry than others to get home for their tea. I decide to stay behind for a little while and try to imagine what it will be like when this historic site closes for the last time. The place empties surprisingly quickly. The Swan Lane East Terrace opposite has emptied quickest and the King Richard Street Main Stand is already almost empty. The M&B Stand has taken a bit longer to thin out but they are nearly clear over there, whilst around me the West Terrace is almost deserted. One or two young lads are scouring the seats looking for any programmes that have been left behind, or perhaps even something with a bit more of an intrinsic value. The stewards are patrolling, encouraging the reluctant departees on their way. I am approached but my reasons for waiting behind are accepted. The steward moves on towards the young lads. I will him to shepherd them out. I want to be the last here. It looks as though I might succeed, though there is still the odd straggler in the Main Stand. What are they doing? Perhaps they are journalists. They don't count. Though the ground appears empty now it isn't really. The players are getting changed, the interviews are being recorded, the cash is being counted. The last people to leave will be the CCFC employees and those business men, women and children who are in the corporate entertainment facilities, meeting players, having a drink, presenting crystal bowls and receiving signed shirts. I've never witnessed these scenes at Highfield Road but have been granted the occasional glimpse of how the other one percent spend their matchdays by the glossy photographs printed in the programme. Fake tan director's wives presenting Robbie Keane, or Dion Dublin, or David Speedie, or Terry Gibson, or Ian Wallace with their thousandth award.

Out here in the stands the place is almost clear. It's vacuous. For the next 3 months it will be unemployed and then, sooner than it expects, it will be pensioned off. The young lads have been caught by the steward and eased on their way. I am on my own. I try to take it all in. There is a sign above my head that thanks me for not using foul and abusive language. Another shows me the way to the exit. This is what it will be like when the last ball has been kicked and the last seat vacated.

I feel a tap on my shoulder. It's the steward. 'Time to move on, son.'

POSTSCRIPT

'From the ashes of disaster grow the roses of success.'
Grandfather Potts, Chitty Chitty Bang Bang

BLIMEY. YOU SPEND FOUR YEARS WRITING A BOOK which eulogises Coventry City's invulnerability and they only go and get relegated while the manuscript is at the publishers. It just goes to show that if you stand on the edge of a cliff staring at the drop for long enough, eventually some little bugger will run along and give you a push. Even experienced fire-eaters sometimes get their tongues burned.

Finally, after three decades of rehearsals, fat ladies all around the globe have been able to unleash their larynxes and partake in a good old sing-song. One of sport's perennial survivors, a team that should have attracted Wilkinson Sword as shirt sponsors such was the frequency of the close shaves, has endured a first ever demotion from the top flight of English football.

So how were things in Coventry in the final week before relegation? Had lepidopterists descended in droves to study the flocks of butterflies? Were there signs in shop windows warning that Bisodol and stomach ulcer treatments had sold out? Was there a localised Diocalm shortage in the city? And since the drop have the Samaritans been forced to recruit extra staff?

In fact the situation is relatively calm. Life goes on much as usual in the city of three spires. The locals have seen it all before. Like the Black Knight in Monty Python and the Holy Grail this mortal injury is seen as little more than a flesh wound. Like an assured wasp in a jar of honey they can be heard to say, "Call this sticky? You should have seen the conserve I was in last year, now that was really a jam." After all, reports of our death have been exaggerated before. Coventry City may be about to embark on a new chapter in their less than golden history (iron pyrites perhaps?), but they do say a change is as good as a rest.

Since we first rose to the upper echelon of English football in 1967 a lot has happened. Back than Eastern and Western Europe were divided by an Iron Curtain. The moon was virgin territory, yet to feel the stealthy footfall of American tourism. Children sang about Old Macdonald's farm without thinking of Happy Meals or foot and mouth. During the intervening decades City have rarely threatened the heights. There have been so many miracle resurrections that we make Lazarus appear like Sleeping Beauty, but Coventry have enjoyed the stay. For many spectators Coventry City seem to have the longest pre-season in the footballing calendar, only really looking remotely interested in trying to win matches in the last two months of the conventional fixture list. The club and the city's names are synonymous with struggle and ultimate victory over apparently insurmountable odds.

But now the one constant in an ever changing world has gone. No longer can lazy journalists refer to Coventry as the Houdini team. No more will we hear that hoary old chestnut that if the Titanic had been painted Sky Blue it would never have gone down. Maybe now observers will feel compelled to draw upon references to that other symbol from the city's coat of arms - the Phoenix. Just like in 1940, the City is being forced to rebuild and replan its future. Coventry's relegation may serve as a warning to those other clubs who feel that their rightful place is in the top flight. If survivors like the Sky Blues can be put down then few other clubs should see their position as irrevocable. The Premier League is nothing like the First Division we ascended to in 1967. Teams are less permanent in all senses of the word. Players and supporters alike are more transient.

Bryan Richardson's visionary plans for a move to a new stadium seem, more than ever, the only way the club can evolve from perennial strugglers into a team that can realistically hope to do more than just keep their heads above water. As is often the case with ambitious goals the plans have had to be modified a fair bit since the original blueprint. The eye-catching spires are no longer a part of the latest design, the price has risen and the deadline has been moved back. The new stadium is now expected to be open by 2004, which would give the club three seasons to develop a side good enough to grace it. Despite rumours of debts and the worry that the club will have to sell off its assets, the sky over the West Midlands is still blue. Sometimes you have to take a step back in order to leap forward. If a short spell in the Nationwide League is the price we have to pay for the development of a stronger side and site, then that would appear a fair deal to make. It seems clear that Coventry City will not sink back into the lower stages of the football hierarchy without a fight. On the eve of this season's relegation Gordon Strachan seemed to echo Dylan Thomas's words,

'Do not go gently into that good night,
Old age should burn and rage at close of day;
Rage, rage against the dying of the light.'

when he urged the Coventry people at their penultimate home match to,

"Lose yourself in singing and dancing. Do what you want - even groan and gripe - but make a noise."

Now our initial adventure is all over despite the shouting and Coventry eyes are scanning the horizon trying to anticipate what sort of future lies ahead. I'm optimistic. The current crop of Sky Blue babes have made a fairly regular habit of reaching FA Youth Cup finals. Those who have already been blooded into the senior squad have looked confident and more than competent. The club are building a young and exciting team. The Sky Blues are aiming high. Shoot at the stars and we may reach the moon. The last thirty years have been fun, if you allow a fairly all embracing definition of the word fun. I've enjoyed being a Sky Blue and the baggage that such a title carries. I've a feeling the next decade may be even more interesting than the last one. The goalposts may have moved but the target remains the same. On a personal front I feel less distraught than in previous seasons, possibly because it seemed so obvious from early on in the season that the game was finally up. Or perhaps my own priorities have changed. Today I enjoyed watching my own children, Oliver and Isabel, kicking footballs in the garden and hardly felt sick about Coventry's relegation at all. I may be back on solid food by the end of the week. Despite my worst fears the world didn't end.

I'm quite looking forward to visiting some new clubs and some older ones that we haven't played for some time. It will be nice to be out of the absolutely shameless casino that is the Premier League. Though hopefully not for too long. My interest in the Champion's League and all European football has totally evaporated away as the national media have tried to persuade me how important these games are. I have also become increasingly jaundiced by the three ring circus that is the Premier League. As clubs have been encouraged to operate like lap dancers, performing for the fattest wallets, I've been left thinking that this isn't really what I wanted from supporting my local football team.

A year or two in the Nationwide may provide a nice rest. I'm looking forward to seeing the young side develop together and forge a team spirit so rare in theses mercenary times. We'll come back a force to be reckoned with, wherever our stadium is.

Play up Sky Blues.